Placuela de Selenque
Calle de los Peregrinos
Calle del Arenal
Calle de la Zarza
Calle de la Vitoria
Calle de la Cruz
Calle de la Gorguera
PROVINCIA
Calle de la Compania
Calle dela Merced
Calle dela Madalena
Duque de Alua
Calle del Calvario
Calle del Olmo

LUCRECIA'S DREAMS

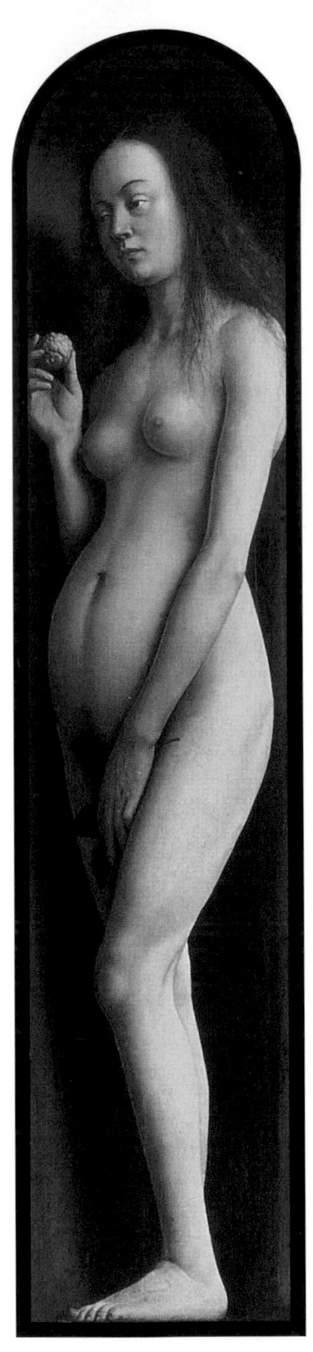

LUCRECIA'S DREAMS

Politics and Prophecy in Sixteenth-Century Spain

RICHARD L. KAGAN

UNIVERSITY OF CALIFORNIA PRESS
Berkeley Los Angeles
Oxford

Frontispiece: Van Eyck, Ghent Altarpiece, right panel, detail of Eve. Ghent, S. Bavone. Courtesy of Giraudon/Art Resource. Upon seeing a copy of this painting in the chapel of the royal palace in Madrid, Ana Ordoñez exclaimed to her daughter, "By Jesus, Lucrecia, look how her body resembles yours . . . especially from the neck down!"

Endpapers: Plan of Madrid's city center in the mid-seventeenth century. The highlighted area on the front endpaper indicates the approximate location of Lucrecia's house, which was situated on the small street opposite the side door of the Convent of the Magdalena and diagonally across the calle de Atocha from the parish church of San Sebastián. From *Topographia de la villa de Madrid descrita por Don Pedro Teixeira año 1656* (Madrid, 1977).

The publisher gratefully acknowledges the Spanish Ministry of Culture and the Program for Cultural Cooperation between Spain's Ministry of Culture and United States Universities for their generous support of this publication.

University of California Press
Berkeley and Los Angeles, California
University of California Press, Ltd.
Oxford, England

Printed in the United States of America
1 2 3 4 5 6 7 8 9

Library of Congress
Cataloguing-in-Publication Data
follows the index.

The paper used in this publication meets the minimum requirements of American National Standard for Information Services—Permanence of Paper for Printed Library Materials, ANSI Z39.48–1984. ∞

For Shreve,
the woman of my dreams

CONTENTS

PREFACE

Lucrecia de León, the young Spanish woman at the center of this book, never kept a diary nor wrote an autobiography. Nor does it seem that she wrote many letters, entered into a notarial contract, or prepared a last will and testament. Nevertheless, we know more about Lucrecia than about most women who lived in the sixteenth century, except those few who were born to privilege or whose autobiographical testimonies survive.

Our knowledge of Lucrecia comes almost entirely from evidence compiled during the course of her trial by the Spanish Inquisition, a *proceso* that began in 1590 and lasted for over five years. These documents, bound in a series of manuscript registers and preserved in the Archivo Histórico Nacional in Madrid, contain oral testimony collected during Lucrecia's trial as well as transcriptions of just over four hundred dreams that Lucrecia allegedly had dreamed in the years immediately prior to her arrest; the trial records of her codefendants have also been preserved. While not all of this material is entirely trustworthy, in the aggregate it offers a wealth of information about Lucrecia's life and times. It is somewhat ironic that the Inquisition, which sought to silence Lucrecia, recorded and preserved those very documents that today enable us to reconstruct Lucrecia's life and share her dreams.

Yet for all the richness of the trial records, Lucrecia remains an elusive figure. Was she a weak woman manipulated by men, primarily the two clergymen who encouraged her to have her dreams transcribed? Was she, in this respect, the sixteenth-century Spanish equivalent of the slave girl in Acts 16:16, whose "spirit of divination" and soothsaying brought her owners gain? Or was she, as other evidence suggests, a woman confident of her own powers of clairvoyance and determined to put them to use? Was she a naive creature, as she sometimes claimed, who did not understand the political implications of her prophetic dreams? Or was she, as others testified, a woman of strong convictions who invented these dreams in order to attract attention to herself and her political views?

I originally conceived of writing a book on Lucrecia de León in 1981. Over time my own thinking about Lucrecia has continued to change. This continuous process of discovering Lucrecia has been aided by numerous colleagues and friends in a variety of contexts, both formal and informal. Here I would like to thank my students, both undergraduate and graduate, and colleagues at The Johns Hopkins University, at the Department of History of the University of Florida, and at the Departmento de Historia Moderna of the University of Santiago de Compostela in Spain. I am also grateful for the comments and suggestions I received at the 1983 annual meeting of the American Historical Association; at a conference sponsored by the University of California, Los Angeles, in 1988, "Cultural Encounters: The Inquisition in Spain and the New World"; and at a seminar in 1989 at the Shelby Cullom Davis Center for Historical Studies, Princeton, New Jersey.

This book could not have been written without the aid and assistance of numerous archivists and librarians, both in Europe and the United States. I am especially indebted to the director and staff of the Archivo Histórico Nacional in Madrid and particularly to the archivists of the Sección de Inquisición, where the documents of Lucrecia's trial are preserved. I also would like to acknowledge with gratitude Gregorio de Andrés, archivist of Madrid's Instituto de Valencia de Don Juan; Mercedes Noviembre, archivist of the Archivo y Biblioteca Heredía Spínola; the staff of the Sección de Manuscritos y Raros of the Biblioteca Nacional in Madrid; and the many *archiveras* of the Archivo General de Simancas.

It is impossible to mention by name all the other individuals who assisted me with this project, although I would like to acknowledge in particular Tomasso Astarita, who worked as my research assistant in 1985–86, as well as James Amelang,

William A. Christian, Jr., David W. Cohen, Patrick Geary, Robert A. Kagan, Fernando Mariás, and Alain Milhou—all of whom offered advice and support at various critical moments. I am especially grateful to those who took the time to read and comment upon earlier versions of this work, notably Gabrielle Spiegel, who taught me how some of Freud's ideas might be incorporated in this study, and Eileen Higham, whose no-nonsense approach to psychology guided me toward a clearer understanding of Lucrecia's complex personality. Jonathan Brown, John Elliott, William Maltby, E. William Monter, Geoffrey Parker, and Orest Ranum improved the book's organization, caught factual errors, and helped me rethink various chapters. Many useful suggestions also came from James Clark, director of the University of California Press, who endorsed this project from its inception, encouraged me to try to make Lucrecia come alive in my work, and then skillfully shepherded the manuscript through to publication. At the Press, I would also like to thank Marilyn Schwartz for her organizational skills and Amy Einsohn for her careful and imaginative editing of the final draft. Marianna Shreve Simpson deserves my deepest appreciation. Her critical mind and superb editorial skills made this a far better, far more readable book.

Finally, I am grateful to the Solomon R. Guggenheim Memorial Foundation for a fellowship that enabled me to spend the 1982–83 academic year in Madrid. The Johns Hopkins University has been equally generous, both with financial assistance, and, more importantly, the time to write.

Richard L. Kagan
Baltimore, Maryland
October 1989

EDITORIAL NOTE

In citing sixteenth-century Castilian documents, I have modernized the orthography, added accent marks, and spelled out abbreviations; for example, Lucrezia de Leon becomes Lucrecia de León, and *q* is rendered as *que.* My translations of Lucrecia's dream registers and various extracts from her trial record are faithful to the original Castilian syntax with one exception: occasionally I have transposed material reported in third person ("she said that the man told her that") into Lucrecia's voice ("the man told me that").

INTRODUCTION

It was in the spring of 1980, while working in the archives of the Spanish Inquisition in Madrid, that I first read about the arrest almost four hundred years earlier of a twenty-one-year-old *madrileña,* Lucrecia de León. The circumstances of her arrest were not mentioned in the archival documents, but Lucrecia was charged by the Holy Office with having "invented" a series of dreams alleged to contain a variety of blasphemous and heretical propositions as well as seditious statements injurious to the honor and reputation of the Spanish monarch, Philip II. My interest in Lucrecia's case was further piqued by references to what the inquisitors described as "dream registers," a set of notebooks containing transcriptions of Lucrecia's dreams from November 1587 until her arrest two and a half years later. I subsequently discovered that the dream registers had not been written by Lucrecia herself, but that she had dictated her dreams daily to several churchmen. A register of more than four hundred dreams was compiled in this manner and later seized by the Inquisition.

Lucrecia's dreams are not, superficially at least, of a type that would necessarily interest a Freudian analyst. Some portions are undeniably autobiographical and can probably be classified as "day-residue" dreams offering glimpses of her daily waking activities. Others can probably be equated with daydreams of the kind described by Freud in his essay "Family Romances," and these do provide some fragmentary insights into Lucrecia's personality and psyche."[1] They suggest that she was a bright, intelligent, although unlettered, ambitious woman frustrated by the inability of her father, a Madrid solicitor, to provide adequately for his family's welfare. In particular, Lucrecia was angry at her father for having failed to give her a dowry or even to help find her a suitable husband. In the dreams, Philip II substitutes for Lucrecia's father and, in an almost textbook case of Oedipal displacement, becomes the target of Lucrecia's wrath, repeatedly faulted for having neglected to arrange for the marriage of his own daughter, the infanta Isabella. For the most part, however, Lucrecia's dreams do not offer what Freud described as "a royal road to a knowledge of the unconscious activities of the mind,"[2] and they do not lend themselves to psychobiographic analysis.

Rather, the real importance of these dreams lies in their social and political criticism of Philip's Spain, and this study approaches Lucrecia's dreams as glosses on historical events. In addition to failing his daughter, Philip is depicted in the dreams as the source of everything that Lucrecia perceives to be wrong with Spain: a corrupt church, oppressive taxes, lack of justice for the poor, and a weak national defense. The dreams also warn of the kingdom's imminent "loss" or "destruction," announcing that Philip's troubles will begin with the defeat of the great Armada—a disaster that Lucrecia predicts almost a year before the *Invencible* set sail for England in 1588. In her dreams she also foresees that Spain will soon be invaded by her enemies, both Muslim and Protestant, and suggests that these calamities are divinely ordained retribution for Philip's personal shortcomings and misguided policies. Lucrecia even presages the deaths of the king and his heir apparent, the infante Philip, the extinction of the Spanish branch of the House of Habsburg, and the accession of a new monarchy that would reconquer the lands lost to the Muslims and ultimately recapture Jerusalem.

The Western tradition of millennial prophecy begins, of course, with the Old Testament, but by the early Middle Ages doomsday prophecies had acquired something of a nationalistic flavor. In the seventh century, for example, Isidore of Seville prophesied that the sins of Spain's Visigothic rulers would result in the kingdom's destruction by the Moors.[3] (The Moorish invasion began in 711, seventy-five years after Isidore's death.) Similar prognostications cropped up periodically thereafter, notably in the Letter of Toledo, a famous doomsday prophecy originally fabricated in 1286, which announced that the destruction of Spain would be followed by an era of restoration in which the religion of Islam would be vanquished.[4] In the second half of the fourteenth century, the tradition was reinforced by the arrival in Spain of the so-called Prophecies of Merlin, originally the invention of the twelfth-century English writer Geoffrey of Monmouth.[5]

At the Spanish court in the Middle Ages, astrologers regularly circulated "fulfillment prophecies" which informed new monarchs that their destiny was to defend the church, to complete the Reconquest, and to destroy Islam. Variants of this prophecy announced that the Reconquest would be entrusted to a *pastor angelicus,* known alternatively as a New David or *El Encubierto* (The Hidden One), a blessed redeemer who would come from the east, rescue the kingdom from its enemies, and forever defeat Islam.[6] Lucrecia's pastor angelicus is a shepherd named Miguel who bests the Muslims, conquers the Holy Land in the name of the Catholic church, and persuades the pope to move the Holy See from Rome to Toledo, the city traditionally regarded as Spain's spiritual capital.

Lucrecia's dreams can thus be viewed as a belated manifestation of a centuries-old prophetic tradition that, according to some observers, was already in eclipse by the time she experienced her first prophetic dreams.[7] But Lucrecia's contemporaries were less concerned with medieval prophetic traditions than with the social and political commentary in her dreams. The Renaissance had its own theories about the interpretation of dreams, and if we are to approach Lucrecia as a historical figure and to understand her and her dreams as her contemporaries would have, we must first appreciate the seriousness that early modern Europe accorded nighttime visions.

Lucrecia's supporters claimed her dreams were divinely inspired prophecies, messages sent by God to caution Philip and his ministers. In early modern Europe prophecies were commonly promulgated to consolidate support for a new monarch or regime, and in Spain royal births were regularly accompanied by the circulation of fulfillment prophecies, similar to those of the Middle Ages, which avowed that the future monarch was destined to complete the work of the Reconquest. Conversely, prophecy was used to establish religious standards by which to judge a secular regime, and in this guise prophecies were often wielded as an ideological weapon by opposition movements and radical groups. Among those who turned prophecy toward political protest, the best known are Savonarola, the radical Dominican preacher whose followers seized control of Florence in 1491, and Thomas Müntzer, the Anabaptist leader who attempted to establish a millennial kingdom at Allstedt and later at Mühlhausen before being defeated by imperial forces in 1525. William Hackett, the former serving man who warned of plague unless Queen Elizabeth reformed her government, was a somewhat less successful prophet: he was arrested for sedition and executed in 1591.[8] As we shall see, word of Lucrecia's prophecies attracted a loose coalition of disgruntled churchmen and courtiers who hoped to use her dreams to goad Philip into changing his ways.

Another decisive factor in the Inquisition's case against Lucrecia was the Spanish church's attitude toward women and women visionaries. Beginning with Deborah and Judith in the Old Testament, Christianity recognized a long line of female seers and religious women who had achieved a state of spiritual grace and were able to receive divine messages, usually in the form of visions. The most renowned medieval visionaries—Hildegard of Bingen, Bridgit of Sweden, and Catherine of Siena—were canonized, but by the mid-fifteenth century the church had grown weary of what the Sorbonne theologian Jean Gerson described in 1416 as "women's enthusiasm."[9] From then on, female seers were suspected of diabolical delusion, and visionaries were more likely to be burned at the stake than elevated to sainthood. A notable exception was Lucrecia's near contemporary Teresa of Jesus (1515–1582), the mystical foundress of the Discalced Carmelite Order. Although some churchmen questioned her orthodoxy, Teresa was canonized in 1622, a brief forty years after her death.

Despite the church's uneasiness, female clairvoyants and visionaries continued to appear, occasionally becoming figures of local veneration and popular pilgrimage. Citing the limits that European society placed on women's conduct, historians generally regard prophetic dreams and visions as an important means for women to exercise autonomy and authority, to gain support for a variety of religious activities, and to attain a voice in secular politics. In particular, the medievalist Caroline Bynum has suggested that mystic or nonorthodox spirituality can be traced to the Church's refusal to allow women to celebrate mass.[10] Although this explanation may pertain to nuns and other religious visionaries rather than to lay seers, Lucrecia's case offers an excellent opportunity to study how an ordinary woman could enter the political arena by drawing upon spiritual gifts.

Even so, the expressly political content of Lucrecia's dreams represents something of an anomaly. Typically, visions and other ecstatic experiences offered religious women in Europe a means of participating in theological debates.[11] Visions also provided these women with a means of consolidating their position within a particular convent, of increasing their convent's prestige, or even establishing a shrine or some other type of new religious institution. To cite one Spanish example, Sor María de la Antigua (1566–1617), a Dominican nun in Utrera, experienced a vision in which she saw three nuns in a new convent, holding a statue of the Virgin that moved and made the sign of the cross. According to her biographer, this vision was a prophecy concerning the foundation of the Convento de Descalzas de la Purísima Concepción, a Dominican house established in Marchena in 1631.[12]

Other women capitalized on the fame of their visions to become spiritual advisors to kings and dukes. The influence of these "spiritual mothers" is difficult to measure, but in Italy nuns and tertiaries such as Luca da Narni, an advisor to Ercole I, duke of Este, and Osanna Andreasi and Stefana Quinzani, both of whom were attached to the court of the dukes of Mantua, achieved considerable notoriety at the start of the sixteenth century.[13] The dukes patronized such women to enhance their own authority, hoping the reputation and spiritual goodness of the "mothers" would redound on their courts. Thus the Italian and other Renaissance princes made a point of publicizing the holy women's ecstasies, raptures, visions, and prophecies, generally in the form of engravings or printed libretti. Spiritual mothers also appeared in Spain, the most famous being Sor María de Agreda (1602–1655), the Franciscan nun who became a close confidante of Philip IV during the 1640s and 1650s.[14]

Most of these spiritual mothers eschewed direct involvement in secular politics, generally limiting themselves to advice on such topics as religious reform, morality, and social justice, but occasionally they did offer counsel on political matters. For example, Bridgit of Sweden was known throughout Europe for her *Revelations,* a copious compendium of several hundred divinely inspired visions. The vast majority of her visions pertained to the corruption of the church and the need for clerical reform; they also advocated the return of the papacy from Avignon to Rome, new crusades against Islam, and a general renewal of Christianity. A few of Bridgit's visions, however, were addressed to secular rulers, notably those of Cyprus and Naples, warning them of the necessity to reform their sinful realms. One vision even expressed a certain sympathy for the English victory against the French in the Hundred Years War.[15] As limited as the political content of Bridgit's visions appears, it was sufficient to galvanize the opposition of Jean Gerson and other French clerics during canonization proceedings at the Council of Constance in 1415. The message was clear: visionaries, particularly female visionaries, were not to stray from the spiritual realm.

Despite such warnings, a number of other late medieval and Renaissance female visionaries spoke to secular matters, often at considerable risk. There was Joan of Arc, of course, but also Elizabeth Barton, the so-called Nun of Kent, whose visions warned that Henry VIII's plan to divorce Catherine of Aragon would lead to his dethronement and to the destruction of England. On Henry's orders, Elizabeth, her spiritual advisor, and several followers were arrested in November 1533 and tried by the Star Chamber on charges of high treason. On the scaffold at Tyburn the following April, Elizabeth confessed her sins, claiming, much as Lucrecia de León would some sixty years later, that she was a "poor wench without learning" who had been wrongfully deluded by "learned men."[16]

A final example of a prophetess who ventured to involve herself in secular affairs is Sor María de la Visitación, prioress of the Dominican Convento de la Annunciada in Lisbon. The Nun of Lisbon, as she was called, is of particular interest because Lucrecia knew about her and she appears in several of Lucrecia's dreams. Beginning in 1575, Sor María experienced a series of ecstasies, raptures, visions, and miraculous levitations. She was far better known, however, for her stigmata, five wounds in her side that dripped blood in the shape of a cross.[17] Sor María also had more worldly concerns: Following the annexation of Portugal by Philip II in 1582, she emerged as a supporter of the exiled Portuguese pretender, dom Antonio. During the autumn of 1588 Sor María made several public statements on Antonio's behalf, and according to one source she boldly announced, "The Kingdom of Portugal does not belong to Philip II, but to the Braganza family. If the king of Spain does not restore the throne that he unjustly usurped, then God will punish him severely." Sor María also presented herself as the living incarnation of Portugal, her wounds the symbol of Portuguese suffering under the Spanish yoke.[18]

Within weeks of these public protests, the royal governor in Lisbon ordered the Inquisition to investigate Sor María's many miracles. The Holy Office soon reported that her famous stigmata were self-induced pinpricks, that her levitations were faked with the aid of sticks, and that her halos had been craftily created by mirrors and lights. On 6 December 1588 the Inquisition pronounced Sor María guilty of "trickery and deceit" and sentenced her to life exile in Brazil.[19] On 25 November, two weeks prior to the publication of Sor María's sentence in Lisbon, Lucrecia had a dream in which a mysterious man told her that "everything she [María] has said is false." Evidently, advance information about the Inquisition's findings had reached Madrid, and Lucrecia, aware of the dangers awaiting false visionaries, hoped to avoid Sor María's fate by establishing herself as a seer who spoke only the truth.

Yet Lucrecia's lack of spiritual credentials sets her apart from the spiritual mothers and the holy women who enjoyed the support and protection of their religious orders. In contrast, Lucrecia exhibited few of the qualities hagiographers traditionally associate with sainthood or a religious calling.[20] As a *doncella,* she was more interested in marriage than a spiritual life of ascetic devotion. Furthermore, she never claimed to have had celestial visions nor any other form of miraculous spiritual experience. Most decisively, perhaps, several months after she was arrested Lucrecia gave birth to a child out of wedlock, an act incompatible with the church's presumption that only chaste women were entrusted with divine messages.

In this respect Lucrecia's career as a lay prophet has less in common with the lives of holy women and more to do with the pursuits of the so-called street or marketplace prophets.[21] Dressed in sackcloth and often carrying a cross, these seers, both religious and secular, publicly preached millennial scenarios. Stock figures in the history of medieval and Renaissance Europe, the street prophets appeared in greatest numbers during times of economic crisis and political unrest. One such period was the 1520s and 1530s, when the squares and plazas of Europe teemed with seers announcing the end of the world. In Catholic districts, at least, they proclaimed Charles V the Last World Emperor, the ruler destined to unite Christendom, conquer Islam, and prepare the world for the Day of Judgment.[22]

But the model of the street prophet suits Lucrecia little better than that of holy woman, since almost all the marketplace seers were men. How, then, we must ask, did this young woman embark on such an unprecedented and politically dangerous career? And why did she do so? Lucrecia's dreams provide an answer to the first of these questions. For the second, we must look more closely at Lucrecia herself.

1

LUCRECIA DE LEÓN

On 25 May 1590 agents of the Inquisition appeared at the house of Lucrecia de León with instructions to arrest her and to take her to Toledo for trial. Following inquisitorial procedure, the officers would not have informed Lucrecia why she was being detained. But Lucrecia, then twenty-one, understood that the Holy Office was troubled by her dreams, some of which, in manuscript copy, had been circulating publicly for months.

Among the hundreds of dreams Lucrecia had dictated for transcription, the most recent was one that had occurred during a Sunday-afternoon siesta on 13 May. The dream begins with the arrival of a man, one of three who regularly appear in her dreams, who wakes the sleeping Lucrecia and takes her into a nearby street. There Lucrecia sees a large processional cart, drawn by three bulls, slowly winding its way through Madrid. The cart carries a large marble statue of a man cloaked in white, with a lance in one hand, a globe in the other. On the statue's head, in place of a hat, is a dove; the statue's mouth is a mirror, and stars serve as its eyes. Flanking this strange figure are two boys. One is dressed in a brown cloak and holds a flask of wine; the other, wearing the long white alb customarily worn by priests, is empty-handed, although in previous dreams he has appeared holding a compass and rule. Lucrecia asks her companion what these boys represent. The man replies that the boy in brown is a symbol of love, the boy in white a symbol of chastity. The latter, he continues, is a sign that the "liberty" which Spain's "bad shepherd" has permitted is soon to end. Lucrecia next encounters an old man, the second of her regular nighttime visitors. Kneeling as the cart passes by, he reaches skyward and proclaims, "Blessed are thou, my Lord, and blessed be the time when we have a king who will be a king, a pope who will be a pope, a farmer who will be a farmer." A young man, the last of the trio of Lucrecia's regular dream visitors, now appears. He instructs her about the coming day of judgment and asserts that God's punishment could have been avoided had King Philip been more devout. But now, he warns, "the angel of the Lord with the scourge of plague must come, but afterward the Lord will send another angel so that the earth will not grieve forever . . . and this angel will banish our sufferings, defeat our enemies, and remove our chains." After a few more words of avuncular wisdom, the dream ends as Lucrecia awakens.

Dreams similar to this one, with its suggestion that Philip II was an irresponsible monarch, were the ostensible reason for Lucrecia's arrest. It is worth recalling, however, that apolitical prophets and visionaries were also persecuted throughout Catholic Europe. Ever since the Reformation, the Roman Catholic church, fearing further heresy, had tried to suppress most forms of individual religious expression. Deviants, eccentrics, and religious ecstatics, all of whom had once enjoyed considerable tolerance, now came under strict scrutiny and control. Nowhere was this vigilance stricter than in Spain, where the Inquisition and its small army of agents kept a close watch over the populace at large. In the 1520s and 1530s the Holy Office ruthlessly persecuted the *alumbrados,* a quasi-mystical sect with followers in Guadalajara, Toledo, and a number of other Castilian towns. Alumbrados were attacked for several reasons. Many were New Christians and therefore spiritually suspect. They were also accused of being Lutherans, a false charge but evidently one connected to their belief that mental prayer was sufficient to achieve a state of spiritual perfection. While practices and beliefs varied, the sect was known for sexual promiscuity and mystical practices, especially *arrobamientos* and *raptos,* two types of spiritual trances. Subsequent targets of the Inquisition included Lutherans, Calvinists, and diverse heretics, as well as anyone who challenged the primacy of the church by claiming to have received direct inspiration from God, particularly in the form of visions or dreams.

Female visionaries, known almost interchangeably as *dejadas, ilusas,* and *videntes,* were particularly suspect because it was believed that women's supposedly weaker nature rendered them especially susceptible to diabolical delusion. Leonor Hernández, also known as Leonor de la Cruz, was arrested on two occasions—in 1547 and in 1559—by the Holy Office in Córdoba on charges of "false revelations."[1] A woman whose visions became public knowledge was suspected of being under the influence of the devil, and sooner or later she was certain to be arrested. This is what happened to Magdalena de la Cruz, a Cordoban nun widely credited with the gift of prophecy until her trial in 1546 revealed that she had been possessed by a demon ever since the age of seven.[2]

Similarly, Francisca de Avila, or Francisca de los Apostóles, a religious ecstatic from Toledo, enjoyed considerable popularity until she, aided by her sister, attempted to establish a new religious order. Francisca, was arrested by the Inquisition in 1574 and charged with heresy. The evidence against her included accounts of various visions in which Francisca confessed to having seen Jesus issue warnings about the sins of the clergy and calls for monastic reform; some witnesses further alleged that she was an *alumbrada* with Protestant leanings. But Francisca's arrest can also be traced to her ties to a small group of Toledan clergymen who were supporters of Bartolomé de Carranza, the controversial archbishop of Toledo who was imprisoned by the Inquisition in 1559. Francisca freely admitted that her celestial visions began shortly after Carranza's arrest and that she then prayed regularly for Carranza's release. For the authorities, thus, Francisca was both a religious heretic and a political subversive—a threat to both church and state.[3]

Suspicion of divine communications in the form of either dreams or visions was so entrenched that some conservative churchmen doubted the orthodoxy of the celebrated Teresa of Jesus, although charges against her were eventually dropped and she was canonized in 1622.[4] Visions were supposed to be kept secret or at most revealed to a confessor for counseling and advice. Thus even Teresa felt distressed after having experienced a series of what she described as "raptures" in church, that is, in public view. "I get so dreadfully ashamed," she wrote to a friend in January 1578, "that I feel I want to hide away somewhere. I pray God earnestly not to let them happen in public."[5]

Despite these precedents, Lucrecia was not merely another female visionary caught in the Inquisition's net. Her case was decidedly different in that her dreams were perceived as a direct threat to the monarchy during a crucial moment in its history. Following the defeat of the Spanish Armada, Philip II felt particularly threatened by his enemies, both foreign and domestic. Though politics was not the Inquisition's usual business, on important matters of state the Holy Office did serve the interests of the monarchy, and its orders to detain Lucrecia came directly from the king. At issue were the explicit criticisms of Philip and his policies contained in Lucrecia's dreams.

Equally troubling to the monarchy was the attention that Lucrecia had attracted at court, where a number of prominent noblemen welcomed her as a prophet. Her dreams concerning the imminent invasion of Spain were so persuasive to the king's architect, Juan de Herrera, that he took time off from his other projects to help design what can only be described as a forerunner of a modern bomb shelter. In hollowed-out caves near the Tagus River, Lucrecia's supporters stocked food, arms, and other supplies that they would need to escape the invasion her dreams foretold (see chapter 5). Among Lucrecia's other noble supporters was Hernando de Toledo, prior of the military order of St. John of Jerusalem and an important member of Philip's Council of State. Beneath his uniform the prior wore a scapular with a cross that was sewn according to a design that Lucrecia had seen in her dreams.[6] Those who wore this garment were to be among the select few to survive the invasion and rebuild a defeated Spain. Lucrecia was, of course, to be among the survivors and in some dreams she envisioned herself as Spain's future queen.

From the crown's perspective, therefore, Lucrecia appeared as one of the leaders of a small but subversive group actively conspiring against the monarchy and publicizing her dreams in order to attract attention and adherents to its cause. Small wonder then that King Philip personally ordered Lucrecia's arrest, an event which elicited the following comment from the Florentine ambassador resident in Madrid:

> Here, and in Toledo, the Inquisition has arrested some important noblemen, among them is the brother of Don Bernardino de Mendoza, ambassador to France, and the prior of the [convent of] San Francisco [in Madrid]. The reason is a woman whom some call a beata and who is said to have had divine revelations in her dreams and to have predicted the defeat of the Armada and now says that the king will soon die.[7]

*

We ought to know more about Lucrecia than we do. The trial record of an individual brought before the Inquisition usually includes a *discurso* or *traza de la vida,* an autobiographical document the accused was asked to provide shortly after the start of the proceedings. This document supplied the inquisitors with information about the accused's family background, education, and religious training. Most of these vitas were brief, but some amounted to full-fledged autobiographies. That of Elena/Eleno de Cespedes, an androgynous surgeon arrested in 1588 on charges of sorcery, was more than thirty pages long.[8]

Lucrecia undoubtedly submitted her statement, but the document is not included in the trial record. Her family background and her life before her arrest must be stitched together from testimony presented during her trial and those of her codefendants. In reviewing this testimony, however, we must recall that much of it was extracted under duress. Also available is testimony provided by Lucrecia's cellmates and other prison acquaintances who spoke up in the hope of obtaining lighter sentences. This testimony, if credible, offers a picture of Lucrecia that differs substantially from the image she projected in court. A final source of biographical information consists of Lucrecia's dreams, although these contain relatively few autobiographical nuggets.

*

Lucrecia de León's father was Alonso Franco de León, a native of Valdepeñas, a small wine-producing town in La Mancha. Little is known about his background except that he was proud of being an Old Christian, free of any trace of Jewish or Moorish blood.[9] A resident of Madrid since at least 1568, Alonso Franco was a *solicitador,* a legal agent who handled the paperwork involved in a lawsuit and generally looked after his clients' interests. Unlike the university-trained *abogado* (barrister), who presented oral arguments in court, a solicitor usually learned his trade through apprenticeship. Alonso Franco probably had no more than the equivalent of a modern secondary school education, but, like most solicitors, he would have been skilled in the minutiae of court procedures and thus indispensable to litigants. His profession would also have brought him in contact with royal judges, legal officers, and other officials attached to the royal court in Madrid. Even so, Alonso Franco's social status would have been somewhat ambiguous. While solicitors were generally regarded as "appropriate and useful," they also had a reputation as bloodsuckers and thieves.[10]

Information about Lucrecia's mother, Ana Ordoñez, is equally sparse. Born around 1550, she originally came from Salinas de Ruso, a small village in La Montaña in northern Spain. It is not known where she met and married her husband, but the couple was already living in Madrid when Ana gave birth to Lucrecia in October 1568. Over the next ten years Ana Ordoñez had four more children—three girls, Ana, María, and María Magdalena, and a boy, Alonso—all of whom survived to adulthood, a relatively rare phenomenon in an era of high infant mortality.[11] Moreover, in a society in which children customarily left home at an early age to serve as apprentices or to work as servants, all the León offspring lived together under a single roof.

Lucrecia and her family resided in the heart of Madrid in the parish of San Sebastián, a district now nicknamed *barrio de las musas* because of the number of famous artists and writers known to have lived there. In Lucrecia's day, these included two court painters, Romulo Cincinnato and Luis de Carvajal, the well-known sculptor Pompeo Leone, and such famous writers as Cervantes and Lope de Vega. Other distinguished parishioners included the counts of Puñonrostro, who lived in a house on the calle de Relatores, the marquis of Viana, and Felipe Centurione, an important Genoese banker residing on the calle de Atocha, the parish's main street. Also in the parish were a number of officers attached to the royal court. By and large, however, San Sebastián in the late sixteenth century was a parish of artisans, shopkeepers, and skilled workers.[12] On the small street where the Leóns lived—that of San Salvador, just opposite the side entrance of the Augustinian convent of la Magdalena—the family's immediate neighbors were Juan Obregon, a carpenter, and Diego Piedra, a shopkeeper.

The Leóns rented the ground-floor apartment (*aposento bajo*) of a small house belonging to the duchess of Feria, an important noblewoman with whom the young Lucrecia seems to have had considerable contact.[13] This dwelling has long since been destroyed, but it was possibly one of the parish's many humble *casas a la milicia,* tenements constructed after the court's arrival in Madrid in 1561. Speculators built these modest dwellings in order to avoid the obligation of billeting individuals attached to the royal court, a charge imposed on larger edifices, the so-called *casas de aposento.* Though the casas a la milicia were criticized as being "of little comfort and authority,"[14] and were considered an eyesore by planners who wanted Madrid to be an architectural showplace, the utilitarian structures accommodated the thousands of Spaniards who, like Alonso Franco and his wife, emigrated to the capital during the second half of the sixteenth century. Between 1550 and 1600 the population of Madrid rose from about 15,000 to nearly 80,000.[15]

From Lucrecia's dreams we may sketch a rough ground plan of the León apartment. The main room was a multipurpose *sala,* a combined living and dining room, and it was here that visitors were entertained. Of the apartment's several bedrooms, one was reserved for Lucrecia, at least when she was ill. The window in this bedroom afforded a glimpse of passersby in the street of San Salvador as well as those on the calle de Atocha, which continued on to the Plaza Mayor, Madrid's main square.

Though these living quarters were relatively spacious for a family living in Madrid, the Leóns were a middle-class household. Solicitors could earn respectable incomes by representing numerous clients, but Alonso Franco's legal practice appears to have been limited to one, admittedly important, client: the Genoese banking community in Madrid. The Genoese were then the principal bankers to the Habsburg monarchs and regularly provided Philip II with the loans necessary to finance his empire.[16] In theory, Alonso Franco ought to have been paid well for his services, yet at various times the León family appears to have been in financial difficulty, or at least Ana Ordoñez felt that her family was needy. To help ends meet, the family took in occasional boarders, and Lucrecia, her sisters, and her mother did a variety of small jobs. Two of Lucrecia's dreams report, for example, that she went from door to door hawking bolts of cloth previously purchased in the marketplace at the Puerta del Sol. In the dream of 17 July 1588 she is mocked for doing so: "Along the streets where I was going," the dream record states, "many people called me mad," an indication that Lucrecia was embarrassed about the thought of engaging in this lowly species of trade.[17] The dreams also suggest that Lucrecia and her mother sold edible herbs collected along the banks of the Manzanares River and in meadows that ringed the town. Nonetheless, the León family appears never to have lacked for food or other basic commodities. Rather, like so many other middle-class households, the family occasionally found itself short of funds. Once Lucrecia became known as a seer, her mother readily accepted alms from admiring nobles.[18]

The testimony of the neighbors indicates that Lucrecia's family was well respected. The widow María Brava described them as "honorable people, good Christians, of good life, reputation, and example," and Mariana Carrasco told the Inquisition that they were a "very honorable family who live honestly." Another neighbor, Juan Obregon, described the León women as "honorable persons, good Christians who respect God and their own consciences."[19]

Lucrecia's own reputation was much the same. Her neighbors described her as an honest *doncella* who lived "recogidamente," quietly and modestly, and attended scrupulously to her religious duties and devotions. She often accompanied her devout mother on her almost daily visits to church. From the register of Lucrecia's dreams, one learns that their first stop was the parish church of San Sebastián, located on the northern side of the calle de Atocha, only a stone's throw from their home. This church, one of Madrid's thirteen parishes, was then under the direction of Alonso de Puebla, an ideal Counter-Reformation parish priest: university-educated, a respectable preacher, and a diligent recordkeeper who maintained exceptionally accurate registers of the parish's baptisms, marriages, and deaths. Puebla seems to have been well acquainted both with Lucrecia and her mother and in general looked after their spiritual welfare.[20]

As important as the parish was for their spiritual life, Ana Ordoñez and Lucrecia divided their devotions among a number of other nearby churches, particularly those administered by the mendicant orders. In Spain, as elsewhere in Europe, preaching was the key to the mendicants' success, and it was evidently the sermons that brought Lucrecia and her mother into these temples. One of Lucrecia's dreams specifically alludes to sermons delivered in the church of the Convento de la Magdalena, an Augustinian convent that had been founded in 1579 for the benefit of former prostitutes.[21] Other dreams suggest that Lucrecia listened to sermons offered in the Jeronymite monastery of San Gerónimo as well as in several nearby convents, including those of Nuestra Señora de la Vitoria (*Clérigos menores*), Santa Ana (Discalced Carmelite), Santo Tomás (Dominican), and La Trinidad (Trinitarian). In addition, Lucrecia and her mother worshiped in the chapels attached to neighborhood hospitals, especially that of Anton Martín, an institution that specialized in contagious diseases and was located only a short walk from the León house. Mention is also made of visits to the church of the Dominican Convent of the Merced, the parishes of San Andrés, Santa Cruz, San Gil, and San Ginés, and even to the chapel of the Alcázar, the royal palace, situated across town, on the western edge of Madrid. Sundays and holidays were occasions for more ambitious religious outings. On these days the dreams indicate that Lucrecia usually accompanied her mother on *romerías* (pilgrimages to shrines), including one to the *hermita* of San Blas "because I had vowed to [visit the shrine] so that the saint would cure me." Yet their favored destination was the shrine of Nuestra Señora de Atocha, whose miracle-working image of the Virgin was the most revered in Madrid.[22]

We cannot, of course, know whether Lucrecia was as deeply pious as her dreams suggest, but her spiritual life seems to have conformed to the model established by the Spanish humanist Juan Luis Vives in his famous book *On the Education of Christian Women* (1524). Women, Vives counseled, should emulate the Virgin and her "holy way of life" by cultivating such virtues as chastity ("the virtue of virtues"), temperance, diligence, and devotion.[23] Though, as we shall see, Lucrecia's sexual behavior deviated from this standard, nothing in the trial record suggests that the Catholicism she practiced was in any way unorthodox.[24] There is little reason, then, to accept the assertion of the historian Beltrán de Heredía that Lucrecia was an *alumbrada,* a member of the heretical sect that the Inquisition had attempted to eradicate early in the sixteenth century.[25] Beltrán de Heredía reasoned that Lucrecia's penchant for dreams linked her to the sect, but none of the witnesses at her trial associated her with the group, nor did the list of charges against her include any such allegations.

Other historians have suggested that Lucrecia was a *beata,* or beguine, a laywoman who had pledged herself to the church and took vows of chastity but who did not officially belong to any religious order.[26] An important aspect of lay piety during the later Middle Ages, the beguine movement in northern Europe peaked in the fifteenth century, although in Spain, as in Italy, it flourished for another two hundred years.[27] During the sixteenth century most Spanish cities continued to support a large number of beatas, living singly as well as in groups, often in special dwellings—*beaterías*—annexed to regular convents. Toledo, an important religious center, had eight such communities in 1575; Madrid nearly as many.[28] Individual beatas, moreover, frequently became famous for their piety and acts of charity. In Toledo, the widow Catalina de Herrera (d. 1616), lauded for her ministrations to the poor, was revered as a near saint.[29]

Madrid had its own share of beatas, one of whom, Juana Correa, a Portuguese woman living in the parish of San Pedro, was a close friend of Lucrecia's.[30] Nevertheless, there is no indication that Lucrecia ever aspired to be a beata, even though the Florentine ambassador described her as such. She is not known to have practiced excessive fasting nor to have displayed any particular enthusiasm for daily communion, two pious practices commonly associated with beatas. Nor did she ever wear a religious habit, another symbol of a beata's life.

Physically, Lucrecia was frail and frequently ill, although the exact nature of her ailments is difficult to determine. Some of her symptoms were quite ordinary, such as the "chills, vomits, and diarrhea" she experienced on the night of 5 December 1587, possibly the result of something she ate and because of which she went to bed early.[31] But, as we will discuss in the context of her activities as a prophet, a long illness, possibly some form of depression, beset her shortly after her first encounter with the authorities in February 1588.

Despite her weak constitution, Lucrecia was reputed to be a beauty. No portrait survives, but trial testimony indicates that she had brown hair, very dark eyes, and a pale complexion. An offhand remark once made by her mother may offer an additional clue about her appearance. During a visit to the royal chapel, Lucrecia and her mother were contemplating Coxcie's sixteenth-century copy of the celebrated van Eyck Ghent Altarpiece, then on display. Ana Ordoñez reportedly told her daughter, "By Jesus, Lucrecia, look how her [Eve's] body resembles yours . . . especially from the neck down!"[32]

Lucrecia's physical appearance, her youth, and innocent ways may well have aided her prophetic career. Her apparent comeliness bespoke her purity and virtue but also helped to attract and to sustain the admiration of a cluster of male attendants, both clerical and lay. The attentions of one of her inquisitors, indeed, appear to have exceeded spiritual admiration. This judge, Licenciado Lope de Mendoza, developed a special fondness for Lucrecia during the course of her trial and, in gross violation of inquisitorial rules, secretly invited her to his house (see chapter 6).

Nonetheless, at the time of her arrest, at the age of twenty-one, Lucrecia remained unmarried. This would not have been unusual in northern Europe, where women were accustomed to marry in their mid-twenties, but in sixteenth-century Spain women had the habit of marrying earlier, often in their late teens,[33] as Ana Ordoñez had done. Ana repeatedly expressed her concern about her daughter's failure to find a husband, particularly one who would be socially advantageous to the León family as a whole. She also believed that Lucrecia's reputation as a dreamer might improve her daughter's marital fortunes. Though Ana had once prayed for the dreams to stop, during the winter of 1587–88, soon after several prominent churchmen and courtiers took notice of Lucrecia and sought to have her dreams transcribed, Ana became Lucrecia's promoter, actively encouraging and supporting her daughter's prophetic career. Early in February 1588, for example, when Lucrecia expressed some reservations about having her dreams transcribed, Ana spoke to Lucrecia "resolutely, urging her not to be afraid," an eyewitness reported, in effect telling her "to get on with it, keep dreaming."[34]

Marriage was also on the minds of visitors to the León household, who often teased Lucrecia about whom she would marry and even suggested that her chances of securing a husband, given her age, were rapidly diminishing. Lucrecia was sufficiently worried about remaining a doncella to raise the subject during confession,[35] and her dreams also indicate that marriage was one of her major concerns. In her dream of 28 December 1587, after it was proposed that she should become a prophet, Lucrecia demurred, answering, "I want to be married," clearly a status she deemed incompatible with that of a prophet. In a dream recorded some two months later, she despaired of ever finding a husband and even toyed with the idea of becoming a nun because "I am already too old [to marry]."[36]

But in February 1590, only a few months before her arrest, Lucrecia had secretly pledged herself to Diego de Vitores Texeda, a twenty-eight-year-old native of Zamora, a city some 150 miles northwest of Madrid. Vitores, a secretary by occupation, was soon employed by Lucrecia's confessor, Fray Lucas de Allende, to transcribe Lucrecia's dreams—a job that led to his arrest by the Holy Office in May 1590.[37] A man of considerable learning, Vitores was skilled in Latin and especially interested in history and poetry. It is reported, for example, that he kept a copy of Petrarch's sonnets in his prison cell.[38]

Vitores had apparently first met Lucrecia the previous October and, according to testimony he later provided the Inquisition, on 20 February 1590 "they gave to each other sworn words and promises of marriage after which they treated each other like man and wife and knew each other carnally, although they did not speak about it to anyone."[39] Two reasons for this secrecy suggest themselves. First, because clandestine marriages of this sort were condemned by the church, the lovers were risking punishments of fine, imprisonment, or both. Second, the decision to keep their union a secret may have been prompted by their desire not to jeopardize Lucrecia's prophetic career.[40] In the Catholic tradition true seers were almost invariably chaste, and thus Lucrecia's prophetic reputation might have been irreparably damaged had news of her relationship with Vitores become public.

As it turned out, however, their secret was not to be secret for long, since Lucrecia was already pregnant with Vitores's child when the two exchanged their private vows. The first hint of her condition occurs in a dream of 18 April 1590, in which she projects, in rather alarming fashion, her anxieties at the prospect of giving birth to a child conceived out of wedlock. The unusual dream begins with Lucrecia in an empty landscape wishing to hear a mass but prevented from doing so by the onset of labor. She then seeks out her mother, asking her to go find a midwife. Alonso Franco appears, carrying a jug of milk in what appears to be a gesture of support, but he challenges the need for a midwife, boldly asserting that Lucrecia cannot be more than seven months pregnant. Lucrecia corrects (and surprises) him by claiming to be well into her ninth month, and then reacts happily when her mother, accompanied by Vitores, appears with a woman who claims to be a *comadre.* Ominously, the woman is brought to Lucrecia hidden in a cape, suggesting the need for secrecy. Now, with the birth about to commence, a voice from inside Lucrecia's womb cries out: "no quiero yo salir ni nacer en tan ruines manos" (I do not want to leave here and to be born in such vile hands). The midwife, shocked and in a near faint, confesses: "You should know that my trade is not what I told you; my intention was only to strangle the infant in order to do harm to you and the man who brought me here." At this point, Alonso Franco, although angry at the prospect of his daughter giving birth to an illegitimate child, relents and miraculously ushers in a second comadre carrying a crown. She assists the birth, which is breach, wraps the infant boy in a sheet, places the crown upon his chest, and sprinkles him with holy water, hoping to prevent a premature death. Lucrecia names the child Carlos and announces that "his life promises more things than death." Ana Ordoñez then arrives with a lunch of bread and cheese "because it was a morning birth." Nine days later the child is baptized and the dream ends with Ana Ordoñez encouraging Lucrecia to nurse the child so that he will be strong and know his mother better.

Just as this dream expresses Lucrecia's guilt and her recognition that an illegitimate child would jeopardize her family's good name, it also suggests that Lucrecia recognized that the pregnancy signaled the end of her prophetic career. But in the dream some of Lucrecia's—and probably her mother's—frustrated ambitions are transferred to her son, whose crown suggests that one day he will become a king.

At Lucrecia's first appearance before the Inquisition on 4 June 1590, the presiding judge noted rather tersely, "She is six or seven months pregnant."[41] Later that summer Lucrecia gave birth to a baby girl, but her name was not entered into the trial record. Apparently the girl lived at Lucrecia's side, confined to a cramped cell in the "secret prisons" of the Holy Office in Toledo.[42]

Despite the difficult conditions, imprisonment seemed only to strengthen the bond between Lucrecia and Vitores. He expressed his continuing love for her in a series of notes that he contrived to have smuggled into her cell. One opened with the phrase "My Lucrecia, my wife" and expressed how much he loved her and his desire for news of their newborn daughter, whose name he still did not know. Vitores also passed on practical information, such as how to make ink out of a mixture of "dirt and cotton" with a little "vinegar or wine," so that Lucrecia could answer. Once he wrote "My Lucrecia, today I received your note and I am sending you another."[43]

As this exchange of notes makes clear, Lucrecia could read, Spanish if not Latin, although she attempted to hide her education from the Holy Office, continually referring to herself as "a simple woman, without substance" and one "without letters."[44] Just prior to her arrest, she also informed one inquisitorial official that she could not sign her name to a document he had just copied because "she did not know how to write," but by 26 June 1595 she was able to sign her name to oral testimony she had just delivered.[45] Vitores's account of her education squares with these incidents: "It is true that Lucrecia de León knew how to read some Spanish, but the truth is that before her imprisonment she did not know how to write except to copy letters that were already written."[46] Alonso de Mendoza, one of the churchmen to whom Lucrecia recounted her dreams, informed the Holy Office that "when she began to have these visions she could only read a little and wrote awkwardly and slowly."[47] Regardless of her actual abilities, the evidence suggests that Lucrecia purposefully portrayed herself as an innocent, unlettered woman, first to enhance her prophetic persona and then, after her arrest, as part of her defense.[48]

In general, Lucrecia's education appears to have been modeled on the prescription that Vives and other sixteenth-century educational writers recommended for girls. Doncellas were to be educated at home, leaving the house as infrequently as possible and scrupulously avoiding contact with males. Girls' instruction was limited chiefly to lessons in piety, obedience, silence, and humility together with the so-called labors of their sex: sewing, weaving, embroidery, cooking, and the like.[49] Little emphasis was placed on book learning, and few educators believed that women needed to be literate. One educational program, outlined by Fray Juan de la Cerda in 1599, specified that girls under ten had only to honor their parents, to avoid contact with Muslims and Jews, and to learn the rudiments of religion and a number of other prescriptive rules. What Cerda described as more "serious" instruction was to begin at the age of twelve, but this included only training in modesty, respect for parental authority, and the avoidance of men.[50] Women of noble birth generally received more education, but Lucrecia's parents did not encourage their daughter to acquire more than rudimentary reading skills, and Vitores testified that he never saw any books in the León household.[51]

Despite this disadvantage, Lucrecia was not nearly as "simple" nor as uneducated as she wanted the Inquisition to believe. In the sixteenth century oral culture was almost as rich and diversified as that available in print. Oral transmission, for example, may well account for Lucrecia's knowledge of the Cid, the medieval hero who appeared in her dream of 13 July 1588. Although various versions of the chronicle of the Cid's life had been available in print since the end of the fifteenth century, he was best known through the *romances,* the cycle of old chivalric tales and *chansons des gestes* that began to be published in the course of the sixteenth century. These ballads may also account for much of Lucrecia's historical knowledge, notably that concerning King Roderic, Spain's last Visigothic ruler, who appears in the dream of 20 April 1590. She also had some awareness of Philip II's father, the Emperor Charles V (1500–1558), as well as of Ferdinand and Isabella, Spain's Catholic Monarchs (1474–1516), who together appear in several dreams as paragons of princely power. Even aspects of Roman history seem to have been within Lucrecia's grasp: she compared the processional carts that appeared in her dream of 3 March 1590 with those the Romans used to celebrate military victories, and she described the large, bare-breasted woman in her dream of 6 December 1587 as "what I have heard called *matronas romanas,*" possibly a reference to Juno or some other Roman goddess.

The dreams also reveal Lucrecia to have been an alert, attentive young woman who learned a great deal simply by keeping her eyes and ears open. For example, in a dream of 6 February 1588 she compares a beast that appeared to her to one "I saw in Madrid, which some call a plow [*arado*] and others a rhinoceros," possibly a reference to an animal she had seen in the royal menagerie at the Alcázar. The dreams also offer illustrations of Lucrecia's excellent visual memory. Her dream of 12 January

1588, which contains a descriptive account of the chapels of St. Ildefonso and Sta. Leocadia in Toledo's cathedral, suggests she had visited that nearby city, possibly on the occasion of the return of Leocadia's relics on 23 April 1587, a celebration attended by thousands of persons from Madrid. Other dreams indicate that Lucrecia was sensitive to the architecture and decoration of churches and chapels she had visited, and the dream of 14 January 1588 specifically makes note of the "figure of Eve painted on the altar," in the chapel of the Alcázar, another reference to the copy of van Eyck's painting then in Madrid. Likewise, the image of Our Lady of the Remedies, housed in Madrid's Mercedarian monastery appears in the dream of 10 February 1588. Lucrecia's ability to remember paintings and sculptures also arose during the course of her trial. When her inquisitors asked how she was able to identify a certain personage who appeared in her dreams as St. John the Baptist, she replied: "by his dress, which was like of the figure of John the Baptist painted in the hospital of the Court."[52]

Her attentiveness and good memory thus enabled her to make the most of whatever information, thoughts, and ideas she gleaned from a long line of informal teachers, the most important of whom was evidently her mother. Ana Ordoñez could not write,[53] but she evidently took care to look after her daughter's spiritual education and material welfare. The relationship between mother and daughter appears to have been extremely close, and in the dreams Ana Ordoñez generally appears as Lucrecia's confidante, companion, protector, and friend.

In contrast, Lucrecia's relationship with her father seems to have been rather chilly. Alonso Franco's work frequently took him away from home for months at a time, leaving his wife to attend to the children by herself. On those occasions when Alonso Franco did involve himself in Lucrecia's upbringing, he was a strict disciplinarian who punished her for dreaming, once even threatening to kill her should the dreams persist. The dreams, he feared, would lead only to Lucrecia's arrest by the Holy Office; they would dishonor his family and discredit him personally. In turn, Lucrecia never expressed much love for Alonso Franco and in her dreams he appears only rarely. Typical is the dream of 20 November 1587, in which he is accused of having failed to help find her a suitable marriage partner.[54] To his credit, Alonso Franco evidently imparted to Lucrecia some knowledge of the monarchy's finances, and in this sense inaugurated Lucrecia's political education.

Lucrecia was also quick to learn from the broad range of individuals she met as a girl growing up in cosmopolitan Madrid. Her informal teachers included friends, neighbors, and relatives, along with the numerous churchmen, mostly confessors and preachers, whom she encountered during her pilgrimages about town. One was Maestro Fray Gerónimo de Aguiar, a Dominican theologian attached to the Colegio de Santo Tomás and a well-known preacher. In her dream of 30 September 1588, Lucrecia recalled a sermon Aguiar had given at the parish church of San Ginés. For a time Aguiar also served as her confessor, and he warned her against having her dreams transcribed. Other instructors included Juana Correa, her beata friend who apparently taught her something about visions, and an unnamed *morisca,* originally from Valdepeñas in La Mancha, who had once run a boarding house in Toledo. This woman, possibly an old acquaintance of Alonso Franco, lived as a boarder in the León household for three or four years and allegedly taught Lucrecia about the Moorish tradition of dreams and prophecy.[55]

Visitors to the León household had other information to offer. Ana Ordoñez's sister María was living in the Yucatan and sent back news and reports of happenings in the New World through friends returning to Madrid. One of these messengers was don Guillén de Casaos, a member of an important Sevilian family and a governor of the Yucatan in New Spain. Casaos returned to Spain in 1585 and subsequently settled in Madrid, joining the swelling ranks of petitioners clogging the royal court. On the side he studied the magical arts, particularly astrology. We do not know when he first visited the León household, but he stopped by frequently during the winter of 1587–88. He discussed dreams and prophecy with Lucrecia, and also taught her about the stars. Chaperoned by her mother, Lucrecia and Casaos stayed up on the night of 13 March 1588 to witness a lunar eclipse.

Though the moralists of the day warned that parents should not allow their daughters to become "amigas de ver gente" (fond of seeing people),[56] the household managed by Ana Ordoñez seems to have been an open forum for the exchange of news, gossip, and information. Friends and neighbors dropped in regularly, and their conversations were enlivened by food and drink. Lucrecia's dreams specifically refer to several of these convivial gatherings in which she took part.

The regular visitors to the León household were mostly women, neighbors such as Ursula Beltrán and María Brava, the wife of a local shopkeeper, both of whom appear in Lucrecia's dreams. The widow Mariana Carrasco was another close friend, as was Magdalena de Jesús, wife of Martín de Ayala, who lived on the nearby calle de las Postas. Ayala, a drycleaner by trade, was known by the nickname Sacamanchas (Mr. Spot Remover). He was also a visionary and had an amateur's interest in astrology, prophecy, and dreams. How much Sacamanchas taught Lucrecia is not certain, but he did tell her about Sor María de la Visitación, a visionary he much admired and someone with whom he claimed to have exchanged letters.

Sacamanchas seems also to have introduced Lucrecia to a rather mysterious group of prophets and faith healers who had gravitated to Madrid in about 1585. One of these was Juan de Dios, a still somewhat mysterious figure previously allied with Francisca de los Apostóles, the Toledan visionary arrested by the Inquisition in 1574. By the mid-1580s Juan de Dios turned up in Madrid, where he spent half his time in the mental ward of the Hospital of Anton Martín, and the rest on the streets uttering prophecies about the coming destruction of Spain.[57] There he identified himself with St. John the Baptist and publicly announced that Spain's sins would soon lead to her destruction by her enemies, a theme later echoed in Lucrecia's dreams. Lucrecia's ties to Juan de Dios remain somewhat vague, but she once described him as "a second [John the] Baptist and royal prophet."[58] Another acquaintance was Miguel de Piedrola Beamonte, a veteran of Spain's Flemish and Italian wars who customarily wore an old military uniform and was known as the soldier-prophet. As we shall see, Piedrola's apocalyptic prophecies apparently served as a model for Lucrecia's dreams about the loss of Spain. Lucrecia was also acquainted with Domingo Navarro, another former soldier who believed that he could heal the sick by making the sign of the cross over their heads.[59]

More fateful was Lucrecia's acquaintance with the two churchmen who arranged for the transcription of her dreams. The first was Doctor Alonso de Mendoza, a member of one of Spain's most illustrious and powerful aristocratic clans. At the time Mendoza first met Lucrecia, in September 1587, he was a canon attached to the cathedral of Toledo, the kingdom's most important church. An expert in Holy Scripture and a skilled theologian, Mendoza was obsessed by dreams, visions, prophecy, and related spiritual phenomena. In masterminding Lucrecia's prophetic career, he contributed to her knowledge of the arts of dream interpretation and divination and other aspects of the occult. Family connections in Madrid and abroad also enabled Mendoza to supply Lucrecia with information pertaining to court business and foreign affairs.

The second of Lucrecia's clerical teachers was Fray Lucas de Allende, head of Madrid's Franciscan convent, one of the town's oldest and most famous religious houses. Allende shared Mendoza's somewhat unorthodox spiritual concerns; as a hobby he gathered news about unusual religious happenings in and around Madrid. His letters, for example, make note of statues that talked and wept, beatas who had experienced visions, and somnolent women who had peculiar dreams. Mendoza introduced Allende to Lucrecia in September 1587, and the following month arranged to have the Franciscan named her confessor and spiritual advisor. In this capacity Allende made regular visits to Lucrecia's house and occasionally arranged for her to visit his cell at the convent. He also shared with Lucrecia his knowledge of dreams, visions, and prophecy. Later, when she was in prison, Lucrecia told one of her cellmates that Allende, along with Mendoza, taught her everything she knew.[60]

From these and other contacts, Lucrecia became familiar with the European tradition of apocalyptic and eschatological thought. Her dreams, for example, explicitly refer to the books of the prophets Daniel, Jeremiah, and Ezekiel, to the Apocalypse of St. John, as well as to the Apocalypse of Esdras. The dreams also indicate that Lucrecia had considerable knowledge of medieval prophecy, especially the vaticinations of Joachim of Fiore (1145–1202) and his many followers, as well as the visions of St. Bridgit of Sweden. References to Spanish apocalyptic literature in Lucrecia's dreams include mention of the prophecies of St. Isidore of Seville; the *Baladro de sabio Merlin,* a fourteenth-century treatise that foretold of the destruction of Islam and the Catholic reconquest of Jerusalem; and the *Encubierto,* the Valencian version of the *pastor angelicus* whose rule was associated with the coming of a universal church. Lucrecia's understanding of this literature may have been rudimentary, but she knew enough to boast to cellmates about her knowledge of St. Bridgit, St. Isidore, and what she described as "the prophecy about the loss of Spain found in the wall of Granada" (see chapter 4).[61]

Lucrecia's political education, like that of many *madrileños,* was largely based on daily gossip about the goings-on in court. Lacking a bishop, a major industry, a university, even a town hall, sixteenth-century Madrid focused its attention on the Alcázar, the former Muslim castle that simultaneously served as the king's residence, the seat of monarchical government, and the locus of the royal court. Access to the palace was limited, but the Alcázar was never isolated from the town that grew up around it. The palace's doors were open to ambassadors, churchmen, and other officials, not to mention hundreds of petitioners seeking offices and favors from the king. By day, moreover, the larger of the palace's two patios—the Queen's Patio—was crowded with artisans and merchants hawking their wares to courtiers. And unlike Versailles, where the courtiers lodged within the palace, the Alcázar housed only a few of the four thousand or so officials attached to the royal household. When the crown's servants left their offices, they carried home news of court business to every quarter of Madrid. In this sense the Alcázar served as the hub of a vast word-of-mouth network, and court gossip was eagerly consumed by the rest of Madrid. The seventeenth-century phrase "Sólo Madrid es Corte" (Only Madrid is the Court) aptly expresses the essential unity that existed between Madrid and the court, although an alternate phrasing, "Madrid is only the Court," underscores the extent to which court life, and its attendant politics, overshadowed the lives of the town's inhabitants.

Indeed, court gossip must have been an important source of information for Lucrecia, for much of what appears in her dreams seems a distillation of what she would have heard in the streets of Madrid. Yet there is also evidence that she had been tutored in political matters by her father. The extent of Alonso Franco's connections at court are difficult to determine, but it appears that he was sharply critical of Philip II and some of his policies. For one thing, Alonso Franco's work as a solicitor for the Genoese bankers inevitably placed him in an adversarial relationship with the crown's lawyers at a time when relations between the monarchy and its foreign financial backers had soured because of Philip's inability to pay off past debts. As Philip's principal bankers, the Genoese had a choice between floating new loans or risking a suspension of payments on past loans and thus the prospect of utter ruin. The extent to which Alonso Franco identified with his client's difficulties is not known, but one witness reported that "Lucrecia's house was not well-disposed to the king."[62]

Lucrecia's political education was further enhanced by a short stay at the royal court in the service of doña Ana de Mendoza, *aya* (governess) to the royal infante, the future Philip III. How Lucrecia obtained this position remains a mystery, although it may have been arranged by the León family's landlord, the duchess of Feria, whose daughter-in-law, Isabel de Mendoza, was the aya's cousin.[63] Apparently, Lucrecia was in doña Ana's service in 1586 and 1587, that is, at the age of eighteen or nineteen. According to court ceremonial, the aya was responsible for "the upbringing and good instruction [of the infante] in spiritual as well as in other areas" and also for managing the prince's household, seeing to everything from his clothes and meals to his attendance at official court functions. An unspecified number of *mozas de cámara y de retrete* assisted the aya, and presumably Lucrecia figured among the maidservants of doña Ana's staff.[64]

Lucrecia's service at the royal palace informed both her testimony to the Inquisition and her dreams, which reveal a detailed knowledge of court ceremonial and the physical layout of the royal household, a restricted area of the Alcázar. Her dream of 26 December 1587, for example, describes a meeting of several *caballeros* of the king's chamber in front of an altarpiece hung in green cloth, and in that of 18 April 1588 Lucrecia enters the palace, visits the prince in his chambers, and then leaves by way of the kitchen into what is described as the *placetilla,* or *plaza del rey,* the smaller of the Alcázar's two courtyards. Other dreams refer to the throne room ("sala larga"), the king's study ("la sala adonde sale a escribir [el rey] Felipe"), the prince's staircase ("la escalera del quarto del príncipe"), and the royal deer preserve ("el cercado que S.M. tiene para los venados") on the grounds of the royal hunting lodge in the Casa de Campo, the park located directly opposite the Alcázar across the Manzanares River.[65]

Likewise, the dreams suggest that Lucrecia was personally acquainted with some of the principal figures at Philip's court. They explicitly refer to García de Loaysa Girón, royal almoner and tutor to the prince; Cardinal Gaspar de Quiroga, inquisitor general and a member of the council of state; and several other influential councillors, including Cristóbal de Moura, Juan de Idiáquez, and the Count of Chinchón. In her dream of 14 January 1590 Lucrecia visits the rooms in the royal palace assigned to don Antonio de Toledo, the king's chief hunter and the individual for whom Vitores had worked on arriving in Madrid.

Lucrecia's dreams further suggest that during her tenure as a maidservant at court she had some contact with the royal family, notably the young infante and the infanta Isabella, who appears regularly in the dreams, always berating her father for having failed to arrange for her marriage. In her dreams Lucrecia also has regular meetings and conversations with Philip, but we cannot be certain she ever met the monarch. Several witnesses at her trial recalled that Lucrecia boasted of having spoken with Philip on several occasions and, in her view, "His Majesty liked her a lot."[66] Lucrecia told Vitores that Philip had offered her a dowry should she ever marry, but there is no evidence confirming such a promise, although Philip, like most Spanish monarchs, was in the habit of granting *mercedes* to maidservants at the royal court.[67]

While Philip may have taken a liking to this young maidservant, Lucrecia's opinion of the king, echoing the views of her father, was decidedly negative. One witness specifically referred to Lucrecia's "great hatred" for Philip, adding that she took "great pleasure when bad things were said about the king."[68] The tenor of Lucrecia's earliest dreams is also emphatically antiauthoritarian, casting Philip in the double role of failed father and failed monarch.

On balance, therefore, Lucrecia was a young woman with strong political views, a clever young woman who picked up information from all the people she met and all the places she went. In modern parlance, Lucrecia was streetwise, versed in the ways of the court and certainly knowledgeable about the topography and traditions of Madrid, a city she knew intimately. In one dream she describes in some detail an old, popular, and apparently somewhat rowdy religious custom of madrileños going to bathe in the Manzanares River on Midsummer's Eve (June 24, St. John's Day), a practice banned in 1588 by the puritanical post-Tridentine church, "in order to excuse some offenses to God and thus to deserve his divine mercy."[69] In other dreams the city comes alive with Lucrecia's vivid accounts of processions of penitents with their whips, street vendors hawking their wares, women working in the washing sheds that once lined the banks of the Manzanares, and gardeners going off to the many groves and orchards on the outskirts of town. Still other dreams describe excavations on the calle de Toledo, where workers accidentally discovered remnants of an old city wall; the altarpiece that once belonged to the Convent of Santa María Magdalena; and curiosities such as the monkey that the royal councillor Alonso de Agreda kept in his house near the church of San Sebastián.[70]

Yet despite such knowledge and the broad range of her contacts, Lucrecia's reputation and the persona she presented to the Inquisition was that of a devout, retiring, and naive doncella. When asked about questions of state, she professed ignorance, asserting that politics could be understood only by men. When asked about prophecy, she claimed to be similarly uninformed. And when asked about dreams, she claimed "not to know anything about them, except that they might tell her if she was going to marry an old man, as some have said."[71] Was this the same Lucrecia who discussed in frank and knowing terms various types of dildos with one of her cellmates in Toledo?[72] Or the Lucrecia whom the Inquisition described as the notorious "mother of prophets" who had invented "visions of war and peace, of pleasure and of terror, together with others of good and bad things to come"? If judged by some of her offhand comments, not to mention the content of her dreams, Lucrecia must have been a far more worldly and politically sophisticated doncella than she chose to pretend. One of her cellmates put it this way: "she has less shame than what she displays in public."[73]

These various sides of Lucrecia's personality may in part reflect her parents' differing, and at times contradictory, expectations for their eldest daughter. On the one hand, the ambitious, hardworking, and outgoing Ana Ordoñez thrust a somewhat reticent Lucrecia into Madrid society, apparently hoping that the dreams would bring her daughter a husband, and bring her family money and recognition. On the other hand, Alonso Franco was a cautious father, fully aware of the dangers posed by the dreams and the risks of attracting the attention of the Inquisition. As both the dreams and the testimony Lucrecia offered to the Holy Office suggest, she thought her father to be not only a harsh disciplinarian but also a poor provider. Her service at court could only have magnified her sense of her father's defects, as each night she returned from the wealth and luxury of the court to her family's humble home.

Thus despite her father's caution, Lucrecia sided with her mother in deciding to publicize her dreams. In September 1587 Mendoza, aided and encouraged by Ana Ordoñez, took Lucrecia under his wing. For the following two and a half years this churchman was a central figure in Lucrecia's life, providing her family with financial support, teaching her about prophecy, and introducing her to the politics of the day. Unlike Alonso Franco, who punished his daughter for dreaming, Mendoza encouraged

Lucrecia to dream and transcribed her dictation. Witnesses testified that they had a warm, almost familial relationship, and it was said that she referred to Mendoza as her true father ("que no tenía otro padre sino a él") as well as "the brother of my soul and of my life."[74] On one occasion Lucrecia sent a letter to Mendoza, much as any daughter would to a father, in which she asked his help to buy some new clothes: "I ask your grace to give me a *merced;* the reason is that I am almost naked and in this city [Madrid] there are many cheap *martiñas* [a type of cloth] and thus I would like your grace to send me what I need to buy a skirt; please pardon my need, your grace. I am too bold, but I don't want to ask you again for this."[75] For his part Mendoza fondly referred to Lucrecia as a sister and also as an angel.[76]

In all, Mendoza seems to have become a surrogate father to Lucrecia, offering her the care, support, and attention she apparently never received from Alonso Franco. By placing their trust in Mendoza, both Lucrecia and her mother hoped to benefit from the patronage and support that his wealth and family connections could provide. In a way, history has proven them correct. Lucrecia would probably never have entered the historical record had the churchman not undertaken the transcription of her dreams. In this sense, Lucrecia is partly Mendoza's creation.

2

DREAMS DIABOLICAL, DREAMS DIVINE

When Calderón de la Barca's *La vida es sueño* was first performed in Madrid around the year 1636, few in the audience could have missed the significance of the play's most famous couplet, "La vida es sueño, / y los sueños sueños son" (Life is but a dream, and dreams are only dreams). Encapsulated here, of course, was the Christian idea that earthly life was only a passing phantasm in which one should not place much trust. More prosaically than Calderón, the moralist Juan de Pineda had commented a generation earlier that "dreams are many, some are vain and nonsensical, others make one foolish, and in still others people place their hopes and come up empty."[1] Popular proverbs offered similar advice: "De los sueños, cree lo menos" (Don't believe too much in dreams).

These admonitions notwithstanding, Spaniards, like most Europeans in the sixteenth century, and indeed most people everywhere, were fascinated by dreams. Dreams, they believed, had two sources, one natural and one supernatural. Regarding the natural causes of dreams, philosophers of the sixteenth century followed Aristotle's explanation of dreams as the product of sensory perceptions upon the anima, or "spirit," during sleep. But Renaissance literature on dreams also included a distinctly non-Aristotelian thesis: that some dreams had a supernatural source, either diabolical or divine. Lucrecia's trial, in effect, was an argument over whether her dreams were divinely inspired prophecies or messages from agents of the devil.

Dream Culture of Renaissance Spain

Just as many modern dream theories are essentially governed by the Freudian paradigm, early modern Europe had its own dream paradigm, the origins of which date to classical times. Though the continent was increasingly divided by religious wars, there existed what amounted to an international dream culture. Catholics and Calvinists, Germans and Spaniards—all shared essentially similar ideas about dreams.

At the core of this dream culture was the belief that dreams had certain practical uses, one of which was medical. Much as modern psychoanalysts use dream analysis as a guide to a patient's repressed thoughts and as an indicator of personality, so did Renaissance physicians use dreams to help diagnose the causes of certain bodily ailments. The theoretical rationale for this practice can be traced to Hippocrates (c. 460–370 B.C.), who regarded dreams as an index of physical health.[2] Some five centuries later Galen went a step further. Believing that disease resulted from imbalances among the various humors circulating through the body, Galen argued that most dreams had humoral sources and that their analysis could provide clues to the precise nature of a particular ailment.[3] Ideas derived from Galen concerning the diagnostic value of dreams changed little in the course of the next fifteen hundred years. Even as Giovanni Argenterio and other sixteenth-century physicians began to question Galen's humoral theory of disease, most medical practitioners continued to employ dream analysis as a diagnostic tool. The practice disappeared only at the end of the nineteenth century, when Freud shifted the medical focus of dream interpretation from the body to the mind.

In Renaissance dream theory, dreams were also viewed as a medium for prognostication. This form of dream interpretation originated in the ancient Middle East and by Hellenistic times had spawned a class of professional oneiromancers who made a living deciphering the confused imagery appearing in dreams and relating them to the life of the dreamer.[4] The most famous of these dream interpreters, and certainly the one most influential for later generations, was Artemidorus of Daldia, a second-century physician from Asia Minor. His treatise *Oneirocritica* was written as a defense of oneiromancy against its critics, but he also offered an elaborate, quasi-scientific typology of dreams and a detailed guide to their interpretation.[5]

By the sixteenth century the *Oneirocritica* was Europe's most popular guide to dream interpretation. Printed in Latin in 1518, it was quickly translated into English, French, and Italian and subsequently pirated and reprinted in a variety of widely circulated "dream-books" that offered stock interpretations for frequent and recurrent images such as water, fire, and blood. These manuals went by many names—*Clef des songes, The Wisdom of Solomon,* and *The Book of Daniel*—but together served as the major source of popular wisdom about dreams and evidently helped make oneiromancy a regular feature of daily life.[6] The León family, for example, regularly gathered to discuss the meaning and importance of Lucrecia's dreams, but similar conversations would have occurred in other houses, both rich and poor.[7]

Nor was talk about dreams limited to the home. Roman Catholic priests were instructed to become knowledgeable about dreams, to inquire about them in the confessional, and to be alert for dreams that might have a divine or diabolical source. Priests, therefore, necessarily served as dream interpreters for their parishioners. Confessors, however, faced competition from free-market dream analysts, village wizards, and "wise-women" who were usually called upon to help the dreamer decide upon some course of action, such as whom to marry or the advisability of undertaking a trip or some other risky enterprise. Juan Luis Vives dismissed these backyard dream interpreters as "soothsayers who predict the future for as little as a *blanca* [a small silver coin]."[8] Nevertheless, these local oneiromancers, mostly women, many of whom dabbled in other types of fortune-telling, were apparently ubiquitous. According to one estimate, Spain alone contained over ten thousand such individuals. The Catholic church, however, viewed these oneiromancers as linked to *conjuros,* or magic, and the Inquisition was asked to stamp them out.[9] Thus Leonor Barzana, a beata from Toledo, was twice arrested, in 1530 and again in 1537, on charges of variously using dreams, omens, stars, and spirits to divine the future.[10]

Secular critics of oneiromancy took their lead from Aristotle's discussion of dreams as natural sensory products whose significance was dubious. If prophetic dreams did occur, a possibility Aristotle was reluctant to admit, their interpretation was extremely difficult.[11] Such doubts about the prophetic value of dreams were seconded by a host of other ancient physicians and philosophers, but even the most skeptical of antiquity's dream critics allowed for the possibility that some dreams might have supernatural causes and that these "message dreams" might have a bearing upon future events.

Several neoplatonic writers of the late antique era pursued this theme, developing elaborate dream typologies. The most influential of these works was Macrobius's *Commentary on the Dream of Scipio,* which classified dreams into five types based on their prophetic content. According to his schema two types of dreams had no bearing on future events: the *insomnium* (nightmare) and the *visum* (phantasm), which Macrobius considered little more than a simple apparition. Prophetic dreams were divided into three distinct types: the *somnium,* or allegorical dream; the *visio,* a more literal, somewhat less enigmatic dream; and the *oraculum,* a message dream in which a warning concerning the future was provided by "a parent, or some other grave or holy person, or a priest."[12]

During the Middle Ages and the Renaissance most writers clung to Macrobius's fivefold division of prophetic and nonprophetic dreams, the only real change occurring when Scipion Dupleix (1569–1641), a French lawyer and amateur oneiromancer, responded to contemporary theological concern about Satan by adding a sixth category of diabolical dreams.[13] Otherwise, the dream typologies of sixteenth- and seventeenth-century Europe were simply variants of Macrobius's work.

Belief in the possibility of prophetic dreams was also reinforced by Christian theology. Taking their cue from the biblical dreams of Jacob and Joseph as well as from Numbers 12:5 ("Should there be a prophet among you, in visions I will reveal myself to him and in dreams I will speak to him"), early Christian writers from Tertullian to Gregory the Great acknowledged that the somnium could serve as a vehicle for divine revelation.

At the same time, however, most of the church fathers, like the ancients before them, had serious doubts about the nature, frequency, and importance of prophetic dreams. Augustine worried about the difficulty of differentiating "divine" dreams from those which had natural, that is, bodily causes, and he cautioned about the difficulty of distinguishing between true revelation and false.[14] Similar reservations about the prophetic uses of dreams can be found in other early Christian writings, but in general the church fathers acknowledged that dreams could serve as instruments of divine revelation.[15]

Medieval theologians basically agreed with the church fathers' position. Aquinas was generally critical of dreams as a tool of divination. He condemned as superstitious and unlawful those who knowingly used "natural" dreams for purposes of divination, attributing the desire to know the future to an express contract with the devil or a tacit diabolical pact by one who sought knowledge beyond ordinary human means. Yet Aquinas acknowledged that dreams had both internal and external causes—the latter including the stars, which had the power to influence the imagination—as well as spiritual causes, both diabolical and divine. He thus left open the possibility that God, either in person or through his angels, could communicate to individuals through dreams.[16]

Later theologians agreed with Aquinas on this essential point, but like Augustine before them found it difficult to distinguish the true prophet from the false. The first writer to establish guidelines for this purpose was Jean Gerson (1363–1429), chancellor of the University of Paris, who sought to provide the Council of Constance (1414–1417) with a way to judge the qualifications for canonization of Bridgit of Sweden. Gerson's contribution to the proceedings was two treatises, *De distinctione verarum visionum a falsis* and *De probatione spirituum*,[17] in which he argued that the only sure way to dispel uncertainty about visions and prophetic dreams was to "test the spirits to see whether they are of God" (1 John 4:1). He therefore recommended that both the contents of the vision and the personality of the alleged visionary be subjected to a series of rigorous tests, which he memorialized in a famous couplet:

Tu, quis, quid, quare,
Cui, qualiter, under, requiere.

You should seek who, what, why,
to whom, what kind, from whence.[18]

In the course of the fifteenth century *De probatione spirituum* and its companion treatise became a vademecum no confessor or inquisitor could be without. Gerson's writings directly influenced Jakob Sprenger, the German inquisitor responsible for the *Malleus Malificarum,* a witch-hunting tract first published in 1493. Gerson also had a profound effect on the Fifth Lateran Council, which in 1516 ordered bishops to investigate anyone who claimed prophetic knowledge on the basis of divine revelation.[19] In the seventeenth century Gerson's rules for distinguishing true visions from false appeared in the "Interrogatorio para la examen de revelaciones, visiones, y sueños," a set of instructions distributed to judges by the Spanish Inquisition.[20]

After Gerson, scholarly thinking about dreams was neither especially inventive nor original.[21] Except for a reaffirmation of the category of diabolical dreams, most of what was written on the subject was little more than a restatement of age-old beliefs. Physicians like Kaspar Peucer (1525–1602) in Germany, Giovanni Argenterio (1513–1572) and Girolamo Cardano (1501–1576) in Italy, as well as the French jurist, Jean Bodin (1530–1596), argued that dreams had multiple causes, both natural and supernatural, and generally acknowledged the possibility of prophetic dreams.[22] But by the end of the sixteenth century some authors expressed new skepticism about divinely inspired dreams as well as the use of dreams for purposes of divination. In 1584, for example, Reginald Scott, an English expert on witchcraft, wrote: "As for dreams, whatsoever credit is attributed to them proceedeth of follie; and they are fooles that trust in them, for which they have deceived many."[23]

From the early medieval period on, Spanish learned writers followed the trends in continental thought. In the seventh century, for example, St. Isidore of Seville included the *somnium* in a discussion of several types of prophecy. The *Setenario,* a book of laws compiled for King Alfonso X "the Learned" in the thirteenth century offered an Aristotelian description of dreams as natural phenomena caused by the "senses" as well as by the movement of the bodily humors.[24] Similar ideas are found in the "Libro del dormir y despertar y del soñar y adivinar y agueros y profecía," a work compiled for King Juan II of Castile in 1449, although its anonymous author allowed the possibility that some dreams might be of divine origin.[25]

Aristotle's influence can also be detected in later Spanish dream literature, notably in Vives's *Commentary on the Dream of Scipio* (1520), in which he argued that dreams should not be used for purposes of divination. Yet Vives, like most Renaissance writers, acknowledged the category of *somnium coeleste*, the dream inspired by God for some particular purpose, and was troubled by the difficulty of distinguishing such dreams from *somnium animale* and *somnium naturale*, let alone those inspired by Satan. A dream that appeared divinely inspired, he cautioned, might, upon close examination, turn out to have a diabolical source. Like Augustine before him, Vives found himself unable to offer any suggestions to help theologians distinguish the source of a dream, and he reluctantly concluded that "great confusion and discord reigns about the interpretation of dreams."[26]

The subject continued to invite learned speculation throughout the sixteenth century. Among the many treatises by Spanish authors, the most influential was Pedro Ciruelo's *Tratado en el qual se repruevan en todas las supersticiones y hechizerías* [Treatise Reproving All Superstitions and Forms of Witchcraft], reprinted eleven times between 1530 and 1577. A humanist who taught both philosophy and mathematics at the University of Alcalá de Henares, Ciruelo believed that dreams had three causes: natural, moral, and theological. Natural dreams were inconsequential, the result of humoral imbalances. Thus, a heavy meal before bed would cause an excess buildup of choler and overheat the body, producing dreams tinged with images of blood and fire. In moral dreams, a category roughly equivalent to Freud's day-residue dreams, the mind rehashes the experiences of the previous day. These moral dreams, according to Ciruelo, occurred especially to "men involved in business or education" who

> all day long expend a great deal of psychic energy in their occupations. Their imaginations are equally wrapped up in their affairs, not only while they are awake but also while they are asleep. At night, the imagination continues to be concerned with the day's preoccupations . . . thus it happens that individuals who are intensely preoccupied with commercial, legal, or intellectual problems often dream of solutions to their problems or make better decisions than while they were awake and weary of thinking about their problems.[27]

Finally, the theological or supernatural dream, the equivalent of Macrobius's somnium, was a revelation, either from Satan or God. Ciruelo cautioned that divinely inspired prophetic dreams were infrequent, occurring "only in a situation which concerns the common good of the people of God," and he warned that only trained theologians had the knowledge to distinguish between these dreams and "diabolic ones" concerned with "frivolous events."[28]

Although other Spanish authors proposed additional criteria for understanding the nature and origin of dreams, they shared Ciruelo's belief that dreams had two possible sources: the imagination, or anima, as affected by the humors, daily preoccupations, and other sensory perceptions; and supernatural forces that had the power to send messages to selected individuals during sleep. But scholarly opinion about message dreams remained divided, with some sixteenth-century Spanish philosophers accepting the notion of prophetic dreams while simultaneously condemning the use of dreams for purposes of divination.[29]

Speculation about the sources and interpretation of dreams was not a topic confined to a learned elite. Lucrecia's trial record indicates that her family and friends defined various categories of dreams that roughly approximated the scholars' typologies. These included *niñerías* (childish fantasies), *borracherías* (alcohol-induced dreams), and others for which there was no apparent explanation.[30] The testimony of Lucrecia's mother included a discussion of dreams as nighttime thoughts about events and ideas experienced during the day and her opinion that the court should dismiss Lucrecia's dreams as trivial childish fantasies because children's dreams are not as orderly or systematic as those of adults.[31] Yet she was disturbed by her daughter's dreams about the deaths of kings and queens, evidently believing that they had a supernatural source. Indeed, the recurrence of these unsettling dreams had once prompted Ana Ordoñez to offer prayers for their cessation.[32]

To Lucrecia's judges as well, the manifest political content of her dreams would have suggested a supernatural source, rather than an internal humoral cause. That the dreams repeated themselves, night after night, also hinted at a supernatural agent.[33] Furthermore, Lucrecia's piety, her reputation as an honest doncella, and the fact that her dreams came "with great calm and tranquillity" and without frightening her implied a divine, rather than a diabolical, source.[34] Her lack of schooling and supposed ignorance of letters pointed to the same conclusion, for she was judged incapable of inventing such complex images by herself. Yet some of Lucrecia's offhand remarks indicate that she may have understood contemporary theories about the source of dreams and cultivated the image of herself as an ignorant, pious doncella in order to enhance her prophetic credentials.

Lucrecia's Dream History

Ana Ordoñez testified that the dreams began when Lucrecia was seven. Similar information came from a neighbor who stated that the dreams started when Lucrecia attained the "use of reason," a stage in life then associated with the age of six or seven.[35] But Lucrecia's own answers to questions about the onset of her dreams were far less precise. More than once she informed the Holy Office that she was only a child ("niña") when the dreams began, yet on other occasions she testified that they started when she reached sixteen.[36] Evidently, she told a similar story to Vitores, who informed the Holy Office that she was seventeen when the dreams began.[37]

These inconsistencies may simply be a matter of terminology. Strictly speaking, in the sixteenth century "niña" applied to girls under the age of ten, and "doncella" to girls and unmarried young women between the ages of ten and twenty. But in popular usage almost any unmarried young woman might be called niña. Another explanation of Lucrecia's contradictory answers, however, would attribute them to her defense strategy. Apparently, she wanted the inquisitors to believe that the dreams were a recent and wholly spontaneous phenomenon rather than fictions she had consciously invented over time.

Be that as it may, Lucrecia's prophetic dreams almost certainly date from early adolescence. Her father testified that when Lucrecia was twelve, in fall 1580, she experienced a dream that he understood to be prophetic. At the time, Philip II was traveling from Madrid to Lisbon in order to lay claim to the Portuguese crown and he had fallen gravely ill in Badajoz. Lucrecia's dream involved a vision of a royal funeral procession in Badajoz. After hearing this dream, Alonso Franco recalled asking Lucrecia whether the funeral was for the monarch, and Lucrecia said no. He reacted angrily, first by punishing her for dreaming—we do not know how—and then by instructing her not to dream any more. Yet Alonso Franco also admitted to having been amazed when, several weeks after this incident, news arrived that Philip's queen, Anne of Austria, had died in Badajoz.[38]

Precociousness similarly marked the lives of many other female visionaries and seers. The visions of the fifteenth-century mystic Margaret of Ypres, for example, began when she was five; Catherine of Siena's started at the age of ten; and Joan of Arc had her first visions at thirteen. The early spiritual awakening of these women is not easily explained, although it may be related to their urge to establish an identity independent of their families.

Despite her father's admonitions and punishments, Lucrecia continued to experience prophetic dreams. As she put it, "Since I was small and began to understand these dreams, my parents beat me for talking about them."[39] Unfortunately, little is known about the subject matter of these early dreams, but, as noted above, they were sufficiently out of the ordinary that her mother felt obliged to pray for them to stop. The implication, then, is that Lucrecia was not punished for the act of dreaming but for the unusual content of her dreams, which her father feared might attract the Inquisition's attention, especially if she talked too much about them. Yet the continuing punishments may also have been motivated by Alonso Franco's desire to exert continued control over his eldest child, to discourage her from mounting any challenge to his paternal authority.

As Lucrecia grew older, the dreams continued and so did her predilection for communicating their substance to others. Friends and relatives visiting her house listened to her recount what she claimed to have dreamed, and it was one of these casual conversations that led to the start of Lucrecia's prophetic career. The fateful discussion took place early in September 1587 when Juan de Tebes, a relative of Ana Ordoñez, stopped by the León household for a drink of water and an afternoon chat. According to one version of this conversation, the talk turned to the subject of Lucrecia's dreams. When Tebes expressed interest in learning more about them, Lucrecia initially replied, "Only some diabolical rubbish."[40] But Tebes wanted more detail, at which she confessed to recently having a strange dream in which a man who resembled Piedrola, Madrid's soldier-prophet, could be seen spewing wheat and then milk out of his mouth.

Tebes, then in the service of don Alonso de Mendoza, one of Piedrola's ardent supporters, dutifully told his master about Lucrecia's unusual vision. Almost immediately, Mendoza summoned Lucrecia to his quarters in Madrid and asked her to recount this dream along with any others she might have had.[41] Fascinated by what he heard, but also worried, Mendoza introduced Lucrecia to Fray Lucas de Allende, another of Piedrola's supporters. At this meeting Lucrecia reportedly told the friar that "I am the girl don Alonso told you about, and I have so many dreams and visions about the loss of Spain that I do not know what to do."[42]

Mendoza first instructed Lucrecia to keep silent about the dreams and especially not to speak about them to anyone "who would not view them in God's service."[43] Then, in quick succession, he arranged for Allende to become Lucrecia's confessor, offered alms to the León family, and made preparations to have the dreams transcribed on a regular basis. He also consulted with his own confessor, a Discalced Carmelite known only as Fray Juan Bautista, in order to determine whether the work of transcription could be justified on theological grounds. The friar, evidently intrigued by the possibility that the unusual dreams might have a divine source, advised that Mendoza should copy them "even though they aren't anything more than chivalric tales."[44]

Mendoza lost little time getting to work. By the beginning of October he was seen entering Lucrecia's house on a regular basis. Lucrecia's sisters stated that he usually arrived in the morning and then, off in a corner of the apartment's *sala* but still within earshot, proceeded to write as Lucrecia recited what she had dreamed the previous night. On 5 December 1587, for example, he wrote, "I went to visit her at 10 A.M. in order to find out if she had dreamed and to write it."[45] Occasionally, Mendoza was heard to ask questions and ask for clarification about specific points, and on some days the work of transcription lasted several hours.

According to Lucrecia, this morning ritual constituted part of confession, or at least this is how she later justified her behavior to the Inquisition: "I told them the dreams in confession."[46] Nonetheless, she told Mendoza and Allende that she was afraid the dream transcriptions could lead to trouble with the Holy Office. Both churchmen attempted to reassure her that nothing was amiss. Allende, an experienced confessor, put it gently, "The Inquisition has no interest in these dreams unless you believe in them; they are not against the faith."[47] Mendoza was rather more blunt, saying that "if there was anything in these dreams that the Inquisition would be concerned about, he himself would personally drag her by the ears to the Inquisition."[48]

Despite these assurances, Lucrecia sought the advice of other clergymen, especially that of Fray Gerónimo de Aguiar, the Dominican who had previously served as her confessor. Aguiar, in line with his order's suspicion of unorthodox spirituality and its attendant superstitions, strongly urged Lucrecia to put an end to the copying, warning that "they would all be arrested by the Inquisition."[49] This advice, however, was countermanded by three mysterious men who appeared with such regularity in Lucrecia's dreams that she called them her "ordinary companions." Her dreams, they told her, were vital to Spain's future and needed to be communicated to the king. They also advised her to trust Mendoza and Allende, both of whom were theologians versed in the rules and regulations of the church. In one dream, on 21 November 1587, two of the Three Men even staged a debate to discuss whether Lucrecia should follow the advice of Aguiar or Allende. The man known as the Young Fisherman argued that Lucrecia should tell Aguiar about the dreams "because he understands these things very well," while his adversary, called the Old Fisherman, insisted that she should trust only Allende. Acting as the judge of this oneiric debate, Lucrecia rendered an initial judgment against Aguiar by stating that "it would not be good to tell everything to him." Four nights later, in her dream of 25 November, the Young Fisherman restated his case and even promised Lucrecia great riches if she opted for Aguiar. But Lucrecia held fast and confirmed her previous decision by announcing, "I do not want to, nor is it my will [to tell Aguiar], because I have been ordered not to do so." Presumably, these orders came from the figure she called the Ordinary Man, the third and, as we shall see, the most influential of the Three Men.

This particular dream marks an important turning point in Lucrecia's nascent prophetic career. Up to this point she had been somewhat reluctant to have Allende and Mendoza transcribe her dreams, and her doubts about the propriety of this unusual enterprise were not entirely offset by her desire to obey the Ordinary Man. In her dream of 6 December 1587, for example, Lucrecia encounters a man, bound in chains, who can be identified as Piedrola, the soldier-prophet she had dreamed about earlier and whose arrest the Inquisition had ordered on 18 September 1587. He warns Lucrecia: "Be careful how you tell these things; you now see what has happened to Piedrola." Despite this admonition, most of Lucrecia's reservations seem by this time to have disappeared. Indeed, Lucrecia became quite eager for night to come "so that she could see her ordinary companions."[50] And, according to Mendoza, she was quite anxious to have the dreams transcribed. "Something I consider mysterious and worthy of considerable reflection and thought," Mendoza wrote in a memo, "is that after she has had a dream and this has not been written within a day or so, she is very nervous on account of her strong desire to tell it and have it written."[51]

Mendoza was also impressed by Lucrecia's extraordinary capacity to remember her dreams. At her trial various witnesses corroborated his description of her particular skills:

> She remembers not only the general themes but also precise words that they [the Three Men] tell her, particulars about the people she sees—their faces, dress, colors of their clothing—animals and birds, the design of buildings, the location of rivers, mountains, valleys, trees, [illegible word], cities, castles, churches, roads, seacoasts, islands, and other places where they take her in imagination, as well as the names of these places, even though most of these things she has never seen or heard about before, because her estate and profession and the conversation she has had with the people with whom she has been brought up have not given her an opportunity to know such things. Yet she recounts them as if she were reading a paper and was a very good reader, but the truth is that when she began to have these visions she could only read a little and could not write with anything like the skill and ease noted above. In any event, once the dream is dictated and transcribed, it is erased from memory, as if she had never dreamed or imagined it. Of this, I am an excellent witness.[52]

Mendoza's high opinion of Lucrecia was obviously colored by his belief that her dreams were inspired by a divine source, but even if Lucrecia did not actually dream everything attributed to her, the dream registers indicate that she had a unique ability to invent what others took to be dreams. In December 1587, the first full calendar month for which we have a dream register, she is recorded as having dreamed at least one dream each night, and for the 28th and 29th, she remembered two dreams. She admitted to finding this nighttime activity somewhat exhausting, and in the dream of 7 December she implored her nocturnal visitors "not to come anymore; I don't want to dream more dreams."

Her protest notwithstanding, the registers show that December 1587 brought Lucrecia thirty-four dreams, and January 1588 brought another thirty-five. In March 1588 she reported thirty-nine dreams, but thereafter the pace dropped off quickly. For May 1588 only six dreams are recorded, and for the next eighteen months her dream production remained well below the levels reached when the transcriptions first began.

This decrease can be partly attributed to a serious illness, the first symptoms of which appeared on 23 March 1588. Allende reported that there was no dream that night because Lucrecia was ill. She was still indisposed the following day, but did have a dream in which she successively saw a procession of flagellants marching through the streets of Madrid, visited the chapel of the Hospital de la Corte in order to receive the holy sacrament, and finally walked to the Puerta del Sol to witness a performance by a troop of Moorish dancers. The following week the illness took a turn for the worse and Lucrecia was confined to bed. By 2 April her condition had deteriorated further, and in her dream that night the Three Men covered her with *lienzos,* the linen cloths in which Castilians traditionally wrapped the bodies of their dead. Subsequently, in her dream of 15 May, after Lucrecia complained of a painful earache ("tengo un dolor de oído muy recio"), the Three Men asserted that her illness would continue until she reached the age of twenty, or for almost another year. In the meantime, Allende wrote to Mendoza on 12 April that "our sister Lucrecia is very ill and very weak," noting that she was suffering from "llagas" (sores) in her throat.[53] Other symptoms included the "achaque de cabeza" (headache) reported on 18 April, and intermittent periods of fever.[54] Alarmed by Lucrecia's worsening condition, the two churchmen arranged to have two prominent court physicians examine her. Lucrecia was subsequently purged and bled, although it is not known to what effect.

In addition to her physical ailments Lucrecia seems to have

been suffering from some kind of mental depression. Allende suggested as much in an undated letter, written sometime in April 1588, which informed Mendoza that "Lucrecia is very ill, filled with sadness."[55] The fragmentary nature of the evidence makes it impossible to determine the cause of her illness, which she later told the Inquisition had lasted for fourteen months. We do know that in February 1588, several weeks prior to the onset of her illness, the vicar of Madrid, alarmed by reports of her prophetic dreams, placed Lucrecia under house arrest. (The details of this incident are related in chapter 5.) Conceivably, Lucrecia's encounter with the vicar triggered a depression that contributed to her illness and also interfered with her dreaming. Alternatively, repression—rather than depression—may have caused her ailments. As we have seen, Lucrecia had been aware of the dangers of talking about her dreams, but the house arrest was the first time that religious authorities punished her for dreaming. Perhaps the headaches and sore throats, then, were induced by the stressfulness of her predicament.

Whatever the source of her illness, Lucrecia was on the road to recovery by fall 1589, at which point the dream registers fill quickly. By March 1590 the number of dreams approached her pre-illness pace. But in May 1590 she was arrested. During her first week in prison, she admitted to one or two dreams, but then the dreams stopped. In total, the records report on 415 dreams, nearly all of which in one way or another concerned the future of Spain.

The Dream Registers

The principal source of information about Lucrecia's dreams is a series of thirty dream registers seized by agents of the Inquisition in the house of Alonso de Mendoza on 21 May 1590. These notebooks contain records of Lucrecia's dreams from 1 December 1587 to 18 April 1590. In addition, the Inquisition confiscated other papers of dreams recorded both before and after these dates.

These registers, which came to form the basis of the Inquisition's trial against Lucrecia, represent a collaborative effort on the part of Mendoza, Allende, and a number of other copyists. Mendoza served as Lucrecia's first amanuensis and recorded the dream transcriptions dating from late September and October 1587. Allende also copied a number of dreams during October 1587, and when Mendoza was obliged to leave Madrid for Toledo, he asked his friend to continue the transcriptions. Within a few weeks, however, Allende developed second thoughts about his involvement in this curious project. After listening to Lucrecia relate a dream in which she described the interior of his cell—supposedly, a room she had not yet seen—Allende destroyed all the dream texts in his possession, asserting that the dreams were only a girl's foolish fantasies. When Mendoza learned about this loss, he immediately rushed back to Madrid and asked Lucrecia to reconstruct at least the general themes of the dream texts Allende had destroyed. But Lucrecia had difficulty remembering what she had related to Allende and was able to supply only fragments of the dreams dating from October and November 1587.

In the meanwhile, Mendoza pressed Allende to resume the work. The arguments he used to convince the friar are not on record, but within a few days Allende apparently regretted his impetuous act. In a memorandum of 17 November 1587, he expressly referred to Lucrecia as "an honorable woman in whom I have full confidence."[56] Mendoza soon returned to Toledo and in a note attached to the dream of 25 November indicated his satisfaction with Allende's work. "From this dream onwards," he wrote, "the copying is done with considerable care and thus things appear more coherent and less confused."[57] So it is only at this point, roughly two months after the first dreams were copied and coincidental with Lucrecia's own decision to trust Allende, that the registers are relatively complete.

For the next nineteen months Allende served as Lucrecia's principal scribe, personally recording over three-quarters of the 415 dreams attributed to her. The other dreams were written down by temporary copyists brought in whenever Allende was ill or otherwise occupied. His helpers included Guillén de Casaos, his astrologer friend; Domingo Navarro, a soldier turned faith-healer; and Juan de Trijueque, a royal police officer (*alguacil de corte*) who copied several dreams in December 1587 and January 1588. Additional assistance came from Sacamanchas, the dry cleaner whom Allende had previously befriended on account of their mutual interest in the visions of the Nun of Lisbon. Sacamanchas copied at least fifty dreams between February and November 1588, but was dismissed after the dream of 6 November 1588 in which one of the Three Men announced that Sacamanchas was guilty of having "diabolical illusions" and failing to copy the dreams correctly.[58] Henceforth, Allende did most of the transcribing himself, often staying up at night to prepare copies to forward to Mendoza in Toledo. But even Allende was prone to mistakes. Mendoza, for example, criticized him for the "disorderly" way the dream of 3 November 1589 had been copied and complained that, because of Allende's carelessness, "this dream confuses me and takes away my interest in interpreting it because I cannot know the exact sequence of events."[59] Despite these occasional errors, Allende remained on the job until March 1590, when he turned to Vitores for aid. Vitores began work on 11 March 1590 and continued as Lucrecia's chief scribe until he was arrested on 25 May 1590.

Despite the intervention of so many hands, the format of the dream registers is surprisingly uniform. Mendoza had evidently prepared a set of instructions (now lost) outlining the form the transcriptions were to follow and the specific information he wanted recorded. He was especially interested in the cut and color of the clothes worn by the Three Men and in the costumes of other individuals. After learning, for example, that a man who appeared in one dream was dressed in the habit of one of Spain's military orders and that this uniform had *lechuguillas* (small, flat collar ruffs), Mendoza drew sketches of the costumes of two of these orders to show to Lucrecia "to see if she could remember exactly what he wore."[60] Presumably, Mendoza wanted this information in order to determine the identity of individuals who appeared in the dreams. He also knew that church authorities would probe for such details before pronouncing her dreams to be authentic prophecies. Further, he wanted visual details so that he could commission paintings of those dreams he considered especially noteworthy—a project that may have begun at Lucrecia's request, since in the dream of 10 November 1589 one of the Three Men ordered Mendoza "to paint all the images I have already sent" as well as "a portrait of Pharaoh crossing a red sea." A few months later, Mendoza wrote to Vitores:

> I have commissioned paintings of [Lucrecia's] principal visions; therefore, it is necessary to know the places indicated, whether to the east or to the north; the hands, whether left or right; the color of hair and of clothes; and the animals and birds that appear. These things often have great significance. Accordingly, you must take note of these things when you write, asking her about these details when she herself does not mention them.[61]

In addition to the visual details, Mendoza wanted to know the precise time at which each dream had occurred. According to oneirocritical theory, dreams that occurred shortly before waking were less significant. Whenever possible, Lucrecia's copyists included this information, and the registers indicate that most of Lucrecia's dreams took place during the night sleep ("at midnight," "at 3 A.M.," "after I fell back asleep"), with some occurring just before she awoke ("at 5 A.M.," "in the morning," "before I awoke," "just before waking," "at 6 A.M. after being up all night with a high fever"). Lucrecia also had dreams during her regular afternoon nap. On 18 April 1590 she specifically remembered a dream that occurred "after eating, when I fell asleep at the table, my head resting on my folded arms." On other days she dreamed "after finishing lunch," "in the afternoon, when I normally fall asleep," or "during afternoon nap, at 5 P.M."

Each time a dream was recorded by someone other than Mendoza, the original copy was dispatched immediately by private courier to him in Toledo. He checked the transcription and marked off portions he considered especially significant; these he later reviewed with Lucrecia in person.[62] During his occasional visits to Madrid he also copied certain dreams that Allende was reluctant to transcribe, such as one of 17 March 1588, which contained the names of many individuals ("personas particulares"), along with dreams of a personal nature that Lucrecia preferred to relate only to Mendoza. In one such dream, which occurred at 6 A.M. on 6 March 1588, Lucrecia and Mendoza had a tiff after she refused to marry Guillén de Casaos, whom Mendoza had designated as her mate. The register reads: "I, don Alonso, wrote this [dream], after she told me that she would tell it only to me because it seemed to her to touch on personal matters and not things pertaining to the king, the destruction of Spain, and its restoration."

Once he had verified the text, Mendoza proceeded to interpret the dream as best he could. The margins of the dream registers are filled with hastily scribbled glosses, written both in Latin and Castilian, that assign names and attach symbolic meanings to the phantasmagoria of figures and images. Mendoza was quick to speculate that the man wearing "lechuguillas" was the royal chamberlain, Alonso de Zúñiga. A more stubborn image was that of an artichoke at the head of the king's bed, its leaves deftly removed by royal tax collectors while Philip was sleeping (dream of 19 January 1588). Mendoza interpreted this image as a sign of ministerial corruption and the theft of "the king's hacienda, which is composed of a thousand different revenues and many taxes." More speculative is his identification of the "boy who sings happy songs" in the dream of 2 March 1590 as "the figure of the just king whom God will send to his people" or the dove in this dream as a hieroglyph of the victory of God. In the dream of 4 March 1590, a woman dressed in widow's black and wearing an emerald collar and carrying a sword informs the monarch: "I come, Philip, to take away your *vara* [staff] of justice." Mendoza identifies the woman as divine justice, her jewels a sign of God's mercy, the vara a symbol of the king's power.

Mendoza cross-referenced the principal images, taking particular care to note figures who appeared in more than one dream. He also compared the visions with those in the Bible, the books of the Apocrypha, and other prophetic texts, again for interpretative purposes and as a means of ascertaining whether the dreams had a divine source. The concordances between Lucrecia's dreams and the Book of Esdras struck him as especially important, partly because Mendoza believed the former could help elucidate the meaning of the latter.[63] Finally, he prepared a special index to the dreams, a notebook later described by the Inquisition as "an alphabetical table of the notable things in the dreams."[64] Once this work was completed, fair copies of the dream texts were neatly entered into a series of special registers.

These fair copies are arranged chronologically, starting 1 December 1587 and ending 15 May 1590. Each dream is dated, although there are occasional mix-ups as to the precise day on which a particular dream had been copied. Some of the dreams fill no more than a page of text; others, four or five. A comparison of the final copies and the preliminary working versions Mendoza used indicates only minimal textual variations.

These registers, the transcriptions of over four hundred dreams in nearly one thousand pages of closely written text, represent a unique historical document. Although Catholics were admonished to tell their confessors about their dreams, only rarely were these dreams recorded. And no more than a handful of Renaissance diarists made a conscientious effort to keep track of their dreams, in most cases transcribing only those they considered unusual or alarming. For example, Girolamo Cardano, a sixteenth-century Italian physician and a specialist in dream interpretation, included a record of fifty-five of his dreams in his study of the dream theories of the ancient writer Synesius.[65] Archbishop William Laud of England kept a diary from 1623 to 1643, but recorded only those dreams, thirty-two in all, he considered particularly unpleasant—one in which the Anglican prelate saw himself converting to Roman Catholicism—or disturbing, one in which the duke of Buckingham climbed into Laud's bed.[66] Another seventeenth-century English diarist who recorded some of his dreams was the Puritan pastor Ralph

Josselin, but he included only disturbing dreams and those he thought might have a divine source.[67]

In contrast, ordinary day-residue dreams and those that touched on matters of sexual fantasy and personal anxieties were considered of minor importance and generally went unrecorded. The husband of Alice Thornton, a seventeenth-century English noblewoman, told her to forget her dreams, and most Europeans of the era seemed to believe that dreams had natural causes and therefore contained nothing worth remembering. The registers of Lucrecia's dreams thus represent a resource without parallel in the annals of European history.[68]

But were the dreams recorded in the registers actual dreams, as opposed to daytime reveries? And were they entirely Lucrecia's or were they, as the Inquisition phrased it, purposely invented with Allende's and Mendoza's help? These questions baffled the inquisitors assigned to the case, and each time they asked Lucrecia to explain whether she had invented the dreams while awake or whether they had come to her during sleep, she avoided giving them a straight answer.

Given the sheer number and repetitive nature of the dreams, it is tempting to assume that some of them were either daydreams or conscious inventions. But Lucrecia, her parents, her neighbors, her friends, as well as Mendoza and Allende, believed that her dreams were true dreams. Even Lucrecia's critics and her inquisitors never totally dismissed the possibility that at least some of her dreams were truly somnia.

A related question is whether the registers are accurate transcriptions of what Lucrecia dreamed or thought she had dreamed. The transcribed dreams manifest many of the confusing and repetitive features of "real" dreams; yet it is hard to imagine that in recounting her dreams Lucrecia abstained from all embroidering. At the very least, she gave them a narrative framework and an internal coherence that dreams so often lack. In this sense, all of Lucrecia's dreams had elements of invention, conscious additions that made her accounts intelligible to others.[69] As for the question of accuracy, her scribes often transposed her first-person narrative into the third person, further altering, however slightly, her actual oral accounts. In this detail, the written dream registers vary somewhat from her dictated statements.

To the Holy Office, however, Lucrecia testified that the dreams in the registers differed from those she remembered as having experienced. She also testified that the two churchmen introduced various details into the dream texts that she had never dreamed. Allende and Mendoza vehemently denied this accusation, claiming that apart from the irregularities in the dreams copied by Sacamanchas, the transcriptions were faithful and precise.

Despite Lucrecia's testimony, the inquisitors were inclined to assign full responsibility for the dreams' contents to her. At one point in the trial, upon discovering a note from Mendoza that referred to the plain style ("estilo llano") in which Lucrecia customarily related the dreams, the inquisitors specifically noted, "Look, it seems that don Alonso cannot be the author of the dreams."[70] But the court's repeated attempts to resolve the issue of authorship were unsuccessful, and in the end the inquisitors decided to sidestep the question, concluding only that they could not be sure who was responsible for what.

Clearly, Lucrecia's knowledge of dreams and prophecy would have influenced the character of her dreams. Perhaps Mendoza added some details to enhance the dreams' authenticity, to endow them with greater authoritativeness and increase their public appeal. But it would be wrong to label the dreams as literary fictions purposely invented for political aims. Lucrecia was known for her dreams long before they were transcribed, and their antiauthoritarian message fits well with what we know of her personality. Still, after Mendoza's arrival Lucrecia may have tailored her dictation to suit what she perceived as the churchman's interests.

Unquestionably, Lucrecia and her scribes intended to make the public aware of the dreams; the registers were not kept solely for Mendoza's private study. We might therefore include Lucrecia's dreams within the genre of fictive dreams, in which an individual uses the dream form to communicate ideas that conveyed by other means might prove dangerous.[71] But for Lucrecia, Allende, Mendoza, Vitores, and Casaos the dream form proved dangerous as well. Whether the dreams were invented or real, whether they were entirely Lucrecia's or partly Mendoza's, their message was readily accepted by many who heard them—and it was the popularity of the dreams' critique of Philip that provoked the arrest of Lucrecia and her associates.

3

"I WAKE UP THE MOMENT MY EYES ARE CLOSED"

The transcribed versions of Lucrecia's dreams are written in what Mendoza referred to as "estilo llano," a plain or unadorned style,[1] a phrase intended to distinguish the colloquial language of Lucrecia's dictations from the consciously artistic, highly mannered style of courtly or literary Castilian. Indeed, in syntax and tone, the texts of the dreams approximate written speech. The syntax is simple, rhetorical flourishes are few, and the diction is generally appropriate to a woman of Lucrecia's age and background. For example, the dreams are filled with references to contemporary dress, such as *chapines grandes* (high-heeled shoes), *gregüescoes* (men's breeches), and *lechuguillas* (lace ruffs); everyday foods like *besugo* (seabream), *chorizo* (a type of sausage), and *rábanos* (radishes); and such mundane items as a *cesta de gallinas* (basket used to carry chickens to market).

The conversational quality of the dream transcripts is reinforced by the essentially descriptive and narrative mode of presentation. The dreams sound less like an artfully designed narrative than a series of dialogues spoken between Lucrecia and the Three Men. Scene follows scene in which Lucrecia states, "The Ordinary Man told me that," "I saw that," "He showed me," and so on. Thus as one reads the dreams, one is also listening to Lucrecia recite them to one of her scribes, and at times it seems almost possible to hear Lucrecia's voice. Nonetheless, we cannot discount the possibility that Mendoza, acting on the premise that simplicity and ignorance can be a sign of divine favor, contrived to have the dream registers recorded in a plain style.

Intermixed with everyday language, however, are terms that

can be described as a prophetic lexicon: *castigo* (punishment), *trabajos* (sufferings), *guerra* (war), *peste* (plague), and other words associated with apocalyptic and millennial writing occur repeatedly. So do words of a redemptive character, among them *misericordia* (mercy), *penitencia* (penitence, repentance), and *restauración* (restoration). How Lucrecia learned these vocabularies, the prophetic and the redemptive, remains a mystery, and Mendoza himself once admitted that "the language of her dreams was different from that of her natural, ordinary speech."[2] In this regard, he was probably correct when he attributed some of Lucrecia's diction and expressions to those she had heard at mass, in sermons, and at other church services.[3]

On balance, though, the dream texts have a chatty, conversational, almost familiar tone. Throughout, for example, Lucrecia and her three night visitors address one another in the second person, *tú* and *os* (*vosotros*), rather than in the more formal third person. The dream conversations between Lucrecia and King Philip and Isabella are also conducted in the familiar, as if to suggest that the customary, more formal mode of earthly address, and the differences in rank and status it implies, is suspended in Lucrecia's imaginary world.

One syntactical aspect of the dream registers deserves comment inasmuch as it suggests that Mendoza did, on occasion at least, play an editor's role. There is little doubt that Lucrecia related all of the dreams in the first person, but some of the earliest dream transcriptions, those from November and December 1587, are recorded in the third person. So instead of "The Ordinary Man visited me," they read, "She said that the Ordinary Man visited her." This disjunction is partly mechanical, a function of the work of transcription. Yet it also relates to Allende's and possibly Mendoza's initial uncertainties about whether the ultimate source of the dreams was divine or diabolical. By employing the third person, the two copyists in effect distanced themselves from the oneiric narrative and insinuated that they were simply the transcribers of what Lucrecia told them.

Yet, as we have seen, by January 1588 Allende expressed new confidence in Lucrecia. Mendoza, who always had been more of a believer in Lucrecia's prophetic powers than his Franciscan collaborator, now wrote, referring to the dreams: "All is divine prophecy about our times and I dare to call her a divine prophet." The churchmen's new resolve exactly coincides with the change in the registers from the third person to the first, a change consistent with what Mendoza believed to be "the style of the prophets of antiquity and especially that of book four of Esdras [now 2 Esdras]."[4] Henceforward, all the dreams are recorded in the first person, and transcripts of the early dreams were redacted to reflect this new prophetic mode.

This change from the reportorial third person to the prophetic first person, then, was motivated by Mendoza's sense of how a divinely inspired dream should sound. Furthermore, the stylistic change was made at the moment that Allende began to circulate copies of these texts among his friends and acquaintances at court. Like other revered prophets and visionaries, both ancient and modern, Lucrecia would convey her heaven-sent messages in the first person.

Some of the imagery of the dreams also partakes of a recognizable prophetic tradition. Angels, beasts, and dragons resembling those in the Book of Revelation, chapter 13 appear in the dreams as do images from 2 Esdras, the apocryphal biblical text that Mendoza mentions as a model of biblical prophecy. In the dream of 18 May 1589, for example, a huge eagle appears, holding the world in its claws, a variation of Esdras's vision of an eagle with twelve wings and three heads. At the trial Guillén de Casaos described a conversation he had with Lucrecia comparing the eagles in Esdras and the eagle on the Habsburg armorial shield. After that talk, he said, "she began to dream about [eagles] without stopping."[5]

Despite such resonances, Lucrecia's dreams are far more than a distilled, bowdlerized version of the standard canon of Christian apocalpytic and millennial literature. The dreams contain a curious and somewhat unusual mixture of images drawn from Lucrecia's experiences in Madrid, court gossip, the oral literature of the *romances,* church decoration and other sacred images, sermons, and religious processions. Medieval legends may have also inspired her: Lucrecia's image of herself atop a white horse, leading an army to rescue Toledo from its enemies, closely resembles various chronicles in which Santiago, Spain's patron saint, miraculously appears riding a white charger to rally the Christians in their battles against the Moors.

This peculiar blend of oral and written, artistic and impressionistic, sacred and profane imagery must be attributed in part to Lucrecia's powers of absorption and imagination. To her contemporaries, the complexity and subject matter of her dreams rendered her something of an oddity, possibly even a prodigy, an unlettered woman endowed with the intelligence of a learned man. According to humoral theory, women were supposed to be more imaginative, but less rational, than men. Intelligence was thought to be influenced by bodily heat; since men, on average, were hot and dry, women cold and moist, the latter supposedly lacked sufficient warmth either to possess true wisdom or to generate rational thought. Yet exceptions to the general rule were believed to occur regularly, especially during adolescence, when the bodily humors associated with adult men and women were not yet fully developed.[6] Excessive sleep was also thought to reinforce natural heat. To her contemporaries, then, a somnolent teenage girl like Lucrecia might have appeared to be a "creative spirit," as defined by one influential writer of the period: "[someone] who can conceive—without art or study—extraordinarily refined, prodigious ideas that have never been seen, heard, or written about."[7]

But was Lucrecia truly an *ingenia,* one of those rare individuals capable of inventing ideas and concepts entirely on her own? This was certainly Mendoza's image of her, and at one point he stated that her *ignorancia,* or lack of letters, represented the source of her knowledge.[8] But even the most skeptical of Lucrecia's judges must have been impressed by the imaginative powers demonstrated in her dream of 24 November 1589, in which she debates three university professors. The dream conversation proceeds as follows:

Professor [speaking to Lucrecia]: Where did you study, [the university of] Alcalá or Salamanca?

Lucrecia: That is the question of an ignorant doctor. Can't you see that I have academic robes from several universities? And if you don't believe me, give me a book and you'll see if I can give you a summary.

Professor: No one from either of these universities has been your master; you have learned supernatural wisdom at night.

Another professor: Who has been your master?

Lucrecia: The Lion Man [a reference to one of the Three Men].

In the dream's next scene she accepts these professors' challenge to debate "casos de conciencia," moral issues whose discussion was reserved for philosophers, theologians, and priests. Her imagination, she implies, affords her knowledge as authoritative as that taught in the universities. That her wisdom was equal to the knowledge of learned men was a point she was also prepared to argue with the Inquisition, as revealed in a conversation with her mother in January 1588.

> I will tell everyone that I dream, and if they take me before the tribunals I will tell them that they [the Three Men] make visions which otherwise I do not see. I will also be happy to tell them that I do not pretend to dream. I don't know where the dreams come from, since I do not solicit them nor do I want them. And then what harm is there in talking about them? If there is anything else involved, I will not rest until God teaches me about it, since I do not wish to separate myself from the church.[9]

Allende, who witnessed and wrote down this discussion, added that Lucrecia spoke with such conviction that "it seems that she is not the one who says these things."

Structure: The Didactic Dream

Despite the apparent originality of Lucrecia's nocturnal imagination, her dreams do have structural and thematic similarities to various literary dreams, especially those found in such classics as the *Romance of the Rose, The Pearl,* Chaucer's *Book of the Duchess,* and Langland's *Piers Plowman.* In this genre the dreamer-author typically encounters an authoritative figure who serves as the dreamer's guide and instructor during a series of special journeys. In *The Pearl* the dreamer is transported by the Queen of Courtesy to the Heavenly Jerusalem, while the poet in *Piers Plowman* is the pupil of such figures as Lady Holy Church, Reason, and Charity. The dreamer, in turn, is expected to convey the didactic message to others by recounting what has been learned.

The guide-instructors in Lucrecia's dreams are three anonymous men, the most important of whom she refers to as "Hombre Ordinario" (Ordinary Man). He plays the role of impresario, single-handedly orchestrating the visions that Lucrecia views during the course of her dreams. Thus nearly every dream begins with the phrase "The Ordinary Man appeared in my bedroom" or "I saw the Ordinary Man." He then proceeds to show Lucrecia images of future events, most of which pertain to Spain's impending destruction.

The Ordinary Man never reveals his identity; nor is Lucrecia able to describe his looks except to say that he was "natural [human] and not frightening."[10] He often appears dressed in animal skins and occasionally in white. When he first appears in Lucrecia's bedroom, he habitually carries such objects as a skull, a globe, a cross, a lantern, a saw, a bloody sword, even a saltcellar, the symbolic meaning of which he is quick to explain. Thus in the dream of 11 November 1589 the Ordinary Man tells Lucrecia that his lantern is intended to warn about the loss of a Spanish silver fleet. He then shows her a vision of three galleons sinking in the presence of enemy ships. Four days later he appears holding a cross, which he says symbolizes the "sufferings" Spain will soon have to endure.

The Ordinary Man has two companions, both of whom carry fishermen's nets. Lucrecia usually encounters these figures on the seashore ("en las orillas del mar"), evidently an imaginary location somewhere on the coast of Galicia, in northwestern Spain, since it is from this vantage point that she witnesses battles between English and Spanish ships. The older of the fishermen, "Pescador Viejo," speaks of issues pertaining to the church and also serves as a dream interpreter, explaining to Lucrecia the meaning of the images before her. He is interchangeably called the Man with the Lion because he often appears leading a lion on a chain. Presumably, in this context the lion represents Habsburg royal authority, and the Old Fisherman is a figure who leashes royal power, taming it to perform good tasks. Because his companion, the so-called Young Fisherman, occasionally paints the images that appear in the dreams, Mendoza compares him to Luke the Apostle. Mendoza also speculates that the Ordinary Man is John the Baptist and the Old Fisherman is Peter.[11]

But the Three Men prefer to remain anonymous, identifying themselves only as divine messengers who have come to reveal to Lucrecia prophetic visions of Spain's future. Thus in referring to the enigmatic quality of the dreams, the Ordinary Man remarks that "our style is that of prophets, who never speak according to the letter and briefly, because God's things are higher than that."[12] Further, the Three Men explicitly and vigorously deny being demons, and in one dream when a devillike figure appears, the Ordinary Man drives him away by chanting, "Verbum caro factum est" (And the word was made flesh, John 1:14).[13]

Despite their self-proclaimed anonymity, the Three Men freely admit that they have come to serve as Lucrecia's instructors and guides. The Ordinary Man claims to be a teacher of wisdom ("maestro de sabiduría"), and he tells Lucrecia that the fundamental purpose of the dreams is to transform her into a seer who will tell others what she has seen and learned. In other instances the Three Men collectively refer to themselves as teachers with a favorite pupil ("discípulo muy querido") to whom they have come to teach "supernatural wisdom."[14] In keeping with their didactic role, they criticize Lucrecia for her ignorance and lack of learning and rebuke her for failing to understand the basic message the dreams are intended to convey. Nevertheless, they also indicate that she has been especially chosen to warn others about Spain's future. Despite her initial reluctance to serve in this capacity, she eventually accepts her role, and in the dream of 14 November 1588 she describes herself as their "instrument."

The Three Men also offer Lucrecia scene-by-scene, image-by-image interpretations of what she has dreamed. An early example of their role as oneiromancers occurs in her dream of 1 December 1587.

> The Ordinary Man came to me, and calling me said, "Stick your head out the window," which I did. I heard a great noise and asked him, "What noise is this I hear?" He answered, "You'll soon see." And then I saw coming from the east a cart pulled by bulls or buffalos in which I saw a tower, on the side of which was a dead lion, and on the top of which was a dead eagle, with its breast cut open. The wheels of this cart were stained with blood, and as it moved it killed many people. Many men and women, dressed as Spaniards, were tied to the cart; they were shouting that the world was ending; and among them I saw [word crossed out] and not having ever seen anything like this I asked, "What vision is this?" and the Ordinary Man told me he could not tell me (although he gave signs that he wished to). In this instant the Old Fisherman appeared, and I asked him, "Why have you left the seashore and come here?" And he responded that it was necessary because this man wanted to tell you about this vision, and I did not want it known until the third night. And I saw that he was carrying a palm leaf, that looked similar to one he had been making, and I asked him, "Who is this palm leaf for?" And he said, "For the new king who will be to God's pleasing. I'll give it to him, but for the moment I cannot say any more." And this was as much as I could remember.

As the Old Fisherman had promised, variations of this dream recurred on three successive nights. On 2 December, after seeing carnivorous birds devour the dead eagle, Lucrecia asks the Ordinary Man if the eagle represents the king; his only reply is to cross himself. On the next night the cart with the bloody wheels appears beneath a sky that has turned red, and the Ordinary Man explains that this is a sign that "your king will die in a year when there'll be a lunar eclipse lasting three nights, followed by the appearance of a red comet with a white tail; as it disappears, the king will die."

On the third night, 4 December, the Old Fisherman appears and offers Lucrecia a complete interpretation: the buffalos mean life, the cart death, the bloody wheels represent the king's bad councillors, the lion and the castle on the cart are the king's arms, and the birds who eat the eagle are heretics who try to seize control once the king is dead. With this, the scene changes rapidly. The Ordinary Man whisks Lucrecia off to England and to the house of Sir Francis Drake, the sea captain notorious for his raids on Spanish territories in the New World and Old. Of Drake's appearance, Lucrecia mentions only his brilliant red damask coat lined in fur. When she sees him, he is writing a letter to the sultan of Turkey in which he states that if the Ottomans win in Poland, "we have Spain in our hands," evidently a reference to Queen Elizabeth's well-known diplomatic efforts to make common cause with the Turks and other Muslim powers against Spain. Upon leaving Drake's house Lucrecia meets a man described as Grumite, the accountant of Henry III, king of France. Finally, the Ordinary Man takes Lucrecia back home, where she awakens with a great thirst.

This pattern is repeated, as night after night, the Three Men appear and reveal scenes depicting the loss of Spain. These mysterious figures speak to Lucrecia directly, and she herself speaks, usually as a curious pupil inquiring about the meaning of the images. On the night of 8 March 1588, the Ordinary Man takes Lucrecia to the royal palace in Madrid, where she sees a widow whose hands have been cut off. The back of her skirt is also cut off, and she weeps as she says, "Woe unto you, Spain and Rome." Then she adds, "Poor Isabella, your hair will become the shoes of your father's enemies." The widow then slashes the veins of her wrists and begins to write messages in blood. At this point, a second woman appears, and the king orders them out of his apartments: "Get out of here, you women." The dream ends with Philip reading various papers by this widow about the loss of Spain. The following night the Young Fisherman explains to

Lucrecia that the widow is the church, and her skirts are cut because the church is poor and has been abandoned by her priests. The widow is handless because the church no longer uses its offices to help the poor; now it serves only the well-to-do. The widow is crying, not for the church, he adds, but for the prophets. And to say that Isabella's hair will become shoes means that she will be so contemptible that no one will recognize her. Finally, Philip's directive to the two old women shows that the king believes these prophecies to be useless women's talk.

A more complex case of analysis occurs within the dream of 10 March 1590. This lengthy dream begins as follows:

> The Ordinary Man came to me and said, "The trumpet is about to sound, and I want you to see what this moment brings." And he took me into the street and blew his trumpet. At the sound, the sky turned very cloudy. As the clouds passed overhead, they turned blood-red, and this lasted quite a long while. Then the clouds went away and three lances appeared, each with bloody points. He then told me, "It is not the blood of the just you see on these lances" . . . the lances then disappeared and the sky was suddenly filled with moons, battling each other, and I saw that many of them fell to earth. The moons then disappeared and the sky was filled with stars, some with lights like torches, others giving forth smoke, and still others grouped like armies. For a long time these last ones fought a battle. These stars did not look at all like natural stars and eventually all of them fell to earth. The Ordinary Man then told me, "The Man with the Lion will explain what this means because, not being new things, I don't have the obligation to tell you." We then walked toward the Palace and he took me into Philip's room. I found him looking very disconsolate, covered with a brown cloak, and the brazier that at other times I saw burning brightly was out at his feet and its ashes had turned into mud. The Ordinary Man then said, "Look and see the placard placed on Philip's head." Looking at it I saw that it read:

> Woe unto you, you who had the time but did not come to understand nor do the things worthy of a king! Woe unto you, who saw yourself placed in an important very high place! Woe unto you, who when you think about the last days will know what you left to fate because you won't have anyone to ring the bells, and this because you failed to listen and earn God's mercy; so it will be in this life and the next, God's justice will catch up with you.

With this he took me out of the palace. . . .

In the next segment of the dream Lucrecia is carried off to the spot on the seashore where she customarily converses with the Young Fisherman. "I don't have to explain the placard on Philip's head because you read it," he tells her, and then he offers the following explication:

The clouds: Philip's sadness when he recognizes that he cannot protect his kingdom in the time of rain.
The blood-red sky: what will happen to Spain when other nations appear.
The moons: the Moors who will invade Spain after the others.
The stars: the grandees who, after Philip's death, will rise in revolt ("harán comunidades").
To see the stars fall: that no one will become king because there will be no one valiant enough to end the wars.
Philip dressed in a brown cloak: the difficult straits to which his narrow-mindedness has led him.
To see Philip with a cold brazier: his life will soon end.
The ashes turned to mud: the time left in which Philip has to do penance before his death.

Analyses of this sort, similar to those offered in the many popular dream books then in circulation, recur often in Lucrecia's dreams. Sometimes, however, the Three Men openly challenge Lucrecia, together with Allende and Mendoza, to interpret the visions themselves. Thus in the dream of 3 January

1590, after explaining that the locusts seen in a previous dream represent Spain's enemies, the Old Fisherman instructs Lucrecia to inform Allende that he should interpret such images himself. The Old Fisherman then shows her a vision of a king on horseback with the figure of death by his side and explains that this scene means that the king will escape a violent death only to die of natural causes during the time of Spain's destruction. Then, as if to help Allende understand the implications of this image, he suggests that the friar consult the works of St. Epiphanius, a fourth-century scholar known for a treatise on heretics.

Some of the dreams entail visits to foreign countries. In most of these the Ordinary Man serves as organizer and guide. On 20 November 1587 the Ordinary Man takes Lucrecia on a journey that begins with a visit to the royal palace in Madrid. Next, in Turkey, Lucrecia witnesses a Spanish nobleman, described as "a traitor to his king," writing a letter to the Queen of England about the true extent of Spanish power. She then visits Paris and compares the streets to those of her own *barrio* in Madrid. Suddenly, she is in England, announcing that Spain would find it impossible to conquer such a prosperous nation. Before returning home, Lucrecia stops briefly to visit the Spanish seashore for a quick consultation with the Old Fisherman about the meaning of her journey. The following month, December 1587, nine of Lucrecia's thirty-four dreams involve trips abroad. On a visit to the English Channel she witnesses the English fleet preparing for war. In London she sees Queen Elizabeth, aided by her Protestant allies, organizing an invasion of Spain. And in France she watches a battle in which Protestant troops commanded by the Huguenot leader, Henry of Navarre, the future Henry IV, rout the forces of the Catholic League, King Philip's allies. The Ordinary Man takes her to Poland to see yet another defeat of Catholic troops, and to Turkey to witness the "great Turk," possibly the Ottoman sultan, Murad III, planning a naval assault against Spain in conjunction with Drake.

In the most memorable journey recorded that month, on 18 December 1587, Lucrecia and the Ordinary Man visit a palace in London. There she sees a fifty-year-old woman, referred to as the Queen, seated on a long bench. In her lap is a dead lamb whose stomach is cut open, its guts and entrails exposed. The Queen is busily shoving her hands into the stomach cavity and scooping up the animal's blood. Next to her sits a woman dressed in widow's weeds. When the Queen asks the woman to drink some of the lamb's blood, the woman refuses. Suddenly, in anger the Queen draws her sword and in a single stroke cuts off the woman's head. The Ordinary Man does not explain the meaning of this gruesome scene, but the dead lamb would seem to refer to Queen Elizabeth's persecution of Catholics, with the beheading of the woman recalling the execution of Mary Stuart, Queen of Scots, on 8 February 1587.

For Lucrecia's contemporaries, this dream dramatized the ruthlessness of the enemy the Spanish Armada would soon have to confront. And it was after studying this particular dream that Mendoza avowed that Lucrecia's dreams "do not proceed from an evil spirit, nor do they appear to be fictions composed either by human or diabolical invention; rather, they are truths advising us about the rigorous justice from heaven that we deserve for our sins."[15]

During the following month, January 1588, only four of the thirty-five dreams recorded involve ventures abroad. But in quick visits to familiar places—the streets outside her house, nearby hospitals and churches, the royal palace, and the city of Toledo—Lucrecia sees bizarre characters and events. The dream of 21 January, for example, begins with the Ordinary Man appearing in Lucrecia's bedroom. He takes her into the street and together they walk to the Hospital of Anton Martín, located a hundred yards from her house. There they visit a man said to be a prophet. Dressed like a saint, with a cross in his hands and another on his chest, this "prophet" tells Lucrecia how he had warned King Philip to kill the moriscos—Spain's population of Muslims who had converted to Catholicism—before they revolted, but that the monarch had refused to heed this advice. He also informs her that part of Spain was soon to be lost, because "we are in the eighth year" (estamos en el año de ocho), a reference to the belief widely held among sixteenth-century astrologers that 1588, owing to a rare celestial conjunction, would be marked by wars, famines, and other catastrophic events. The prophet quickly adds, however, that Spain's "sufferings" would last for another six years. The prophet is not identified, but his circumstances resemble those of Juan de Dios, a seer known to have been forcibly detained in the Hospital of Anton Martín during the late 1580s. He also warns Lucrecia that she too is likely to wind up in jail.

The Ordinary Man now takes Lucrecia into the streets, which are piled high with corpses, a sign that the destruction of Spain has already begun. Suddenly, a monster with the features of an elephant, lion, porcupine, and horse appears, turns quickly into an angel, and disappears, informing Lucrecia that he is leaving in order to rescue Toledo from its enemies. The scene changes abruptly to a seashore location, where the two fishermen show Lucrecia a vision of several old women gathering and bundling wild herbs and grasses that they apparently intend to sell. Two tax collectors appear and order the women to pay the *alcabala,* the royal sales tax from which the crown derived much of its income. The women object, claiming they have no money, and one says she hopes the king will soon die for his sins. A voice cries out: "You'll live to see his death in nine months, followed by an invasion that will last three years, and finally prosperity." With this, the dream ends and Lucrecia awakens.

The motifs and structure of this dream—with its rapid shifts in scene—are typical of those recorded in the registers, though the reference to the herb-gathering women complaining about taxes may well be autobiographical. Another noteworthy feature of Lucrecia's dreams is their interconnectedness: figures appearing in one dream frequently return in others. For example, two angels who first appear in the dream of 24 February 1588 reappear in three dreams in March 1590. In the early dream, one of the angels says that his mission is to punish those priests who have mistreated the poor, and the other claims, "I have come to punish Philip and not only him but his entire Monarchy." Two years later they have names—"the angel of the priests" and "the angel of anger"—but their mission remains essentially unchanged. Thus in the dream of 6 March 1590 the angel of the priests informs Philip, "You have been a bad governor of your church, because you have awarded clerical offices in your gift to ignoramuses and to men who have violated their vestments."

Another figure who makes regular appearances is a man named Miguel. He shows up in various guises: first, as a masked man imprisoned in a tower; then as an anonymous seer to whom Lucrecia says, "May God save you prophet; do your office"; and subsequently as Piedrola, the soldier-prophet. Miguel also appears humbly as a shepherd who has taken refuge from Spain's enemies in a cave, and more triumphantly as a "New David," a reference to the medieval prophecy of El Encubierto, which announced King David's return as the monarch who would complete the Reconquest against the Moors. In other dreams Miguel is a redeemer dispatched by the Lord to liberate Spain from her enemies with the help of an army wearing white crosses; a monarch who will "reform God's Church" and eventually usher in "the golden century and the time of God"; and a crusader who conquers Jerusalem and establishes the Church "in places which have never known the faith of God." Finally, Miguel appears as Lucrecia's husband, with the implication that she will one day become queen of Spain.[16]

Miguel's varied personae are difficult to interpret, but it seems likely that Miguel-Piedrola represents Lucrecia's conception of the good governor, compared to Philip, the bad governor. If one chooses a Freudian interpretation, Lucrecia's marriage to Miguel and her elevation to queen reads as an Oedipal fantasy in which Lucrecia rejects her evil dream father, the king, and displaces him by marrying Miguel, the ideal governor-father.

As the dreams discussed thus far illustrate, Lucrecia is not simply a narrator or a passive witness to the images she sees, but an active participant in the dramatic sequences. In some dreams her role is similar to that of a Greek chorus: she comments on the scenes she witnesses and asks the Three Men to explain the meaning of the images she sees. In others she plays the role of protagonist. In the dream of 29 December 1587, she appears as

Philip II's lawyer, counseling the monarch to prepare his will inasmuch as his death is soon to occur. In another dream (18 July 1588), she is the king's spiritual advisor, criticizing him for having neglected his subjects and boldly asserting that Philip insulted his own patron saint, St. Lawrence, because he built El Escorial—a building dedicated to this saint—with "the blood of the poor." Once, too, Lucrecia appears as a learned astrologer who impresses Philip after having successfully challenged one of his sages to a debate about the significance of a solar eclipse that they had just witnessed (dream of 28 November 1589).

The dreams also portray Lucrecia as a participant in the destruction that she forsees. In that of 31 December 1587, for example, she becomes a hapless victim of war who is taken captive by a squadron of Turkish invaders. Conversely, she sometimes appears in the guise of a Spanish Joan of Arc, a *doncella guerrera* or warrior woman who helps to rescue Spain from its enemies.[17] Thus in the dreams of 9 February and 21 March 1588 she assists in the defense of Toledo and, riding a white horse, leads a successful cavalry charge against an enemy army. This image of Lucrecia as Spain's savior appears in other contexts, notably the dream of 18 March 1588, in which she discovers a two-year-old boy in a well near Madrid. He asks her to pick him up and carry him. She responds that he is too heavy. The boy, hinting that he is the infant Jesus, says, "Christopher can carry me." Lucrecia then places the child on her back and carries him off to safety in the cathedral of Toledo, forty miles away.

Each of the dreams recorded in the registers possesses its own dramatic and psychological structure, yet together they suggest that Lucrecia was engaged in a form of mythmaking in which an otherwise neglected adolescent appears larger than life. To her contemporaries, however, the psychological aspects of Lucrecia's wish-fulfillment fantasies were of little or no interest. The dreams' prophetic quality, their immediate relevance to the future of Spain, and their source—divine or diabolical—these were the aspects of Lucrecia's dreams that captured the attention of Mendoza, Allende's friends at court, and ultimately the Holy Office.

The Loss of Spain

As Lucrecia told Allende when she related her first dream to him in September 1587, the persistent theme of the dreams is the loss or destruction of Spain. Her comment is corroborated by surviving fragments of some of the earliest dreams. For example, in the first dream on record—that of 7 November 1587—Lucrecia has a complex vision in which she sees two armies fighting, enemies arriving in the streets of Toledo, and a wounded marquis of Santa Cruz, the admiral Philip had named to command the Armada.

In a dream two days later, Lucrecia visits the royal palace in Madrid and enters the kitchen. The fire in the hearth is extinguished, and Lucrecia is informed that this is a sign of Spain's poverty. She then sees flames envelop a great monastery—clearly, a simulacrum of the Escorial—and hears a mysterious voice crying out, "Many will die of plague." This threatening message is echoed in the dreams of 20–25 November 1587, with talk of new "comunidades"—a reference to the revolt of the Castilian cities against Charles V in 1520—and a strange vision of the sultan of Turkey promising to make one of his wives "ruler of Castile and queen of Spain." On 23 and 25 November Lucrecia sees Drake defeating Santa Cruz, and on 14 December 1587, eight months before the defeat of the Armada, Lucrecia witnesses a naval battle in which an English fleet routs a Spanish armada commanded by Santa Cruz:

> I saw two strong fleets fighting a fierce battle. Because I had seen them fight before, I knew that one was the fleet of the marquis of Santa Cruz, the other of Drake. This battle was the fiercest and loudest of all those I had seen in other dreams. Previously, I had seen them fighting in a port; this one was on the high seas and lasted all afternoon because before it began I heard a clock strike one; it lasted three hours, until sunset. Once the sun was down, I saw the defeated fleet of the marquis of Santa Cruz fleeing toward the north, having lost many of its ships and men, and

> I saw Drake's fleet returning to England to take on more troops. I saw Drake writing letters, asking for more men. He also wanted to forward a request for troops to the Great Turk, but one of his knights said, "Do not send it, the men we have are enough to secure victory." And with this I woke up.

Not all of Lucrecia's dreams about the Armada were accurate. In the dream of 9 February 1588 the Ordinary Man announces that the Armada will leave Lisbon within the week; it did not leave that port until 28 May. But he is almost correct when, in the dream of 16 January 1588, he predicts the death of Santa Cruz, the Spanish commander, within a few weeks; the marquis died on 9 February. And in late August, when Madrid is anxiously awaiting news of a Spanish victory, the Ordinary Man boldly states that it is wrong to assume that the Armada had sailed under the protection of the cross, clearly a warning that something was amiss (dream of 26 August). Not until early September, a month after the battle, did news of the Armada's defeat reach Spain. In a subsequent gloomy proclamation, on 30 September, the Ordinary Man asserts that the Armada's defeat is only the beginning of Spain's "punishment" and "ruin."

Once the Armada has been defeated, the emphasis of the dreams shifts to the conquest of Spain by her enemies. Lucrecia sees various portents of this defeat: the death of the infante Philip, marking the end of Habsburg rule in Spain; a revolt of moriscos in Avila and Medina del Campo, an uprising which is interpreted as Philip II's failure to eradicate heresy in his own kingdoms; and the death of the monarch, who, by having failed to respond to the warnings contained in these dreams, is accused of abandoning his kingdom and incurring the wrath of God. Spain's enemies then launch a simultaneous invasion through the kingdom's four "doors": the French from the north, through Navarre; the English by way of Lisbon; the Turks from the Levant, through Valencia; and the Moors of North Africa from the south, through Seville. Eventually, the entire kingdom, including Madrid, is lost. Moors take up residence in the royal palace, churches are looted, and their contents destroyed.

"This is the time of tears," the Ordinary Man asserts. "Time is short for Spain," its "punishment" is at hand. The sounds and images in the dreams portend death and destruction: Lucrecia hears cannon assaulting Madrid's St. Isidro gate; she sees enemy captains rampaging through the streets of Madrid; and she learns that the effigy of St. Isidro, Madrid's patron saint, will be ground up and transformed, oddly enough, into a salad. The destruction is accompanied by plagues of locusts and flies, by famine and pestilence. Fierce bulls, wolves, and other wild animals roam Madrid's streets. She sees fighting moons and falling stars, rivers of blood and blood-red skies, and blood dripping from the clouds. In three dreams (23, 24, and 28 December 1588), she sees a seven-headed dragon—the seven deadly sins—breathing fire across Spain.

Particularly striking is the dream of 17 April 1590, in which Lucrecia sees a huge woman dressed as a warrior riding a bull through the center of Madrid. The arms of this amazon are covered with snakes, her breasts are bared, and she brandishes a sword to decapitate the children she finds in the streets. In a subsequent dream Lucrecia encounters the female warrior in a garden near Madrid. On this occasion the woman is unarmed. Holding a lantern and leading a black bear on a leash, she openly laments Spain's fate, "Woe unto Spain, and the Spaniards, the forgotten ones." On her back, inscribed in blood, are the words "I am the suffering of Spain and I come as a woman to show you the little strength you have to defend yourselves." Spain's defenselessness is also depicted in a dream in which Lucrecia sees a vision of Spain as a castle, a lion, and an eagle—the images depicted on the Habsburg armorial shield. As she looks more closely, however, she realizes that the lion has only one foot, the eagle lacks claws, and the top of the castle is collapsing.

The schedule for these horrific events is vague, although the Three Men drop occasional hints. The loss, they claim, will occur in the month of July during a year with a solar eclipse; it is also suggested, in a dream of 26 December 1587, that the destruction will begin within three years. In the dream of 21 January 1589, Lucrecia sees Spanish elms perishing in a violent storm, and the Ordinary Man explains that the falling leaves and downed trees are "a portrait" of the king's life. The Young Fisherman becomes a bit more specific in a dream of July 1589, when he announces "in the eighth year [1588] you lost the Armada; in the ninth year [1589] you'll lose your cities [cabezas de reinos]; and in the tenth year [1590] you'll see the end."[18] And in a dream of 30 March 1590 the Ordinary Man announces, mistakenly, that Philip is to reign only for another 150 days.

Accompanying these messages of death and destruction are the traditional millennial visions of rebirth and renewal: after the conquest, the reconquest. The Ordinary Man and his companions reveal that one city—Toledo, the city traditionally regarded as Spain's spiritual capital—was to escape destruction thanks to the timely intervention of an army concealed in caves along the Tagus River. This army is to include Lucrecia, her mother, brother, and sisters, as well as Allende, Mendoza, Casaos, Vitores, and a number of other friends and supporters, all of whom wear black scapulars embroidered with a white cross. This army, led by its captain, Miguel, will emerge from its hiding place just as Toledo is about to fall, break the enemy siege, and in a series of battles expel the invaders and eventually reconquer Spain. Miguel will then be elected king by popular vote. He will marry Lucrecia, father several children, and establish a new monarchy blessed by God.[19] His crusade will "bring God's faith to the remotest parts of the earth," and he will ultimately deliver Jerusalem from the grip of Islam. This sequence of miraculous events ends with the transfer of the Holy See and its relics from Rome to Toledo. Miguel's monarchy is also portrayed as the "last monarchy," which inaugurates "a terrestrial paradise, a Golden Century, a time of God" that is followed, presumably, by the end of the universe.

This particular scenario resonates with images from the Apocalypse of St. John as well as Spain's centuries-old tradition of prophetic lore.[20] The variation on the New David prophecy is obvious, and the dreams also resemble a number of older fulfillment prophecies which had announced that a Spanish monarch would ultimately complete the work of the Reconquest by expelling the Muslims from the Holy Land.[21] Yet the dreams also indicate that Lucrecia was much influenced by the *romances,* particularly that cycle of tales concerning Roderic, the Visigothic king whose sins led to the defeat of Spain by Islam.[22] Similar ideas appear in Spanish historical literature, and the image of a national savior appearing from a cave harks back to Pelayo, the mythic king who began the Reconquest from a base of operations in a secret cave located in the mountains near Covadonga, in northern Spain.[23]

These concordances suggest that Lucrecia drew the basic conquest-and-reconquest pattern from a diversity of sources, both oral and written. Yet the dreams were also directly inspired by court gossip as well as by Lucrecia's personal knowledge of the Alcázar. Compared to medieval prophecies, which were usually worded in vague allegorical language and rarely referred to specific individuals by name, Lucrecia's visions are distinguished by their immediate relevance to the politics and personalities of the day. Names are named, and Philip and his ministers are held personally responsible for Spain's impending loss.

Indeed, the list of those blamed for the imminent calamity reads like a who's who of the Spanish court. Included are Juan de Idiáquez and Cristóbal de Moura, two influential members of Philip's Council of State and among his closest advisors. In the dreams, however, they are described as traitors guilty of "ruinous thoughts" and a refusal to heed Lucrecia's prophecies. The marquis de Auñón, a courtier notorious for his gambling and one associated with the moral corruption endemic to Philip's court, is similarly accused of treachery.[24]

Other prominent individuals singled out for criticism include the marquis of Santa Cruz; Alessandro Farnese, duke of Parma, Philip's general in Flanders; and the Inquisitor General Gaspar de Quiroga, archbishop of Toledo.[25] Quiroga is depicted as an unqualified prelate who is so greedy and avaricious that even as Spain's enemies enter Madrid, he cares more about burying his own treasure than looking after his church. Two other churchmen who come under attack are García de Loaysa, the royal almoner and the king's chief advisor on ecclesiastical appointments, and Fray Diego de Chaves, the royal confessor, who, as we shall see, orchestrated Lucrecia's arrest by the Inquisition.

The dream that best dramatizes the criticisms of Philip's

court is that of 27 March 1590, in which Lucrecia sees eight ministers joined together in a diabolical dance intended to demonstrate that "all of Philip's counselors are involved in dirty and abominable things" (todo lo que en los consejos de Felipe anda es cosas sucias y abominables). The dancers include the marquis de Carpio, who is criticized for his evil ways; García de Loaysa, singled out for his lack of charity and service to God; and Juan de Idiáquez, who appears "with his head up his ass" (metida la cabeza por las tripas).

The criticisms of Philip are stronger still. In an early dream (11 November 1587) he is referred to as "the powerful one" (el poderoso) who has become so weak that Lucrecia can sneak into his bedroom while he is sleeping and steal his sword. Four nights later (15 November) Lucrecia has a dream that begins with a frightening image of the king's corpse lying in the mud. The corpse slowly rises and is greeted by a chorus: "Do you remember the harm and injustice you have done? . . . Just look at the alcabalas and the people you have destroyed. And don't you remember having appointed a bishop who did not deserve that office?"

From this dream onward, Philip is damned. Most often referred to simply as Philip, instead of the respectful Your Majesty or His Majesty, the king is subject to wholesale contempt: "He's tyrannized the poor"; "there would not be so many prostitutes if it weren't for the poverty he's brought to us"; "he is responsible for the evil and ruin of Spain."[26] The Young Fisherman's attacks on Philip are particularly bitter. In one dream he speaks of "the cruelty of Philip's heart, because, knowing what you [Lucrecia] said about the Armada and the coming wars, he never attempted to learn more, mainly because of an evil counselor who warned him that if he talked to either don Alonso or to Fray Lucas he would have to reduce the alcabalas and other taxes" (4 November 1588).

The Ordinary Man also maintains that Philip has a "cold, cold heart" because he failed to listen to the messages of God contained in Lucrecia's dreams.[27] So angered is the Ordinary Man by Philip's conduct that in the dream of 14 January 1590 he fights his way into Philip's bedroom and decapitates the monarch with a saw. Apparently, the Ordinary Man was accustomed to dispatching kings in this manner, for he boasts that he does it "for fun, as a hobby," particularly when he has an opportunity to attack those like Philip who have committed "many injustices."

These many injustices are both spiritual and secular. In the spiritual realm they include the appointment of unqualified bishops and tolerance for nonresidency among prelates, a practice prohibited by the Council of Trent. Another principal injustice is Philip's construction of the monumental Escorial; in one dream a serpent holds aloft a placard reading: "Stop work on the Escorial, since it is not pleasing to God" (15 January 1588). In the secular realm, the king is attacked for having ignored the concerns of the poor by failing to administer justice properly, by selling to private individuals the *tierras baldías* (common lands) that poor villagers had traditionally worked in common, and by having raised taxes, notably the alcabala, to a level at which his vassals were "destroyed."[28] After the Armada's defeat, Philip sought new taxes, later known as the *millones*, in an effort to rebuild the royal navy. In the dream of 7 July 1589 Philip is specifically attacked for requesting these taxes despite having been advised that the new levies would lead to the "destruction of the poor." A few months later the Young Fisherman delivers a similar message, claiming that the Lord is about to punish Philip because he taxed and oppressed the poor, rather than caring for them as a good shepherd should (1 October 1589).

Criticism of Philip's policies alternates with images of the king as an isolated, unpopular monarch who is afraid to leave the royal palace. In actuality, Philip attracted admiring crowds wherever he went up through 1591, when the millones tax led to riots in Avila, Madrid, and other cities. Uncannily, Lucrecia's dreams prefigure the popular unrest. In one, Philip is harassed by a mob shouting for justice "because he took away their money and fields in order to feed his court" (3 February 1588). In another, Philip's appearance sparks a protest among the fruit vendors of Madrid, who shout, "We'll desert you as you deserted us," and a group of orphans joins in, "Philip has abandoned us; we're forced to eat grass because we've no other food" (4 February 1588).

In other dreams Philip appears as a weak, aging, decrepit monarch whose subjects impatiently await his demise. In the dream of 30 December 1588 the Ordinary Man accompanies Lucrecia to the royal palace. There she sees the ailing Philip, seated in a chair. With trembling hands he reaches for a glass of water, spills its contents and thereby extinguishes the brazier at his feet. At this moment, a crowd gathered in the plaza outside the palace begins to shout, "Long live the [new] King, already Philip's hands are shaking." To dispel rumors that he is dying, Philip appears at a window and announces, "yo soy vivo" (I am alive), but the crowd roars back, "We have no ears, just like you, who has been deaf to things of God, and how you have refused to listen to the counsel given you, and therefore it is good that no one knows or helps you."

Echoing court gossip, Lucrecia's dreams insinuate that the king arranged for the murder of his son, the unfortunate don Carlos, who died in mysterious circumstances in 1569. Additionally, in a dream among those destroyed by Allende but known as the "dream of the four queens," Philip is blamed for the deaths of his four wives, María Manuela (d. 1545), Mary Tudor (d. 1558), Isabel de Valois (d. 1568), and Anne of Austria (d. 1580).[29] Furthermore, contrary to the historical image of Philip as a warm family man, the dreams depict him as a father who has failed to look out for his children's welfare, notably the future of his favorite daughter, Isabella. Lucrecia envisions the unmarried infanta worrying that the king will soon die, leaving her an orphan without a kingdom.[30] Isabella is also depicted rebuking Philip for having failed to heed Piedrola's advice as well as Lucrecia's warnings about the fate of the Armada. Angered by his daughter's outburst, Philip threatens to burn her. To which an indignant Isabella retorts, "If so, Your Majesty will burn the truth."[31]

Isabella's most trenchant criticism occurs in the dream of 12 March 1590, in which the infanta tearfully reminds the king that he will never deserve a glorious place in history:

> Look, Your Majesty, Spain is lost. You will not achieve the fame of my grandfather. Past kings enlarged their realms, and at the moment of their death they recognize the truth. The worst thing that can happen to a king is to discover that no one wishes to write his history, either because they do not wish to uncover the faults or to lie. . . . Your Majesty is aware of the fame my grandfather, Emperor Charles V, left behind. The name of the Catholic Monarch [Ferdinand] also lives, even though he has been dead many years, and the names and glories of the holy kings of France are known everywhere. As for you, it is only said that you have impoverished your kingdom.

To the extent that Lucrecia shared Isabella's unmarried plight, a modern observer cannot help identifying Isabella as an imaginary projection of Lucrecia, and Philip as Alonso Franco. But sixteenth-century dream theory did not account for projection. For Lucrecia and her contemporaries, these dreams were visions whose historical truth or falsity would be known once their source was determined. A supernatural origin was likely because the dreams involved, as Ciruelo had suggested, the "common good of the people." It was disturbing, therefore, that the dreams presented Philip as a monarch who had failed God, his kingdom, and his family, and therefore would never achieve glory either on earth or in heaven.

Official portraits of Philip show a proud, aloof, and somewhat haughty monarch, dedicated to the service of the church. A portrait of quite a different kind appears in Lucrecia's dream of 2 March 1588: Philip, asleep in a chair, in his right hand holds a placard inscribed "El Descuido" (The Negligent One). Insects crawl in and out of his mouth. On his forehead is written "Corto ha quedado en el fe" (He did not do nearly enough for the faith). His left hand holds another placard: "Codicia" (Greed). At his feet is another: "Largo en seguir pasos de bestia" (He follows the path of idiocy). And on his head, another: "Variedad te lleva a lo hondo" (Your lack of constancy will carry you to hell). In yet another dream Philip appears as a new Roderic, the corrupt and licentious Visigothic king whose sins were believed

Alonso Sánchez Coello, *Philip II*. Museo del Prado, Madrid. This portrait, dating from around 1580, depicts Philip dressed soberly in black, adorned only by the insignia of the Order of the Golden Fleece—symbol of his commitment to the defense of the Catholic religion. In contrast, Lucrecia's dream portraits of Philip portrayed him as a decrepit monarch who "tyrannized the poor" and "impoverished" his kingdom.

to have been responsible for the first loss of Spain to the Moors in 711 A.D. The next loss, the dreams warn, is imminent unless Philip recognizes his sins, offers public repentance, and placates the wrath of God.

In sixteenth-century Spain such messages were tantamount to sedition. Castilian law defined as *alevoso,* or seditious, "anyone who speaks badly of the king and his family." The minimum penalty for such statements was the confiscation of one half of one's goods. But if it was determined that the accused had advised or counseled anyone to rebel against or refuse to obey the king's law, the penalty was death.[32] In her testimony before the Inquisition, Lucrecia maintained she was a loyal subject who never intended to do the king any harm. If there was anything seditious in her dreams, she swore, it was the fault of the two churchmen who had recorded the dreams and publicized them.

The inquisitors believed otherwise, and the final indictment against Lucrecia included accusations of seditious acts. The dreams, the Holy Office charged, were subversive misdeeds expressly designed to foment opposition to the king. The would be prophet was to be tried as a traitor.

4

POLITICS AND PROPHECY

Prophets rarely act alone. For prophecy is a social act, a collective enterprise, a public endeavor, though its origin is quintessentially a private experience, such as a divine revelation in the form of a dream or vision.[1] By voicing aloud the supernaturally inspired warning or promise, the prophet hopes to move listeners to take specific actions. Often allied with a cause or group, the prophet is a mediator between that group and the general public as well as a transmitter of a message received through a miraculous medium: a mysterious voice, an angel, a heavenly vision.

The vast majority of medieval and Renaissance prophecies addressed religious issues. The dominant theme was the reform of the church, which was accused of corruption and immorality. Other sectarian prophecies were uttered in support of the establishment of new religious houses and new religious orders. Of prophecies with more secular purposes, many were intended to convince the populace that a king or some other important individual had received divine approval and would achieve momentous or long-awaited results. Typical of this genre of fulfillment prophecies were those describing Philip II as a New David and, later, those naming the children of Philip IV (1621–1665) as princes destined to complete the Reconquest by returning Jerusalem to the Roman Catholic faith.[2]

These fulfillment prophecies essentially served to confirm or bolster the existing political and social order. In contrast, protest prophecies were intended to effect some form of social, religious, or political reform desired by an ignored, neglected, or otherwise marginal group. The prophet faulted the existing ecclesiastical or political establishment for failing to meet high, generally religious, standards and insisted on certain reforms, warning of divine chastisement if these demands were not met. Fundamentally, then, protest prophecies represented a bid for power and legitimacy and were a medium for public exposition of grievances that could otherwise only be whispered behind closed doors.

The later Middle Ages had a strong tradition of self-proclaimed street or marketplace prophets, typically friars who used the pulpit to advocate or protest a particular cause. Laymen dressed in sackcloth and carrying crosses also brought their doomsday messages into the streets. The most famous street prophet of the Renaissance, and probably the most successful, is undoubtedly Savonarola, but nearly all the Italian states hosted a series of street prophets up through about 1530.[3]

The history of street prophets in Spain has yet to be written, but there is ample evidence of their activity. At the start of the fifteenth century, for example, the fiery Dominican preacher Vicente Ferrer (1350–1419) cited Jeremiah 23:16 to warn against the horde of prophets inundating Spanish streets: "Do not listen to the words of the prophets who prophetise and deceive you. What they tell you are their visions; it does not come from the mouth of God."[4] Despite the future saint's admonitions, a Savonarola-like street prophet known popularly as "el bachiller Marquillos" claimed to have been inspired by the Holy Spirit and collected a sizable following during the anti-*converso* riots that erupted in Toledo in 1449.[5] Other prophets surfaced in Valladolid during the tumultuous years immediately preceding the outbreak of the comunero revolt in 1520, among them Fray Juan de San Vicente, a Franciscan who made public pronouncements about the "bad government" of Spain.[6] Two years later, during the Germanía revolt in the Valencian town of Játiva, there appeared a hermit who described himself as *el Rey Encubierto.* Dressed in animal skins, possibly to identify himself with King David, the hermit claimed to be a redeemer sent by the Holy Spirit to destroy "the swamp of this kingdom." Promising riches for his followers and rewarding some with noble titles, this "king" was soon dispatched by assassins hired by the royal viceroy.[7]

The 1580s constituted another moment in Spanish history when street prophets suddenly proliferated, in part prompted by the expectations raised by Philip II's conquest of Portugal. In 1580 there surfaced in Albuquerque, a small town near the Portuguese border, a widow who claimed to have experienced a vision which revealed that Philip would not realize his goal unless he first vowed to lead the Portuguese on an African crusade.[8]

Yet most of the decade's prophetic activity was centered in Madrid and should be linked to the monarchy's mounting economic and political difficulties. In particular, after 1585 many believed that the ailing Philip could no longer defend the kingdom against its enemies, either domestic or foreign. The first street prophet who voiced dissatisfaction with the monarchy itself was probably Juan de Dios, who publicly announced that Spain's sins would soon lead to her destruction by her enemies, a theme later echoed in Lucrecia's dreams.

As noted earlier, Lucrecia's ties to Juan de Dios remain somewhat vague, but Mendoza was among the street prophet's supporters and was reputed to be his biographer.[9] Lucrecia also had connections with a loose coalition of dissident courtiers, each of whom, for various reasons, had grievances against the monarch. Could this young woman have dreamed what these men dared not say aloud? The Holy Office thought so, charging that the dreams were intended to foster opposition to the king and his policies. Lucrecia, the inquisitors suspected, was no divinely inspired prophet, merely the mouthpiece of a fledgling conspiracy of disloyal malcontents.

To understand the political context of Lucrecia's arrest we must trace the crisis of confidence that beset Philip's court in the late 1580s, beginning with the so-called Pérez affair, which involved the arrest and trial of the royal secretary, Antonio Pérez. During the 1560s and early 1570s Antonio Pérez had been one of the most influential figures at Philip II's court, although his power derived less from his office—he was responsible for Spanish affairs in Italy and Flanders—than from his intimate knowledge of court business and his close, personal ties with the king. For a time the young Pérez (b. 1540) was Philip's closest confidant, all the while misappropriating his knowledge of the king's secrets to acquire a small fortune and a substantial art collection. For all his influence, Pérez could not escape the tumultuous and often unpredictable factional struggles of the Spanish court. He himself belonged to the "peace" faction headed by Ruy Gómez de Silva, prince of Eboli, which favored a negotiated end to the Dutch revolt, begun in 1566. The opposing faction, led by the duke of Alba, argued that the revolt should be suppressed by force. By the mid-1570s the "war" faction was in the ascendant, and it was only a matter of time before Pérez began to lose influence with the monarch.

The story of Pérez's downfall has been told many times. In brief, the secretary's detractors arranged for him to be charged with corruption and malfeasance and also to have him implicated (probably rightly) in the murder of Juan de Escobedo, a royal official stabbed by unknown assailants in the streets of Madrid on the night of 1 April 1578. The following year Philip suspended Pérez from office pending a full investigation of all charges levied against him. For the next five and a half years Pérez, aided by various members of the old Eboli faction, attempted to clear his name. His friends included the Mendoza family, the powerful clan of Castilian grandees to which Eboli belonged by virtue of his marriage to doña Ana de Mendoza, princess of Eboli, as well as Madrid's powerful community of Genoese bankers, a group to which Pérez had been particularly close. Also working on his behalf was Cardinal Gaspar de Quiroga, inquisitor general and a member of Philip's Council of State.

Philip was generally inclined to be conciliatory toward his former friend, but in February 1585, after receiving reports that Pérez was complaining "too openly about the affront done to him by the king," the monarch ordered Pérez's arrest.[10] Pérez only made matters worse by attempting to elude two royal officers sent to arrest him. His enemies, among them the royal confessor, Fray Diego de Chaves, now charged that he was guilty of the greater crime of lèse majesté. Pérez was subsequently sentenced to two years' imprisonment, exile from Madrid, and the permanent loss of the emoluments of his office. Yet Philip, still inclined to leniency, soon reduced this sentence and in March

1586 had Pérez brought back to Madrid under house arrest to await the outcome of the inquiry into Escobedo's death.

While Pérez remained hopeful of receiving a royal pardon, by this point his detractors had the king's ear. Early in 1590 Pérez was imprisoned again and under torture asked to confess to the murder of Escobedo. On the night of 19 April 1590, before sentence could be passed, Pérez escaped from Madrid with the help of his wife and a number of accomplices, and fled to Zaragoza, in his native kingdom of Aragon. There crowds greeted him as a hero, and his arrest by the Inquisition the following July prompted riots in the streets. In 1591, however, Pérez escaped once again and fled to safety in France and in England, where he eventually wrote a series of books and pamphlets harshly critical of his former king, master, and friend.[11]

The Pérez affair has been extensively documented, yet most accounts treat the attempts to secure Pérez's pardon primarily as a matter of court intrigue.[12] But interest in his affairs extended well beyond the court, for Pérez cut an enormously popular figure in Madrid. Even during his confinement, his elegant villa, La Casilla, served as a meeting place for distinguished courtiers, nobles, diplomats, and bankers. Pérez also maintained close ties with ordinary madrileños, and as a parishioner of San Sebastián—the same parish in which Lucrecia lived—he had the reputation of being generous and charitable to the poor. It mattered little, therefore, that his enemies criticized this lowborn official for living in greater luxury than the nobility. In the eyes of many, Pérez was the victim of the king's arbitrary and unjustified abuse of power, and this was the version of his arrest disseminated in and around the court by his friends and supporters. Through their efforts the Pérez affair entered the public arena as one aspect of a diffuse political dissatisfaction with Philip's rule.

The causes of this dissatisfaction are difficult to unravel, but what seems certain is that the sense of *desengaño* (disillusionment) traditionally said to have beset the whole of Spain immediately after the Armada's defeat in 1588 actually began somewhat earlier.[13] For one thing, the aloof and retiring Philip was never a truly popular ruler, at least not in comparison with his convivial father, the Emperor Charles V.[14] Early in his reign Philip's reputation was enhanced by a combination of prosperity at home and a series of military triumphs abroad, climaxed by the great naval victory over the Turks at Lepanto in 1571. Also aiding Philip was his popular French queen, Isabel de Valois, his third wife, who organized a string of lavish court entertainments designed to curry favor with Spain's haughty grandees.

The conquest of Portugal (1580–1582) and the reconquest of the south Netherlands (1582–1585) by the duke of Parma subsequently created an atmosphere of euphoria, at least in Spanish political circles, but the optimism prompted by these military victories proved short-lived. Parma was unable to follow up on his 1585 capture of Antwerp, and hopes for an immediate end to the war in Flanders quickly ebbed.

The monarch's military adventures abroad were sustained by seemingly inexhaustible supplies of silver from Mexico and Peru, but only a small portion of these riches ever reached Castile, the heartland of Philip's empire. By the mid-1580s, moreover, prosperity had given way to economic stagnation, and thousands of hungry peasants flooded into Madrid, Toledo, and Seville looking for work. Castilian industry was also in trouble, owing in large measure to Philip's tripling of the *alcabala* in 1574. Throughout the kingdom, and especially in the cities, taxes increasingly became the source of grumbling and unrest.

Other bad omens came from France, where the power of the anti-Catholic Huguenot faction was growing, and from England, as Elizabeth I encouraged Drake, Hawkins, and other sea dogs to attack Spanish ships and shipping in the Atlantic. The economic losses caused by these raids was relatively minor, but the "English scare" during the 1580s undermined confidence in Philip's government and its ability to defend the kingdom against foreign attack. The French ambassador Longlée reported that the court was "scandalized" after learning of Drake's raid on Galicia and the Canary Islands in October 1585, and news of Drake's attack on the island of Santo Domingo the following month gave rise to urgent demands for the restoration of the monarchy's defenses, both in the Old World and the New.[15]

Faith in Philip's ability to protect his kingdom was further undermined by his failing health. An unsustainable blow came on 18 April 1587, when Drake, having been ordered by Elizabeth to "singe the beard of the king of Spain," dared to attack the Spanish mainland, raiding the Atlantic port of Cádiz and destroying many of the supplies intended for the Armada. Foreign ambassadors reported that Madrid was consumed by rumors of the kingdom's "defenselessness."[16] The Cortes, Castile's national assembly, urged Philip to seek an immediate "remedy" to prevent further attacks and to defend the Indies' trade, and the governors of Cádiz wrote a particularly urgent letter warning that their city "was in great danger of being lost" unless the monarch immediately appropriated money for new defenses.[17]

Given such pressures, the only hope for Castile was that Philip would prove himself to be his father's son, for Charles V never hesitated to take up the sword against an enemy. But Philip, "the Prudent" had never been a man of action, and his illness left him more indecisive than ever. "He [the king] looks old, more pensive," wrote the Venetian ambassador in 1586, "with less resolution and dispatch."[18] Philip thus appeared to dither at a moment when his kingdom demanded heroic deeds. As the Venetian ambassador put it, "The Spanish say the king thinks and plans while the Queen of England acts and that in earnest."[19] The repeated postponements that delayed the sailing of the Armada in 1587 and early 1588 further frustrated and alarmed Philip's subjects.

The king's isolation from his own court made matters worse still. Traditionally, Castilian rulers had made themselves available to their courtiers; grandees had easy and immediate access to their monarch, and the king met his other subjects in regularly scheduled audiences. This open-door policy ended in 1548, when Charles V reformed the etiquette governing the operation of his son's household, partly as a way of protecting the young prince from the factional divisions of the court. So long as Philip was prince the new ceremonial, a complex etiquette modeled after that of the Burgundian court, did not cause much of a stir. But complaints began soon after Philip returned from the Low Countries to Spain as its monarch in

1559. As early as 1562 the Florentine ambassador alluded to the dissatisfaction "this pretension of precedence" had aroused among the grandees.[20]

In principle the new ceremonial was designed to augment the king's authority, but it also had the effect of isolating him from his courtiers and enhancing the influence of a small inner circle of household officers who controlled access to the royal person. To be sure, such isolation probably suited Philip's melancholic temperament; but as he grew older and his health deteriorated, he gradually withdrew from any active involvement in life at the court. As the duke of Infantado explained, Philip's illness led him to "retire more" and "not allow the grandees so much entrance."[21] Now Philip preferred to make most decisions independently, aided only by a small coterie of advisors that included Mateo Vázquez, the royal secretary, and Cristóbal de Moura and Juan de Idiáquez, two members of the Council of State. This clique, soon known, somewhat sinisterly, as the "Junta de Noche," assumed many of the daily tasks of governance that Philip previously handled himself. The paperwork flowed more smoothly than before, but the emergence of this inner circle provoked additional complaints about the king's isolation, among them a satirical note by one disgruntled courtier who described life in the royal palace as nothing less than "withdrawn."[22] By 1587, then, Philip had retired into a royal cocoon, protected by a carapace of advisors whose ambitions and motives were becoming increasingly suspect.

The depth and extent of this crisis of confidence in Philip's ability to govern his kingdom remains open to debate, but by the late 1580s many Spaniards feared that the king's reign was nearing its end. Despite his age and ill health Philip ruled another ten years, but they were years marked by the spread of apocalyptic ideas and various doomsday scenarios. In Madrid, Fray Alonso de Orozco, a prominent Augustinian preacher widely revered for his prophetic gift, publicly expressed his concern that the Armada would end in defeat because "our sins are great."[23] Millenarian ideas were also fomented by the discovery, in a tower in Granada in March 1588, of the *plomos de Granada,* lead boxes holding a series of parchments written in Arabic and Greek. Among these documents was an Arabic version of St. John the Evangelist's prophecies about the end of the world, as well as others that scheduled the millennium for "the years just short of 1600."[24] Although the parchments were later proven to be forgeries, interest in them indicates that the current of millennialism had spread well beyond the royal court.

Astrological forecasts added yet another dimension to doubts about Spain's future. In 1566 Michel Nostradamus announced that "in the year five hundred fourscore more or less, there shall be a strange age." Other astrologers were more precise, predicting that 1588 would be a year of cataclysm because of one solar eclipse, two lunar eclipses, and a grand conjunction, a rare astronomical alignment of Saturn, Jupiter, and Mars. Since biblical times, these conjunctions had been associated with wars, revolutions, deaths of important persons, and other momentous events. In sixteenth-century Europe printed almanacs and popular *prognostica* helped to spread these astrological ideas among street prophets and soothsayers. Throughout the continent, therefore, 1588 was anticipated as the "wonder year," a time of great changes, perhaps even the end of the world.[25]

Spanish astrologers tended to interpret celestial phenomena primarily in nationalistic terms. Guillén de Casaos, the astrologer who offered Lucrecia instruction concerning lunar eclipses, spoke openly about Spain's troubled future. So did such street prophets as Juan de Dios and Miguel de Piedrola, both of whom warned madrileños of the dangers 1588 was certain to bring. But Piedrola's prognostications were coupled with criticism of Philip as an unjust, arbitrary ruler whose continued presence on the throne jeopardized the entire future of Spain. And Piedrola was not merely another doomsayer caught up in Spanish millennialism. As it turns out, Piedrola had ties to Antonio Pérez, and his prophecies may well have been intended as political stratagems designed to press Philip into ordering the former secretary's release. Lucrecia's dreams were evidently used to similar purposes, but in order to understand her connection with Pérez, it is helpful first to examine Piedrola's prophetic career.

Piedrola, the Soldier-Prophet

Miguel de Piedrola Beamonte was a native of Navarre, in northern Spain. Although he claimed noble descent, in his youth he worked as an itinerant tinker (*ollero*). He later joined the army, serving for a time as a foot soldier in Italy. There, by his account, he was twice captured by the Turks and twice ransomed. After serving briefly in the campaign to suppress the *morisco* revolt in Granada, Piedrola drifted into Madrid in about 1570, hoping to secure a royal pension. Shortly thereafter he began writing a series of *arbitrios* (memorials) to the king, offering advice about the "conservation of his kingdoms" and suggestions for ending the war in Flanders.[26] Such missives were a commonplace means of communicating with the monarch, but Piedrola's messages had a macabre twist: he warned that Philip's children would die unless the monarch heeded his advice. For a while Piedrola was evidently considered harmless, and he was left alone.[27]

Official attitudes changed, however, some time late in 1578, when Piedrola began to deliver similar messages in the streets of Madrid. Identifying himself with the biblical prophets Elijah and Malachi, Piedrola publicly asserted that the advice he was offering the monarch had a divine source.[28] Soon after, one of Philip's secretaries advised Piedrola to abandon Madrid. This he did, sometime in 1579, coincidental with Antonio Pérez's first fall from the king's favor. But the only connection between Pérez and Piedrola at this time was that both favored a negotiated end to the war against the Dutch.[29]

Piedrola's precise movements over the next few years are difficult to trace. He seems to have rejoined the army, arriving in Naples sometime before January 1580.[30] By 1584 he had returned to Madrid and resumed his career as the soldier-prophet. Piedrola's reputation as a seer rested on the (mistaken) belief that he was an illiterate soldier who had miraculously memorized the entire Bible with divine assistance. He further claimed that his knowledge of the future derived from a series of dreams—seventy-two in all—which he attributed to God. No records of these dreams survive, but evidently they dealt with contemporary political events and openly criticized the king and his ministers. Some spoke of the "great events of the year 1588," which would result in the "imminent destruction of Spain." The soldier-prophet also proclaimed that at the moment this destruction began, his supporters were to seek refuge in a cave called la Espelunça. There, like a later-day Pelayo, the mythical eighth-century king who had planned the Reconquest, Piedrola would organize Spain's deliverance from her enemies and establish a new Spain governed by a limited monarchy under a constitution—an open challenge to the absolutist principles of Habsburg rule.

The source of Piedrola's radical ideas remains unknown, although they may have a basis in the medieval constitutionalist traditions (*fueros*) of his native Navarre, which limited the powers of that kingdom's monarch. Piedrola's adopted second surname—Beamonte, or Beaumont—further identifies him with a fifteenth-century Navarrese tradition of resistance to kings thought to be unjust. The Beamontes were an aristocratic faction opposed to Juan II (1431–1479), the Aragonese ruler who in 1451 deposed his son, Carlos, prince of Viana, as ruler of Navarre. The leader of this faction, Luis de Beamonte, branded Juan II a despot who had violated the kingdom's fueros. Piedrola is not known to have expressed an opinion on this particular point of Navarrese history, but his identification with the Beamontes, coupled with his criticisms of Philip II, suggest that he considered Philip the Castilian equivalent of Juan II—a tyrant who ruled without popular consent.

The extent of Piedrola's following is difficult to determine. In 1588 the papal nuncio in Madrid reported to the Vatican that Piedrola "was esteemed by many persons of great and small estate" along with other "wise persons of quality" who compared his prophetic powers with those of Isaiah and Jerome.[31] No list of these supporters has survived, and Piedrola himself referred to his friends only by a series of mysterious aliases such as "Dr. Silence, the Strong Knight of the Golden Key, Pastor Anastasio, and Lady Obstinate."[32] Other sources indicate that his partisans included Mendoza and Allende, along with Lucrecia's astrologer friend, Guillén de Casaos.[33] In addition, Piedrola appears to have had a number of supporters among royal officers and others directly associated with the court. Alonso de Orozco alleged that Piedrola deceived "many honorable *letrados,*" a group which seems to have included Juan de Herrera, the royal architect, and even Quiroga, the inquisitor general.[34] The royal chronicler Jerónimo de Sepúlveda also attested that Piedrola "fooled and deceived . . . not just anyone, but very important people," among them the dukes of Medina Sidonia, Nájera, and Pastrana, the marquis of Carpio, as well as Lady Jane Dormer, an English Catholic who, as the duke of Feria's widow, frequently meddled in the politics of the Spanish court.[35] In sum, Piedrola successfully gathered a small but influential band of followers, many of whom were evidently prepared to enter Espelunça once the millennium began.[36]

The agenda of Piedrola's followers also included the prompt release of Antonio Pérez. In this respect the apocalyptic message of Piedrola's prophecies and his demand for governmental reform can be interpreted as part of an attempt to rally popular support for the imprisoned secretary. Another aim was to have Piedrola officially designated as Spain's national prophet, a new and previously unfilled post. Oddly enough, this scheme almost succeeded, owing to worries about the worsening economy and increasing disapproval of Philip's government. At the urging of Piedrola's well-placed allies, the Castilian Cortes appointed a special commission to investigate Piedrola's prophetic credentials and the implications of his dire prognostications for Spain's future.

Thus during the summer of 1587, at a moment when Piedrola's reputation as a prophet and seer reached its height,[37] the national assembly sent the head of a parliamentary commission, a certain Gaspar Gómez, to meet with Piedrola. Apparently, the two engaged in a learned discussion about Holy Scripture. In a report delivered to a plenary session of the Cortes on 22 August 1587, the commission acknowledged that many "important churchmen and preachers . . . consider him [Piedrola] a prophet, as in times past" and recommended that the king establish his own royal commission to determine "if Piedrola justly deserves the title of Prophet, and if the prophecies he publicizes are sincere and true." During the subsequent debate in the Cortes on the merits of this proposal, Dr. Guillén, a representative of Seville, maintained that "one of the most important issues facing the kingdom is to determine whether Piedrola is a prophet."[38]

Yet Piedrola also had powerful detractors, among them Fray Alonso de Orozco, a rival prophet, and Fray Juan Baptista, an Italian Franciscan then resident in Madrid.[39] Beginning in June 1587, Fray Juan denounced the soldier-prophet as an "evil spirit" and an "agent of Lucifer"; in one sermon the friar claimed that Piedrola "was possessed by a demon which was responsible for everything he said and did."[40] Within a matter of weeks the controversy sparked by these denunciations spread to the royal court and apparently led Philip II to name a commission to investigate Piedrola's prophetic career.

The three commissioners—Quiroga, the inquisitor general; Chaves, the royal confessor; and García de Loaysa, the royal almoner—met in late July and gathered a series of reports concerning Piedrola. Fray Luis de León, the famed Augustinian theologian and expert in prophetic discourse, advised that Piedrola's "spirit of prophecy" should not be doubted. But the vicar of Madrid accused the soldier-prophet of speaking only to those "a quien tocar" (that is, his friends) and of treating many important people with "poca modestía" (little respect).[41] The commission also heard testimony that Piedrola's prophecies included ideas that "our Holy Catholic Faith cannot tolerate," and it was apparently this allegation that persuaded its members to recommend that the proper venue for a detailed inquiry into Piedrola's prophetic credentials was not the Cortes but the Inquisition. Thus, on 18 September 1587, precisely at the moment the Cortes was publicly debating the merits of Piedrola's prophecies, the Holy Office ordered the soldier-prophet's arrest and, the following day, spirited him off to Toledo for trial. The arrest, the secretary of the Florentine ambassador in Madrid noted, caused "great murmurings" at the royal court.[42]

In the months that followed, the individual who worked hardest to secure Piedrola's release was none other than Alonso de Mendoza. Aided by Allende, Mendoza prepared a series of documents and reports attesting to Piedrola's prophetic spirit. On 19 September 1587, only a day after the arrest, Mendoza appealed to Cardinal Ascanio Colonna in Rome, comparing Piedrola's arrest and imprisonment to Darius's order to cast Daniel into the lions' den.[43] In the meanwhile, Piedrola saw to his own defense with a claim of insanity as well as a confession, offered in May 1588, in which he asserted that his visions were nothing more than "illusion and deceit." Later that year the Holy Office decided that Piedrola was indeed a "false prophet" and on 18 December 1588, at an auto da fe staged in Toledo, sentenced him to two years' seclusion followed by perpetual exile from Madrid.[44]

Piedrola's case illustrates several points relevant to our understanding of Lucrecia's fate. The Spanish Inquisition, it appears, treated false prophecy as a relatively minor offense. (In Elizabeth's England, by way of comparison, William Hackett's prophecies and public criticisms of the queen's government led him directly to the scaffold.) In theory the Spanish church, following the general tenets of the Counter-Reformation, took a dim view of any lay person who claimed to have the "prophetic gift." Yet in practice most seers were either tolerated or ignored, so long as they did not openly espouse heretical concepts or ideas.

The Spanish crown also tolerated the vitriol of self-proclaimed street prophets—for years the monarchy virtually ignored Piedrola's presence in Madrid—as long as the prophet had only a scattered following. But once a prophet appeared to pose a political threat to the power of the throne, once the Cortes was on the verge of transforming Piedrola into a national figure, official tolerance ceased. To deny Piedrola a public pulpit for further criticisms of the monarch, the crown decided to have him arrested by the Holy Office rather than by civil authorities, for the Inquisition was the sole tribunal that could guarantee a secret trial. The essentially political, rather than religious, nature of Piedrola's arrest was evident to his supporters, one of whom wrote to another that the political implications of the case required the Inquisition to handle the trial in an "extraordinary" fashion.[45]

Even then the crown went to extraordinary lengths to ensure

that Piedrola be kept in strict isolation, a policy it enforced long after his sentence was announced. Ordinarily, the Holy Office sent those condemned to a period of seclusion to any convent or monastery willing to take them. In this case, however, the crown instructed the Suprema, the Supreme Council of the Inquisition, to undertake a thorough investigation of a number of sites in order to make certain that security for this seditious prisoner was adequate. After considerable deliberation it was decided that Piedrola would be confined to the fortress of Guadamur, situated in a small, relatively isolated village six miles west of Toledo.

Given this story, what are we to make of Piedrola's recurrent presence in Lucrecia's dreams, both as the prophet whose advice Philip had rejected and as the redeemer who would restore a defeated Spain? And what of the similarities in the content of their dreams: Spain's imminent destruction, Philip's failures, and the cave—Piedrola's la Espelunça and Lucrecia's Sopeña—as the headquarters of Spain's restoration? First, we know that Sacamanchas, a mutual friend, arranged for Lucrecia to visit Piedrola in his lodgings at Madrid's Trinitarian monastery on at least one occasion. Second, we know that Allende, Mendoza, and several other members of la Espelunça numbered among Lucrecia's supporters. More to the point, in a letter of March 1588, Mendoza named Lucrecia as one of the "spirits" who, following the arrest of Piedrola, "have appeared at God's order to spread his secrets."[46] Thus it was not a coincidence that Lucrecia's first dreams about the "loss of Spain" were announced at virtually the moment of the soldier-prophet's arrest. Evidently, Lucrecia was willing to inherit the prophetic mantle that the Inquisition forced Piedrola to relinquish.

But did Lucrecia share Piedrola's political agenda and his alliances with the Pérez faction at court? The evidence is mostly circumstantial, but surely Lucrecia's ties to the Mendoza family and, through her father, to Madrid's Genoese bankers, as well as her own grudges against the monarch, were motives for allying herself with the faction supporting the former secretary. And in his testimony to the Holy Office, Vitores stated that Lucrecia had once boasted of having publicly defended the former secretary in the presence of the king.[47] However, to appreciate the full extent of Lucrecia's connection with the Pérez affair, and to determine whether her dreams were exploited by Pérez's supporters to secure his release, we must look more closely at the individuals with whom she cast her lot: Mendoza, Allende, and Casaos.

Alonso de Mendoza

Members of the Mendoza family were among Pérez's staunchest supporters. The nominal head of this rich and powerful clan of grandees was Alonso's first cousin, the duke of Infantado, but the large family counted among its various branches the dukes of Pastrana and the counts of Ceñete, Coruña, Priego, Saldaña, and Tendilla. Alonso's father, Alonso Suárez de Mendoza, second count of Coruña, was a soldier who served under the Emperor Charles V.[48] He married Juana Jiménez de Cisneros, niece of Cardinal Jiménez de Cisneros, the famous archbishop of Toledo and the founder of the university at Alcalá de Henares. Together this couple had twenty children. The eldest brother, Lorenzo, inherited the family title and was later appointed viceroy of Mexico, but it is Bernardino (d. 1604) who is best remembered, as a scholar who chronicled the Dutch revolt and as Philip II's ambassador to London (1578–1584) and Paris (1584–1590).[49]

While Bernardino was abroad, he kept in close touch with Alonso, buying foreign books not available in Spain and forwarding to Toledo news of international events. Bernardino's increasingly gloomy assessment of Spanish power, particularly in the period immediately following the Armada disaster, seems to have shaped the political opinions of his younger brother. Other members of Alonso's family were at court—his sister Ana was *dama de honor* to Queen Anne of Austria and, after 1584, royal governess to the infante Philip—and most likely provided Alonso with up-to-date news of the king and his policies.[50]

Born in Guadalajara in 1537, Alonso, as a younger son, was destined for an ecclesiastical career. He studied liberal arts and theology at Alcalá de Henares and in 1558 entered the university's prestigious Colegio Mayor de San Ildefonso. A specialist in biblical studies, he was elected to the university chair of Holy Scripture in 1566. Alvar Gómez de Castro, a leading humanist, described Mendoza as a scholar of "rare intellect" and a "skilled theologian." He was also an accomplished preacher and in 1568 was asked by the university to deliver the sermon honoring Queen Isabel de Valois after her death. Ten years later the powerful cathedral chapter of Toledo appointed Mendoza magistral canon, an important position that required him to deliver weekly Bible lessons. In addition, Mendoza was nominated Abad de San Vicente, a largely honorific but lucrative dignity. The combined revenues from these two offices amounted to approximately 5,500 ducats a year, a substantial income roughly equivalent to that of a minor nobleman.[51]

Once in Toledo, Mendoza rapidly became known for his erudition as well as his charity, eventually earning a reputation as a "great almsgiver."[52] In 1585 he served as rector of the foundling hospital of Santa Cruz, an institution established in the late fifteenth century by his great-grandfather, Cardinal Pedro González de Mendoza. In this capacity don Alonso was reputed to "serve the poor personally, feeding them and making medicines for them with his own hands, and even attending to them at night."[53] Meanwhile, Mendoza's theological expertise enabled him to forge close links with the local tribunal of the Inquisition, which occasionally employed him as a *calificador* (theological advisor). In this capacity he helped censor the 1570 edition of the breviary printed by Plantin in Antwerp.[54]

Yet the charitable and studious Mendoza had another side. Although his reputation was generally that of "a good, virtuous man" who was, in the opinion of one prominent Toledan, among "the most exemplary clerics the cathedral of Toledo ever had,"[55] during his trial several of Mendoza's old acquaintances testified that he was mentally unstable. Dr. Alonso Serrano, who apparently had known Mendoza since their years at the university, mentioned an occasion on which Mendoza dressed in secular clothes and white shoes and walked openly about the streets of

Alcalá. Law professor Tello Maldonado reported that Mendoza "does not have all his senses" and remembered when he had created a scandal by shouting inside the Toledo cathedral.[56]

Mendoza's eccentric attire and behavior had caused him trouble with the cathedral chapter in 1582, and he was criticized for a close and somewhat unbecoming relationship with a certain Gerónima Doria, the daughter of a prominent Toledan merchant family of Genoese descent.[57] Mendoza also raised eyebrows when his study of alchemy led him to seek out mines, both in Spain and in England, that produced the best tin.[58] Astrology, divination, and oneiromancy were among his other pastimes, and it was evidently these preoccupations that led him to begin writing a biography of the street prophet Juan de Dios and to take an interest in Piedrola and Lucrecia.

To the Inquisition, Mendoza defended his involvement with Lucrecia on strict theological grounds. His task, he explained, was to determine whether her dreams might be of divine origin. Mendoza also claimed his right as a churchman to have Lucrecia's dreams transcribed, justifying his actions by reference to the Lateran Council of 1516 which, in his opinion, allowed theologians to examine and study dreams and, if they turned out to be "good," also to publicize them.[59] Thus Mendoza compared his transcriptions of Lucrecia's dreams to the work of the fourteenth-century cleric who wrote down the revelations of St. Bridgit as well as to Fray Luis de Granada's hagiography of the Nun of Lisbon.[60] Furthermore, he claimed that the transcriptions were "an act of charity."[61]

As noted earlier, Mendoza was also keenly interested in the parallels between Lucrecia's dreams and the Book of Esdras. In a note appended to the dream register for 20 January 1588, he explained that "from here on I will juxtapose one with the other, noting the concordances that exist between them . . . for the glory of God and the defense of his truth."[62] In this sense, Mendoza sincerely believed that he was doing God's work when he interpreted the dreams, and in a revealing note, written at 3 A.M. on 7 February 1588 and appended to the dream register, he made the following confession:

> it is not my intention to differ in anything from the doctrine professed and taught by the Holy Mother Roman Catholic Church, whose faith I received thanks to the mercy of God in Holy Baptism and which I have attempted to keep, although as a bad Christian and vile sinner, until the age of fifty years and ten months less three days.

Despite these assertions of scholarly detachment and religious orthodoxy, Mendoza's attitude toward Lucrecia was clearly that of a partisan. He regularly referred to her as a *vidente* (seer) and to her dreams as "divine prophecy," "heavenly inspirations," and "works of God"; other notations in the dream registers indicate that he believed her prophetic spirit was "manifest," and in one he specifically refers to her as a "divine prophet."[63] The intensity of his conviction is also evidenced by his painstaking labors to copy and annotate her dream visions and his efforts to create Sopeña, by converting some caves near Toledo into a protective bunker.

One might be tempted to view these exertions as demonstrations of the mental instability described by Mendoza's trial, but it is worth remembering that virtually everyone in the sixteenth century believed in prophecy, visions, magic, and the occult. Still, on the face of it, the extent of Mendoza's preoccupation with Lucrecia bordered on the obsessive. From the hastily scribbled notes in the margins of the dream registers, however, one can infer that Mendoza's eagerness to accept Lucrecia's dreams as prophetic messages was deeply rooted in religious conviction, notably his belief that Philip had betrayed the ideals of the Counter-Reformation church as expressed in the canons and decrees of the Council of Trent. Apparently, Lucrecia's oneiric portrait of Philip as cruel, unjust, and tyrannical matched Mendoza's view of the monarch. Mendoza made few public statements against the king; to do so might have cost him his life. But in the privacy of his study Mendoza dropped his guard and vented his grievances in notes appended to the dream registers.

Crucial to Mendoza's distrust of Philip was the churchman's interpretation of the Tridentine doctrine of good works and the need for every Catholic, layman and cleric, to perform charitable deeds. Mendoza wholeheartedly embraced this doctrine and censured Philip for paying only lip service to charity. The focus of Mendoza's criticism was the Escorial, the royal monastery whose construction took fourteen years and cost nearly five million ducats, a sum roughly equivalent to one year's treasury receipts from the Indies, or almost as much as Philip expended on the Armada.

Mendoza's grievances against Philip's monumental edifice first appear in a lengthy note appended to Lucrecia's dream of 22 January 1588. In this dream the Ordinary Man expresses the view that the monastery "was not pleasing to God because St. Lawrence did not want so many towers [built] at the cost of the poor." Mendoza's initial reaction to this statement was terse: "His judgment is just." Then, he catalogued the king's sins in having undertaken the work: "pride, ambition, and celebration of his name in future centuries." "God can be served," he wrote in a tone reminiscent of Erasmus's earlier criticisms of clerical ostentation, "with fewer high walls and haughty towers, slate roofs, brocades, gold, silver, precious stones, pearls, and extraordinary marbles." God could be better served, he continued, through "moderation in all that involves the divine cult, the construction of his churches, and altar services, as one finds among the Discalced Franciscan and other poor religious orders and churches where their finances do not permit vessels of silver." But at Philip's Escorial, "the humblest goblets in the sacristy are made of silver" and the "iron and stone and metal of the grilles, altars, retables, and chapels are gilded with gold." Such extravagance, Mendoza complained, did not induce prayer but served only to "mock God" (hacer burla de Dios). The Escorial, he concluded, was nothing less than a dishonor to St. Lawrence, a saint "who distributed church treasures to the poor instead of building a haughty temple to himself at the cost of the blood of the poor." That the monastery's construction had been financed by money derived from "unjust taxes and increases in the alcabala" made the Escorial the oversized emblem of Philip's lack of Christian charity.[64]

Mendoza's list of grievances against Philip did not end with the Escorial. Like other churchmen, he took issue with Philip's taxation of the clergy and the sale of ecclesiastical jurisdictions and villages, a policy that had adversely affected the cathedral chapter of Toledo.[65] At the heart of this particular grievance were the *escusado* and *subsidio,* two levies upon church revenues that Pope Pius V had granted to the Spanish monarchy in 1572 in order to help Philip defray expenses in his wars against the Turks. Originally intended as temporary measures, these taxes were subsequently renewed every five years, and the rates were the source of bitter and frequently protracted negotiations.

As it turned out, Mendoza was the *presidente* of the church congregation that convened in Madrid in 1586 in order to discuss the fourth and latest installment of the church tax.[66] As the head of this congregation, Mendoza represented the clergy in its dealings with the crown. The negotiations proved difficult and spilled over to include other causes of friction between clergy and crown, notably certain privileges Philip had granted to the Society of Jesus. A tough negotiator, Mendoza at one point during the summer of 1587 refused to hand over certain papers to the king and was arrested by a royal official. His arrest, however, was surely not unrelated to documents he had circulated that not only attacked Philip's fiscal policy but alleged that "while other kings, your ancestors, have given to the church, Your Majesty only takes things away."[67] Claiming benefit of clergy, Mendoza immediately appealed his arrest to the papacy, and the papal nuncio soon secured his release, but this incident appears to have turned Mendoza permanently against the king as well as García Loaysa de Girón, the royal almoner whom Mendoza considered directly responsible for his arrest.[68]

Mendoza also disapproved of Philip's failure to adhere to the decree by the Council of Trent that priests and bishops were to reside in their churches. Mendoza subscribed to this doctrine and made every effort to obey it. But Philip flouted it by appointing churchmen to royal office, among them two members of his own cathedral, García de Loaysa and Quiroga. Yet another source of irritation was the king's policy toward the moriscos, a group that Mendoza, along with many other conservative churchmen, regarded as "the greatest enemies we have."[69]

The king's refusal to expel the moriscos, Mendoza feared, could only lead to a general revolt.

A further point of contention was the king's failure to curtail corruption among officials involved in the collection of royal taxes. As Mendoza explained to Guillén de Casaos: "I am not bothered so much by the fact that these officials get rich, but that the king does not reject any advice or counsel they give him about additional taxes; the money serves only to make them rich and to impoverish the kingdom."[70] Mendoza's assessment of the king's imprudence in spending his ill-gotten tax revenues informs an invidious portrait of Philip in his gloss of Lucrecia's dream of 3 February 1588. The appearance of some deer in this dream led Mendoza to recall the day when, traveling from Madrid to the Escorial, he had encountered some royal deer. This idle recollection suddenly arouses Mendoza's impassioned ire:

> This king wants to be a king of animals rather than men, because he gives more to those beasts than to his vassals, since he does not kill the former for erecting fences and barriers and if anyone kills his deer they are whipped. On the other hand, after the church gave him 600,000 ducats for one hundred galleys to defend the coasts, he did not want to do it until the enemies came to seize captives and to rob the land, as in Cádiz and elsewhere.

Drake's raid on Cádiz, Philip's misappropriation of church subsidies, and the stringency of the monarchy's protection of game in royal hunting preserves—Mendoza's complaints against the monarch were all-encompassing. And, of course, there was the matter of Antonio Pérez. Mendoza was outspoken in his support of the imprisoned secretary. Upon learning of Pérez's escape from prison in April 1590, Mendoza noted ironically that this "important news" will serve as an invitation to Spain's enemies since it reveals the many "divisions among the rulers of our kingdom."[71]

Yet for all these disagreements over policy, Mendoza's animosity toward the king and ministers must also be attributed to frustrated ambition. Ordinarily, an ecclesiastic with Mendoza's family background and academic credentials could have expected promotion to a bishopric. Several of Mendoza's ancestors had been prelates, notably his grandfather, Pedro González de Mendoza, and his great-uncle, Jiménez de Cisneros, both of whom served as archbishops of Toledo. According to some witnesses at his trial, Mendoza harbored similar aspirations, and he once told Lucrecia that the king was personally responsible for not having recommended him for an episcopal see.[72] Given the politics of the day, however, Mendoza's prospects for promotion were few. Ecclesiastical appointments during the 1580s were controlled by the royal secretary Mateo Vázquez, as well as García de Loaysa, who, as a fellow member of Toledo's cathedral chapter, knew Mendoza and apparently disapproved of his eccentric habits. Furthermore, according to the court historian Cabrera de Córdoba, the entire Mendoza clan, including the powerful duke of Infantado, was out of favor with the king, undoubtedly a result of the family's having sided with Antonio Pérez.[73]

Personal disappointments, therefore, seem to have compounded Mendoza's objections to the king's policies. Frustration mingled with resentment, enhancing the churchman's professional concern with prophecy and his avocational interests in oneiromancy and divination. In the street prophets Juan de Dios and Piedrola, he may have been seeking divine confirmation of his disenchantment with the monarchy. In Lucrecia, the frustrated cleric may have hoped he had found a means of rallying opposition to the king.

Fray Lucas de Allende

Assisting Mendoza in this seditious enterprise was Lucas de Allende, the prior of Madrid's Franciscan convent, one of the largest and most important religious houses in the capital. Born in about 1545 of humble origins in the village of Villarrubia de Ocaña, near the site of the caves at Sopeña, Allende, like Mendoza, was trained as a theologian. He became a Franciscan at about the age of sixteen and was educated in Toledo, Alcalá de Henares, and finally in Coimbra, where he resided in the College of St. Bonaventure in 1574–75. He subsequently taught theology in a Franciscan convent in the Canary Islands and then served as the prior of the convent in Mora, a village near Toledo. According to various members of his order, Allende was a "skilled preacher," "very lettered," and a "good theologian," qualities that helped to account for his promotion to the position of *guardián* of the Franciscan convent in Madrid in 1585.[74]

As the head of this important religious house, Allende easily established close connections with the royal court. Among his friends were various members of the royal household, notably Antonio de Toledo and Alonso de Zúñiga, both royal chamberlains; the royal secretary Francisco de Idiáquez; and Hernando de Toledo, prior of the Order of St. John of Jerusalem and a ranking councillor of state. Allende was also in touch with two of Philip's architects, Juan de Herrera and Francisco de Mora. His other friends included the marquis de las Navas (Alonso de Zúñiga's brother), the count of Lemos, and the dukes of Medinaceli, Medina Sidonia, and Nájera, all of whom had designated Allende as their confessor.

Outside the court, Allende's interests in astrology and prophecy brought him into contact with Guillén de Casaos and Pedro de la Hera, another well-known astrologer. In addition, he collected news of monstrous births and other prodigies, of beatas known for their prophetic gifts, as well as information about a variety of street prophets, including one, possibly Juan de Dios, who claimed to be El Encubierto and warned about Spain's future. Also in Allende's circle were Piedrola, Sacamanchas, and Juan de Trijueque, a court warden who claimed to have experienced prophetic visions about the future of Spain.[75]

Because the Franciscan order was traditionally associated with a variety of unorthodox spiritual movements, Allende's interests cannot be considered unusual. Like Mendoza, however, Allende had a list of grievances against the king. Having witnessed English pirates sack the Franciscan convent on the island of Gomera in the Canaries in 1585, Allende believed that Philip was not doing enough to defend Spanish interests in the Atlantic.[76] Allende was also angered by royal attempts to tax the clergy, and he vigorously resisted Philip's tax policy when he served as the representative (*comisario de corte*) of the Franciscans at the royal court. Allende, moreover, was a fervent supporter of Antonio Pérez and deeply involved in efforts to secure his release. The two had a number of mutual friends, including the Genoese banker Jacome Marengo and Fray Gerónimo Paez, head of the Franciscan convent in Villarejo. Allende even claimed to have visited the famous prisoner on several occasions, once for unspecified reasons in his capacity as comisario de corte. Allende's relationship with Pérez was sufficiently close that he learned about the prisoner's escape plans four months in advance, and Pérez entrusted Allende with certain "goods and jewels," along with a cot that his friends retrieved just prior to his flight in April 1590.[77]

These contacts suggest that Allende, much like Mendoza, hoped to turn Lucrecia's dreams to political purposes. He later informed the Inquisition that he had never believed in her dreams, but in a note scribbled to Mendoza in January 1588 he assured him that "it seems I have nearly all the moral [?] evidence I need to prove that this business [i.e., the dreams] is from God."[78] Soon, Allende was comparing Lucrecia's dreams to those of Daniel, Job, Joseph, and other biblical figures, and he described Lucrecia in a letter of February 1589 as an "honest doncella in whom I have total confidence."[79]

Allende also introduced Lucrecia to some of his powerful friends. He may have done this simply to present her as some type of curiosity or natural prodigy, but more likely he intended to draw attention to the political messages in her dreams. In December 1589 Allende's confidence in the substance of Lucrecia's dreams was strengthened by news of the impending victory of the Protestant faction in France and an alliance between Queen Elizabeth and Protestant leaders in Germany. On 21 December, after informing Mendoza of these developments, Allende added, "it appears that everything you and I know about is well underway."[80]

Guillén de Casaos

Allende's closest collaborator was the astrologer Guillén de Casaos. Born in 1541, Casaos belonged to an important hidalgo family originally from Seville. His father had served as governor in Nicaragua and Costa Rica. Casaos was similarly attracted to the New World. Trained as a soldier, he initially served as an infantry captain in Andalucia, but in 1577 he was appointed captain general of the Yucatan, an important position that he exercised for seven years. In 1583 Casaos took leave of his wife and returned to Madrid in order to gain royal support for a planned expedition to New Mexico.[81] Philip, however, was preoccupied with European affairs and so Casaos was obliged to join the throng of petitioners milling around the royal court.

While he waited, Casaos began writing a series of arbitrios to the king about "his honor and hacienda" as well as "matters touching on the government of the realm, including what should be done in the planned armada to England."[82] In the form of a long poem, Casaos reminded Philip of his responsibilities to his subjects, likening the monarch to a pastor charged with the welfare of his flock. "The defense of the realm depends less on soldiers than upon justice, equity, and well-treated vassals," Casaos wrote, and the tone of the poem suggests that he, too, had by the late 1580s lost faith in Philip's ability to rule.[83]

By 1587 Allende was already serving as Casaos's confessor. The two had apparently met in 1586, discovered their mutual interest in astrology and prophecy, and quickly become friends.[84] The two also shared a fascination with visions, a phenomenon Casaos claimed to have experienced firsthand. His visions, he explained at his trial, had begun in 1574 and continued after his arrival in New Spain. In 1583 he had had a vision of his mother, "white like a cloud and blessing him," which he took as a sign of her death. When this premonition was later confirmed by letter, he thought that the vision might have had a divine source. His other visions and dreams, especially those he experienced while in Madrid, pertained to "more substantial" topics, notably "matters of government" and the "bad government" (mal gobierno) of Spain. In a dream he had in 1585, which he attempted to relate to the king, he heard a voice announce that Philip would become ill during his forthcoming trip to Aragon. Some of his dreams were apocalyptic, concerning "the chastisement of the world, but not its people," but most had political content, including mention of the corruption of the representatives of the cities at the Cortes, the death of Henry III of France, and the defeat of the Armada.[85]

Casaos's letters to the king were ignored and his plans for expeditions to northern Mexico were shelved. Like Mendoza and Allende, then, Casaos had both personal and political grievances against Philip and a marked antipathy toward the royal ministers. Philip's government was inherently corrupt, or as Lucrecia testified, the three of them once agreed that "everything about the king is wrong, even the time of His Majesty's three clocks."[86] With Piedrola in jail, Mendoza, Allende, and Casaos—all charter members of la Espelunça—were denied a spokesman. But at precisely the right moment Lucrecia appeared, a young, innocent, unlettered woman whose dreams could be understood as divine messages in support of the campaign against Philip.

When called before the Inquisition, Casaos denied that he ever considered any of Lucrecia's dreams as prophetic and steadfastly maintained that he had dismissed them as a product of "women's unsteady spirit": "The spirit of women," he claimed, "is a marketplace of lies, filled with nonsense and lots of ups and downs." He attributed Lucrecia's dreams to women's illness ("la enfermedad de mujeres"), further testifying that he never considered them anything but a joke ("burlería").[87] Yet in at least one letter, a note to Mendoza, he admitted that "the dreams are proceeding in an extraordinary manner every night; they are of such substance and the words so exemplary and inspiring that there is nothing to do except give thanks to God."[88]

Such comments by Casaos, Mendoza, and Allende would seem to refute any attribution of purely cynical motives to the men who transcribed and publicized Lucrecia's dreams. Though the dreams were used to political ends, the disgruntled churchmen and courtiers closest to Lucrecia did believe in her prophetic gift.

As we have seen, Lucrecia knew the dangers of speaking out and initially refused to do so. She soon capitulated, however, and by November 1587 had agreed to have the dream texts circulated for political purposes, a decision consistent with her own animosity toward the king as well as her mother's ambitions for the León family. This fateful decision launched Lucrecia on a course that ultimately led to the Inquisition's jail.

5

LUCRECIA THE PROPHET

As Casaos's remarks about women's unsteady spirit suggest, women who claimed to be seers or prophets were at a decided disadvantage in sixteenth-century Europe. A century earlier the Sorbonne theologian Gerson had warned churchmen to be skeptical of women who claimed to have prophetic dreams and divine visions. Women's "enthusiasm," he wrote, "is extravagant, changeable, uninhibited, and therefore not to be considered trustworthy." The "curiosity" and "excess fervor" of young women made them particularly susceptible to imagining religious experiences, he cautioned, and their claims to having visions and prophetic dreams required especially close investigation.[1]

Spanish philosophers and theologians also lectured about women's "natural propensity" for false illusions. In the *Book of Examples* (ca. 1420), Sánchez de Vercial warns readers to "watch out for the deceit of women" and "not to believe in visions."[2] A century later Fray Martín de Castañega, a noted Franciscan, concurred in his *Tratado de las supersticiones y hechicerías* (1529), a treatise expressly commissioned to condemn superstition and witchcraft. He warns his readers of women's natural curiosity about superstition and the occult and repeats the commonplace that women are particularly attracted to the devil because, lacking the physical strength of men, they are apt to rely on diabolical powers for purposes of revenge.[3] Similar ideas inform Diego de Simancas's *Institutiones catholicae* (1552), an influential handbook widely used by Spain's inquisitors,[4] as well as the writings of Fray Domingo Bañes, the Dominican responsible for the censorship of the autobiography of Teresa of Jesus, a work that described in detail many of her visions and revelations. Such matters, wrote Bañes, are "always to be feared, especially in women."[5]

Theologians of Lucrecia's generation harbored similar opinions. In 1588, for example, Juan de Horozco y Covarrubias published his *Tratado de la verdadera y falsa prophecía,* an important antisuperstition tract that was directly inspired by the activities of a number of street prophets, Piedrola and Lucrecia among them. Citing Eve as the archetypal woman, Horozco argues that the devil is always ready to exploit women's "lack of resistance" and use them to in order to deceive "not only a town but also an entire kingdom." He also mentions Magdalena de la Cruz, the prophetic nun from Córdoba who was revered almost as a saint until 1546, when she confessed that the source of her visions was diabolical rather than divine.[6] Confessions of false revelations had also been secured by the Inquisition from Leonor de la Cruz—sentenced to perpetual imprisonment in 1556—and Francisca de Avila, the Toledan beata arrested by the Inquisition in 1578.[7]

Criticism of female clairvoyants also appears in the works of Pedro de Rivadeneyra (1527–1611), one of the most influential Jesuit thinkers of his time. Writing in 1589, Rivadeneyra condemns the "mujercillas," the "crowd of deceived, evil women whom we have recently seen in many of Spain's most illustrious cities; those who with their trances, revelations, and stigmata have excited and deceived their priests and confessors."[8] Misogyny of a different sort surfaces in Pedro Navarro's hagiographic account of Sor Juana de la Cruz, the well-known sixteenth-century visionary from Illescas. In arguing for the uniqueness of Sor Juana's spiritual qualities, Navarro explains that relatively few female prophets appear in the Bible because of women's "natural instability and weakness—an ideal instrument to fabricate trickery and deceit."[9]

The Inquisition's seventeenth-century manual on dreams and prophecies reiterates the notion that women are more "melancholic" than men and therefore women have more active imaginations, which make them more susceptible to diabolical delusion.[10] The manual prominently features St. Teresa's warnings about female visionaries:

> "It should be remembered," she wrote, "that the weakness of our nature is very great, especially in women, and that it shows itself most markedly in the way of prayer; so it is essential that we should not at once suppose every little imagining of ours to be a vision; if it is one, we may be sure that the fact will soon become clear. When a person is subject to melancholy, much more caution is necessary; fancies of this kind have come to me and I have been quite alarmed to find how possible it is for people to think they see what they do not."[11]

The Holy Office also held women to be "less prudent" than men and lacking the mental and physical strength to resist temptation. Immediate suspicion was to fall upon any woman who claimed to have experienced a prophetic vision.[12]

Also working against Lucrecia's credibility was her lack of a religious vocation. Bridgit of Sweden, Catherine of Siena, Teresa of Jesus—traditionally, female seers were nuns or beatas who benefited from the protection and support of a religious order. The asceticism, chastity, and moral reputation of these holy women helped overcome suspicion about the source of their visions. Possibly inspired by the celebrated visions of her Portuguese contemporary, Sor María de la Visitación,[13] Lucrecia either misjudged or misunderstood the dangers of claiming herself to be a prophet: it was difficult even for pious nuns to be credited with having a prophetic gift, almost impossible for laywomen—most of whom, sooner or later, wound up in jail.

A further disadvantage was that Lucrecia's millennial image of Spain's future came to her in dreams rather than visions. Theologians since Augustine argued that the preferred medium of divine revelation was the *visio,* a vision of ineffable character that directly enlightened the intellect and infused it with divine understanding. Such "true" visions were thought to be extremely rare and generally reserved only for those who displayed other forms of divine favor. More common was the "imaginary vision," in which the visionary imagined having seen something or heard a voice communicate a miraculous message. Theologians tended to view this type of vision with considerable suspicion. Rivadeneyra, for example, explains that the devil cannot "enlighten our understanding," but does possess the power "to represent in our imagination various images, to make a voice, and to change objects, colors, etc." The Jesuit thus advises that "when anyone says he is a prophet and has some imaginary visions, or hears a voice speak to him, one must be very suspicious and examine the truth of his prophecy as carefully as possible."[14] Dreams were even less credible than imaginary visions as they were considered particularly susceptible to diabolical manipulation as well as an inappropriate vehicle for a true understanding of divine wisdom.

Thus Lucrecia's chances of gaining wide acceptance as a seer were fairly remote, although she herself may not have completely understood the finer theological points. Rather she seems to have subscribed to Allende's notion that "the dream is often the instrument God uses to reveal his will," along with his argument that "dreams have told the truth in Holy Scripture."[15] What is certain is that she used this particular argument as part of her defense, or as she once remarked to one of her cell mates, "By this road I hope to exonerate myself."[16]

In the final analysis, however, the insurmountable obstacle to Lucrecia's prophetic career was the overtly seditious message of her dreams. Many holy prophets had announced dreams and visions that pertained to questions of dogma and clerical reform: Hildegard of Bingen's visions concerned the reform of the church; those of St. Bridgit called for the return of the papacy from Avignon to Rome; and St. Catherine of Siena addressed papal politics and the start of a new crusade. But such visions rarely contained direct personal criticism of a prelate or king.[17] In Renaissance Spain the visions, raptures, and ecstasies of Sor Juana de la Cruz revealed "occult and invisible things, not only present, but future," but Sor Juana concerned herself with the health of the church and specifically with the welfare of her flagging nunnery, the Convent of Santa María de la Cruz, whose fortunes she helped to revive by attracting the interest and financial support of a number of wealthy patrons.[18] Teresa of Jesus achieved even greater renown as a visionary, but her visions were primarily "intellectual visions" involving Christ, the

Virgin, and the celestial court. Limiting herself to questions of faith and to the establishment of her new religious order, the Discalced Carmelites, Teresa avoided direct involvement in secular affairs.[19] Lucrecia's pointed attacks on Philip, in contrast, almost guaranteed that her prophetic dreams would lead to prison rather than a privileged position in paradise.

The Vicar's Court

Lucrecia's first encounter with the authorities occurred in February 1588, less than five months after she began dictating her dreams to Mendoza and Allende. This incident was clearly the result of the publicity she and her dreams had already received.[20] Lucrecia had never hesitated to speak freely about her dreams to others, including her beata friend, Juana Correa, and other neighborhood women. Nor were Allende and Mendoza circumspect in sharing their knowledge. Indeed, Allende gave copies of the dreams to his powerful friends, presumably for further distribution at court. By early February 1588, rumors about the girl whose dreams foretold the Armada's defeat and Spain's imminent destruction had reached the ears of Philip's principal advisors. Within days a preliminary investigation of Lucrecia was under way, ordered, perhaps, by Fray Diego de Chaves, the royal confessor.

Chaves (1507–1592), like other holders of this important post, remains a shadowy and somewhat sinister figure, known only for his role in ecclesiastical appointments.[21] A doctor of theology from Sigüenza, one of Spain's second-rank universities, Chaves exemplified the stern and rigid spirituality of the post-Tridentine church. A Dominican, he shared his order's intolerance of unorthodox spirituality of any sort. He also upheld the practice, if not the doctrine, of *raison d'état,* and had demonstrated his determination to pursue perceived enemies of royal authority by his active role in the arrest of Bartolomé de Carranza, the archbishop of Toledo, in 1559, and that of Antonio Pérez twenty years later. Chaves's combination of religious zealotry and political Machiavellianism also led him to play a prominent role in the attack on Piedrola during the summer of 1587.

Lucrecia, Chaves now urged, deserved to be punished for "trickery and sedition." The official entrusted with the investigation was Juan Baptista Neroni, who had been recently named vicar of Madrid, the town's ranking ecclesiastical office. On 10 February 1588, the vicar began questioning some of Lucrecia's neighbors and friends. Beata Correa told him that Lucrecia's dreams warned of impending wars, a Moorish invasion, and the death of the prince. A similar story came from María Núñez, a resident of calle del Pozo, who testified that Lucrecia "dreamed great things" about the loss of the Armada as well as a new outbreak of *comunidades* in which everyone would die except for a small contingent hidden in the cave known as Sopeña.[22] This mention of the comuneros revolt of Castile's cities against Charles V in 1520–21 would have immediately suggested to Neroni that Lucrecia, following the example of the friars who had preached against Charles in 1517, was using her dreams to foment opposition to the king.

Neroni had heard enough. On 13 February he had Lucrecia arrested and detained in the house of one of his notaries on the pretext that her dreams were stirring up the "masses" and becoming a source of scandal in Madrid. Lucrecia spent some ten days at the notary's house, during which Neroni continued his investigation and interviewed her about her dreams.[23] At her first audience with the vicar, Lucrecia professed innocence, reportedly telling him that "if they [the dreams] were from the Devil, pray to Our Lord to remove them, and if they were from God, then she did not deserve them."[24] But she freely admitted that her dreams indicated that Philip and his heir would die "because of the sins the king, our lord, has committed in killing his sons and the Queen Isabel [de Valois] and taking lands away from the *labradores* and other things, like the administration of justice and lack of charity for the poor."[25]

At this point Neroni, a canon lawyer, called upon a number of theologians for advice. Learned testimony came from Fray Juan de Orellana, one of the Inquisition's theological advisors, as well as from Diego de Chaves, both of whom considered the dreams' political rhetoric to be potentially inflammatory. On 14 February the two theologians filed a preliminary report indicating that Lucrecia "does not have the spirit of prophecy but rather one of trickery and sedition." Two days later, after interrogating Lucrecia personally, they wrote a more comprehensive report:

> There is no doubt that it is possible for divine revelations to occur both in dreams and in waking visions. But the dreams of Lucrecia are not from God, nor from ignorance, nor from her own sense of vanity and wish to be esteemed. They do not even come from the devil, who might have pretended to use this little woman to upset Spain and to disrupt plans for the holy armada against England. . . . As we have seen, she contradicts herself, often denying what she once said; she consequently says false things. She herself confesses that she does not believe in the dreams and has told the same to her accomplices and, as they have testified, they persuaded her not to believe in them either. This evil dreamer ["negra soñadora"] does not want these things to be told to the king, our lord, to whom it would matter if these things were from God. Rather she tells them to the common people in order to stir them up.[26]

In accordance with established opinion, Chaves and Orellana concluded that the dreams could not be divine because true prophets never contradict themselves. Lucrecia had invented the dreams for political purposes, they inferred, and she should be punished by the "via ordinaria," that is, by civil justice, presumably for sedition.

This harsh judgment of Lucrecia was counterbalanced by the conciliatory report of the celebrated Augustinian theologian Fray Luis de León (1527–1591). A victim of university politics, Fray Luis had himself been arrested by the Inquisition in 1572 and held prisoner for five years. As it turns out, Fray Luis was an acquaintance of Alonso de Mendoza, possibly because of their mutual interest in prophecy. Fray Luis had met Lucrecia the previous October, just after the work of transcribing her dreams had begun. At that time, after a brief meeting, he announced—much to Mendoza's disappointment—that the dreams, while interesting, were not worth transcribing. For the vicar's investigation, the aging friar interviewed Lucrecia more extensively, examined several dream transcripts with care, and concluded that the source of the dreams was neither "melancholy nor illusion." Unable to discover in them "any sure sign of God," he suggested that the dreams were caused by a "vertiginous spirit" and recommended that Lucrecia be exorcised rather than punished.[27]

Before Neroni could file his own report, his investigation was brought to an abrupt halt engineered by Mendoza. The canon had been in Toledo at the time of Lucrecia's arrest but returned hurriedly to Madrid to secure her release. He was angry that his friend Fray Luis did not find Lucrecia's dreams "the work of a good spirit," yet also told him that if the exorcism would bring an end to the dreams, it would be a boon to Lucrecia "because she wants the dreams to stop."[28] Undeterred by Fray Luis's report, Mendoza appealed Lucrecia's case to Neroni's superiors. On 20 February he wrote to the papal nuncio in Madrid, Cesare Speciano, protesting that Neroni was treating Lucrecia like one of Madrid's "fallen women" and that the vicar's method of determining the source of Lucrecia's dreams was totally misdirected. Prophecy, he wrote, belonged to the spirit, not the will, and the vicar was wasting his time questioning her directly about the dreams; he should rather devote himself to a close study of their contents.[29] He wrote a similar letter to Quiroga, the inquisitor general, justifying his own involvement with Lucrecia on theological grounds and advising that further study was required to determine whether the dreams were diabolical or divine.[30]

Mendoza's efforts were well directed. As a personal friend of Quiroga and a member of the cardinal's own cathedral, the canon persuaded the archbishop to read several of Lucrecia's dreams, particularly one that had correctly predicted the death of the Armada's commander, the marquis of Santa Cruz. Apparently, Quiroga was sympathetic to Lucrecia's cause, for he ordered her immediate release on the condition that she be secluded in a convent and that her dreams be transcribed only for purposes of theological study.[31]

Not surprisingly, Quiroga's intervention on Lucrecia's behalf provoked immediate reaction from Chaves, his long-time enemy. The two were already at odds over Quiroga's support of Antonio Pérez as well as Quiroga's handling of the trial of Piedrola. Chaves, alleging bias on Quiroga's part, had written a memorandum to Philip in which he attacked the archbishop for having publicized details of the Inquisition's supposedly secret case against Piedrola.[32] To Chaves, Quiroga's release of Lucrecia was further proof that the aging inquisitor general—Quiroga was nearly eighty—was losing his grip and failing to prosecute deviants and heretics as vigorously as he should. Chaves also implied that Quiroga, as an ally of Pérez, was predisposed to treating both Lucrecia and Piedrola leniently because of their ties to the former secretary.

Equally upset with Quiroga's order to release Lucrecia was Neroni. Soon after, he summoned Lucrecia to his quarters and, in the company of Pedro de Valle, a secretary of the Inquisition, staged a little drama intended to intimidate her. Neroni sarcastically announced to Valle: "Here is the prophet; look at her." To which Lucrecia responded modestly: "I am not so good as to merit such a great name; anyhow, I have never claimed to be a prophet." At this point Valle, placing his hands on Lucrecia's head, threatened her: "I have undone many prophets with these hands." Neroni then instructed Lucrecia to keep silent about her dreams, dismissed her, and sent her home.[33]

Quiroga's plan for Lucrecia to go into seclusion, however, was blocked by Ana Ordoñez, who was reluctant to have her eldest daughter leave home. As a compromise measure, Mendoza proposed that Lucrecia move to Toledo and live with his friend Gerónima Doria, whose house was adjacent to a convent, the Franciscan community of Santa Ana. There, he claimed, it would be easy for him to record, interpret, and ultimately determine the source of her dreams, a project he estimated would require another six months.[34] But now Lucrecia's father entered his objections. Alonso Franco had been away on business in Valladolid and had learned only belatedly about his daughter's arrest. By the end of February, Alonso Franco had returned to Madrid. Angry and embarrassed by the dishonor Lucrecia had brought to the family's name, he singled out Mendoza for blame, calling him a "loco" (madman). In a letter to Mendoza, he adamantly refused to allow Lucrecia to be sent to a convent and argued that "although he lacked a son, he did not wish to have a daughter missing from his house." The letter also expressed his wish to keep Lucrecia at home, "without scandal and out of harm's way."[35] In an emotional meeting with Lucrecia, Alonso Franco made a startling threat: "Daughter, in my family nobody has ever believed in superstitions because dreams are only dreams, and if you believe in them I will give the order to have you killed."[36]

Despite Alonso Franco's hostility, Mendoza still hoped to work out a settlement that would allow for the transcription of Lucrecia's dreams to resume. Afraid of further trouble, Alonso Franco continued to refuse. But Ana Ordoñez had always been favorably disposed toward Mendoza and appreciated the alms the wealthy canon provided her family,[37] and she tried her best to persuade her husband to change his mind. Ana's arguments and the fact that he would be unable to control Lucrecia once he returned to Valladolid left Alonso Franco little choice. He reluctantly agreed to have the transcriptions proceed so long as Mendoza and Fray Lucas promised not to publicize them.

The Cult of Lucrecia

With her father's consent, Lucrecia and her transcribers were free to resume their work, but now she became mysteriously ill. The number of dreams she recalled dropped precipitiously and remained at a low level for the next eighteen months. Yet neither her arrest nor her illness dampened her reputation as a seer. Indeed, according to Guillén de Casaos, her encounter with the vicar "left her with more credit than before."[38] And shortly before or after her release from house arrest, her most ardent supporters began work on Sopeña, the refuge she envisioned in her dreams.

On property belonging to Fray Lucas de Allende's brother, Cristóbal, in the side of some cliffs overlooking the Tagus, near the town of Villarrubia, Mendoza began directing preparations to transform several caves into a survivalists' bunker.[39] In March or April 1588 the caves were reportedly enlarged and stocked with stores of wheat, oil, and wine, even some firearms. Mendoza's correspondence confirms the purchase of these and other provisions, along with shipments of various church ornaments intended to furnish a small chapel that was reportedly designed by Juan de Herrera, the royal architect.[40] Permission of the papal nuncio to have mass said in this chapel was also secured.

Whether Lucrecia participated in these preparations we do not know. But she visited the caves on at least one occasion, apparently brought there by Mendoza, who later described Sopeña "not as a cave, nor a fortress, but the place and house of God."[41]

As these preparations for Armageddon proceeded through the summer of 1588, Lucrecia's reputation and credibility soared when her well-publicized dreams concerning the defeat of the Armada came true. New sympathizers were drawn to her side by her vision of the Armada's defeat as a symbol of Spain's vulnerability and Philip's inability to protect his vassals. Her various dreams of Queen Elizabeth conspiring with Spain's enemies bespoke the fear then on every Spaniard's mind: the prospect of England using its newly won seapower to seize Spanish treasure ships or to launch new attacks upon the Spanish mainland.

The "Year after the Armada" was Spain's *annus infelix.*[42] Much of the Spanish navy had been destroyed; the royal treasury was almost empty; the English were bold enough to sack the mainland city of La Coruña in April 1589 and then attempt an invasion of Lisbon the following month;[43] and the assassination of Henry III on 1 August paved the way for the succession of Spain's long-time enemy, Henry of Navarre, to the throne of France. In the meantime Philip found it difficult to raise the revenues needed to strengthen his wobbly defenses, especially since the Cortes of Castile put obstacles in the way of the new millones tax.

In autumn 1589, Lucrecia dreamed of an English fleet sailing off, unimpeded, "to fish in the Indies"; she saw repeated images of Spain's certain loss and Elizabeth gloating over the silver her ships had captured.[44] Though these events never came to pass, Lucrecia's view of a Spain sorely wanting in power perfectly captured the temper of the times. By placing the blame for Spain's troubles squarely upon Philip's shoulders, Lucrecia's dreams articulated what many Spaniards undoubtedly felt but were afraid to say aloud.

The monarchy's continuing misfortunes almost guaranteed Lucrecia an audience, and by the end of 1589 she herself placed great stock in her prophetic powers. This self-confidence is reflected in her health, which began to improve dramatically in June 1589, prompting one of her supporters, Domingo López Navarro, to write: "Lucrecia is healthy; they even tell me she is fat, although she doesn't talk as much as before."[45] After the summer of 1589 she began to dream more and the dreams transcribed during the winter and spring of 1590 are among the longest on record. Even Lucrecia's personal life took a turn for the better: in October or November 1589 she first met Diego de Vitores.

This stage in Lucrecia's prophetic career also marks her debut as a court celebrity. During the winter of 1589–90 Lucrecia gained access to some of Madrid's most elegant salons, as more and more courtiers began to express interest in meeting the "doncella de buena vida," the honest young girl who had dreams about the loss of Spain. A favorite meeting place for those in sympathy with her cause was the house of Lady Jane Dormer, an English Catholic who had married the duke of Feria in 1558. Following the duke's death in 1571, Lady Jane became a Franciscan tertiary, and consequently became acquainted with Allende. Through her son, Lorenzo Suárez de Figueroa, the duchess had close ties with the Mendoza clan. Though known to wear the habit of the third order to St. Francis, the Poor Clares, Lady Jane did not lead the withdrawn life of a beata. She

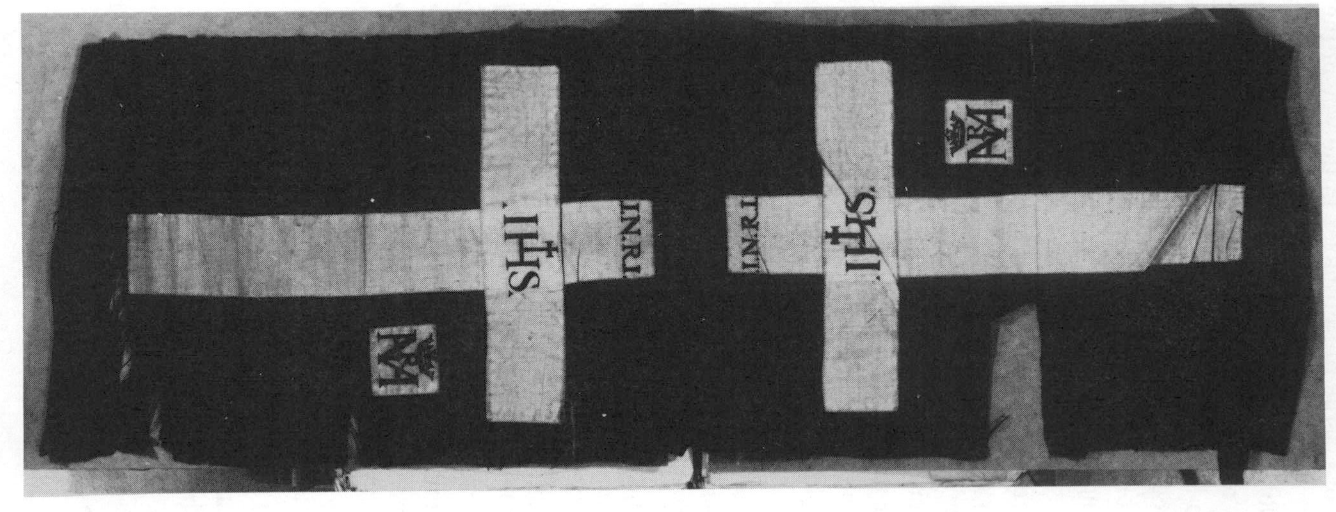

Cloth scapular. Archivo Histórico Nacional, Madrid. This simple black garment emblazoned with a white cross was fashioned after a scapular Lucrecia envisioned in her dreams. Lucrecia's followers wore it beneath their ordinary clothing as a symbol of their belief in her millennial vision of Spain's future. The Inquisition seized several of these garments for use as evidence against Lucrecia and later bound them into the registers containing the transcript of her trial.

lived in Madrid in a large palace located near the Plaza Mayor and regularly entertained a wide circle of courtiers and writers, among them, Pedro de Rivadeneyra, the Jesuit scholar.[46] As the León family's landlady, Lady Jane seems to have had considerable contact with Lucrecia, who frequently visited the duchess's house and, at her request, related the contents of her dreams to selected groups of invited guests.[47] Reports of these gatherings are scattered throughout the record of Lucrecia's trial, and in a dream of 25 December 1589 Lucrecia sees herself being formally presented to the duchess's assembled household.

Gradually, a cult coalesced around Lucrecia. Her dream of an army bearing white crosses marching to defeat Spain's enemies evidently inspired Guillén de Casaos to establish a confraternity known as the Holy Cross of the Restoration. The statutes of this organization, a copy of which is dated 19 September 1589, required its members to wear a black scapular emblazoned with a white cross, a garment fashioned precisely after one Lucrecia had seen in her dreams. Members were also expected to defend God against heretics and infidels, foster the spread of Catholicism, make a pilgrimage to Jerusalem, help the poor, and promote justice.[48] It is said that Casaos even planned a journey to Rome in the hope of persuading the pope to establish a new religious order *de la cruz* modeled upon the new confraternity.

Little else is known about this organization save that Mendoza once referred to it as "our Christian guild [gremio]"[49] and its members addressed one another as brother and sister. In addition to Mendoza, Allende, and Casaos, the group's adherents included Sacamanchas, Domingo López Navarro, Juan de Trijueque, Allende's brother Cristóbal, and Vitores.[50] A small cluster of sympathizers wore or possessed the confraternity's scapular, though they cannot be said to have been active members. The prior Hernando de Toledo figured in this group, along with the dukes of Medinaceli, Medina Sidonia, and Nájera, all of whom were friends of Allende. Other officials aware of the confraternity's existence included Juan de Herrera, the king's chamberlain Alonso de Zúñiga, and the royal secretary Martín de Idiáquez.[51] The duchess of Feria and her son were also involved. Lucrecia was another *cofrade,* but appears to have worn the scapular only in her dreams.

Most of the members of the Holy Cross of the Restoration had been among Piedrola's supporters; the new confraternity rather resembled a reorganized version of la Espelunça. The members were also allied with or at least sympathetic to Antonio Pérez. Indeed, Allende's activities on behalf of Pérez suggest that the brotherhood may have helped to coordinate efforts to free the former secretary, perhaps even assisting in his escape. More importantly, however, the confraternity seems to have united various courtiers and other individuals who, for various reasons, believed that the monarchy's policies required urgent reform. In this respect the confraternity may have constituted the nucleus of a court faction whose members faulted Philip for having strayed from the fundamental principles of justice, defense of religion, and aid to the poor—the principles articulated in the brotherhood's charter. Lucrecia's dreams, of course, articulated a similar program, and she seemed to have served as the brotherhood's public voice. Aware of the risks the group was running, she warned Mendoza on 26 March 1590 about the carelessness ("poco cuidado") with which Allende was circulating copies of the dreams and her letters, which were filled with court gossip and other information.[52]

Nonetheless, Lucrecia openly continued her prophetic activities in direct violation of the terms of her release from the vicar's prison in 1588. Despite pledges made at that time, her dreams continued to be publicized and openly discussed, and her supporters continued to represent her as a divinely inspired prophet. That she was not immediately silenced by the Holy Office, which usually acted quickly and decisively to suppress any heresy or ideological deviance, implies both the relative orthodoxy of her message and the limits of her influence.[53] From the crown's perspective, a dream-prone doncella whom a small group of courtiers credited with revelations hardly represented a serious threat to the monarchy, and it is very likely that Philip simply dismissed early news of Lucrecia's activities as inconsequential. When discussion of the "public abuses" emanating from various "prodigies and divinations," arose in a meeting with the papal legate in March 1588, Philip reportedly said, "It was the practice of the emperor, my father, not to believe in or to act upon such things."[54]

Lucrecia's liberty can also be attributed to Quiroga's reluctance to order her arrest. Quiroga was no liberal. A forceful proponent of the Tridentine reforms and a staunch enemy of Protestantism, he was responsible for revising the *Index of Prohibited Books* in 1583, adding hundreds of new titles to the list of those already declared heretical.[55] But Quiroga was also a supporter of Antonio Pérez, and he was frequently at odds with the inner circle of royal ministers—Chaves, Loaysa, and especially Vázquez. (In 1594 Quiroga would die in virtual disgrace owing to the machinations of these ministers against him.) Thus Quiroga may have been somewhat sympathetic to Lucrecia's critique of Philip's counselors. According to Chaves, Quiroga had indulged Piedrola,[56] and Lucrecia appears also to have enjoyed the inquisitor general's tacit support and protection.

Quiroga's influence may also explain Philip's disinterestedness in Lucrecia's conduct. When asked on 26 July 1589 by Mateo Vázquez what should be done about "that woman who does not remember the ire and justice of God" and who promulgated many "very false revelations," Philip responded, somewhat enigmatically, "You should not be afraid of what she says but of what she does not say."[57] Refusing to take any action against her, the king simply noted that "while she does not tell the truth, she is wrong to talk about it [i.e., Spain's apocalyptic future]." Some nine months later, however, on 19 April 1590, Antonio Pérez escaped from Madrid—an event that persuaded the monarch to change his mind about this young dreamer and the activities of her admirers.

Chaves and the Inquisition

Pérez's escape was more than an embarrassment for Philip. There were fears, soon realized, that the former secretary would use his base in Aragon to stir up opposition to the king, perhaps even to provoke an uprising against royal authority. Already hard-pressed abroad, the monarchy could not afford any domestic disturbances, and efforts were redoubled to scrutinize the activities of Pérez's friends and supporters at court. The political crisis created by Pérez's escape thus raised new questions about the motivations of the group surrounding the woman whose dreams were so ominous. In some quarters Lucrecia's predictions of a new wave of popular rebellions were construed as signs that Lucrecia and her associates, aided by Pérez, were actively plotting against the king.[58]

Although there is no proof that such a plot existed, by early May 1590 Philip's closest advisers decided that it was time to silence Lucrecia. The principal instigator of this new policy was Lucrecia's old nemesis, Chaves, the royal confessor. Thwarted in his previous attempt to get her off the streets, Chaves seized upon Pérez's escape as an opportunity to be done with Lucrecia while gaining an edge on his old rival, Cardinal Quiroga. Quietly at first, he began collecting information.

Chaves's principal source was Juan Ortiz de Salvatierra, one of the Inquisition's *comisarios* in Madrid. Comisarios were charged with keeping an eye open for unorthodox religious behavior, and Ortiz de Salvatierra, a university-trained cleric, did his work well. A friend of the duchess of Feria, he questioned Lady Jane's servants about Lucrecia's performances at the duchess's house; doña Mayor Méndez de Soto, chief lady-in-waiting, proved an excellent source. Ortiz de Salvatierra also visited Allende, who said that Lucrecia's dreams could not possibly be her own "because she is a young, ignorant woman"—an ambiguous statement that may have been Allende's way of indicating that he thought the dreams were divinely inspired.[59] The comisario then arranged to meet with Lucrecia. With her characteristic openness, she spoke freely to him about her dreams, mentioning that she had ignored them until Piedrola's arrest.[60]

Sidestepping standard inquisitorial procedures, Ortiz de Salvatierra reported what he had learned directly to Chaves, and only later did Chaves inform the Suprema (the Supreme Council of the Inquisition) about the investigation he had initiated. On 8 May 1590 the Suprema voted to undertake its own investigation and ordered Licenciado Lope de Mendoza, one of three inquisitors attached to the Holy Office in Toledo, to collect Alonso de Mendoza's papers "quickly, with surprise, avoiding all publicity." But this inquisitor, an old friend (and possibly a distant relative) of don Alonso, sat on these instructions for nearly two weeks, alleging that the Suprema failed to send him the proper orders.[61] Ten days later a new set of instructions arrived, obliging the reluctant inquisitor to act. On the night of 20 May he entered don Alonso's house and found many sets of papers hidden behind a cupboard.

Don Alonso immediately wrote to Quiroga and to the king, protesting this intrusion and demanding the return of his papers, especially his "libro de memoria," which he used to remember things told to him in confession, along with a notebook containing his poems.[62] On this occasion, however, don Alonso was unable to persuade Quiroga to intervene on his behalf. Apparently, Quiroga recognized the gravity of the situation and decided that this was the moment to distance himself from his former friend, just as he had earlier dropped Piedrola. The prosecution of the case against Lucrecia and her supporters was now fully in Chaves's control.

We do not have a complete list of the papers of don Alonso that were seized by the Inquisition, but reports forwarded by Lope de Mendoza to the Suprema on 22 and 23 May indicate that he was both shocked and surprised by what he found. He inventoried thirty notebooks containing records of Lucrecia's dreams from 1 December 1587 to 18 April 1590, another notebook described as "an alphabetical table of the notable things in the dreams," and two black taffeta scapulars with a white cross inscribed with the letters JHS, MARIA, and INRJ.[63] In addition, there were copies of Sacamanchas's visions, materials relating to the prophecies of Piedrola, a copy of the prophecies of St. Isidore of Seville, and "letters from England . . . in code." He also found diverse papers about the loss of Spain and other topics "which I cannot write about except with pain and even with shame as my pen copies them." All in all, the material amounted to nothing less than "sedition in disguise."

Armed with this information and prodded by Chaves, the

Suprema moved quickly. Although the Holy Office did not usually involve itself in political matters, the royal confessor arranged to have Lucrecia's case discussed on 23 May at a meeting with Quiroga, several members of the Suprema, and Mateo Vázquez, who also served as the secretary of this council. No records of this meeting survive, but Chaves got his way, for two days later the king was asked to sanction the arrest of Lucrecia and her associates. According to Vázquez, Philip gave his immediate consent ("S.M. lo ha aprobado") during a meeting on 25 May, and that very evening the royal secretary, acting on Philip's direct orders, instructed the Inquisition to carry out the arrests.

Later that night Lucrecia, Allende, Vitores, and other prominent members of the confraternity were taken into custody in Madrid; in Toledo don Alonso was arrested quietly ("con mucha quietud") at 11 P.M., according to one report. Casaos, who was visiting Mendoza in Toledo, was arrested the following day, and by 31 May all the suspects were in the Inquisition's prison in Toledo.[64] Philip expressed satisfaction at the efficacy and speed with which the arrests had been handled. A few days later, on 4 June, the Inquisition officially began its inquiry into Lucrecia's dreams.

With her arrest Lucrecia's prophetic career ended, but the dreams did not. The dream registers run almost to the moment of her arrest, and it appears that she continued to have dreams for some time thereafter. Soon after the start of her trial, however, in June or early July 1590, the dreams seem to have stopped, or at least she stopped recounting her dreams to others. Perhaps Lucrecia felt the need to exercise caution, although, as we shall see, her conduct in prison was hardly prudent or restrained. Or perhaps the dreams no longer came to her, unlike Joan of Arc, whose visions continued throughout the course of her trial. Or perhaps Lucrecia's sudden isolation from family and friends deprived her of the audience she needed to inspire either the dreams or the recounting of them.

What is certain is that Lucrecia's incarceration had no immediate effect on her imagination. Her trial was well under way when she related to a fellow prisoner a prophetic dream at once apocalyptic and seditious, both in tone and imagery. Lucrecia, perhaps wisely, refused to discuss this dream with her judges, but a summary provided by the fellow prisoner tells of a horrific seven-headed dragon, a creature reminiscent of the satanic monster that battles the archangel Michael and then declares war on all of Christendom in the Book of Revelation 12:4–17. Lucrecia's dragon, though, directs its wrath at Philip and his kingdom: "Woe unto Spain," hisses the dragon, "you must be destroyed and conquered by Vendôme, king of Navarre [the future Henry IV of France, a Protestant]; and woe unto you, Philip."[65]

The message was not a new one, but to discuss it while in prison constituted a bold act of defiance, a challenge to the authority of the king and the Holy Office. In repressing Lucrecia's creative spirit, arrest and imprisonment were only partially successful. Lucrecia the prophet had been silenced, but Lucrecia the dreamer eluded everyone's grasp.

6

TRIAL IN TOLEDO

The inquisitorial tribunal selected to try Lucrecia and her compatriots was among the most important in Spain. Founded in 1483, five years after the papacy authorized Ferdinand and Isabella to establish an inquisition independent of Rome, the tribunal's jurisdiction was roughly equivalent to that of the archdiocese of Toledo, a sprawling region encompassing most of New Castile and a population of just over two million souls. So large was this province that in 1573 the tribunal's judges complained about having too few agents to police the spiritual life of "one thousand towns."[1] To focus their limited resources, Toledo's inquisitors had all but abandoned the practice of visiting small villages and other remote areas, leaving the inhabitants of isolated regions such as the Montes of Toledo virtually free of inquisitorial scrutiny and control.[2]

The cities were another matter, for they traditionally harbored the church's principal enemies: Muslims and Jews; conversos and moriscos, the suspect population of recent converts to Catholicism; and Protestants. So while agents and familiars in rural areas were spread fairly thin, the Toledan tribunal constructed a dense network of monitors to watch over the spiritual life of urban dwellers. In 1562 the city of Toledo, with a population of approximately sixty thousand, had more than seventy such agents.[3]

Some twenty-four or twenty-five officials worked in the Holy Office of Toledo. Heading the tribunal were three inquisitors (*oidores*) whose chief tasks were to interrogate those accused of heresy and other religious crimes, determine the extent of their guilt, and assign the appropriate penalty. Assisting the oidores was a prosecuting attorney (*fiscal*), an attorney for financial matters (*juez de bienes confiscados*), three recording secretaries, several notaries, and a handful of assistants. Other officials worked in the tribunal's prisons (*cárceles secretos*): a warden (*alcaide*), a sheriff (*alguacil*), a quartermaster (*dispensero*), and their helpers. Part-time employees included a physician and various *calificadores,* experts in canon law and theology brought in to evaluate the heretical content of books and to offer advice on complex issues of religious doctrine. Toledo was home to many of Spain's best-educated churchmen, and the tribunal's calificadores included such eminent scholars as Juan de Mariana, a Jesuit historian and theologian, and Pedro Salazar de Mendoza, a canon lawyer known for his historical and genealogical writings.[4]

The cost of running this tribunal is difficult to estimate, partly because the salaries of the inquisitors and the prosecuting attorney came from church prebends whose rents had been set aside for this purpose. Otherwise, the tribunal's annual expenses amounted to approximately six thousand ducats, nearly all of which came from the sale of goods confiscated from convicted heretics. In 1590, however, these condemnations provided for only two-thirds of the tribunal's needs, and the oidores urgently requested financial assistance from the Suprema in Madrid.[5]

The financial shortfall was caused by an acute shortage of cases. Following the persecution of Spain's converso population—a great wave of terror that rolled on unabated from the beginnings of the Holy Office in 1479 until the mid-1530s—the number of cases prosecuted by the Inquisition had dropped off.[6] In Toledo the docket fell from a record 373 cases tried between 1551 and 1555 to 150 for the period 1586–1590. By the end of the century the tribunal dispatched an average of only 30 or 40 cases a year, about half of which involved such relatively trivial charges as blasphemy, fornication, and scandalous remarks.[7] So diminished was the supply of *reos* (offenders) that the tribunal often found itself hard-pressed to stage an auto da fe, the public ceremony at which heretics were formally reconciled to the church. Thus in April 1587 the inquisitors, needing "penitents" for an auto da fe scheduled to coincide with a visit by the king, asked the Suprema for permission to import "six or eight persons from another inquisition"[8]

Despite these problems, the Toledan tribunal still enjoyed considerable prestige. Its oidores were seasoned inquisitors with experience on one of the lesser tribunals; nearing the peak of their power and reputation, they looked forward to promotion to the Suprema. At least two of the judges initially assigned to Lucrecia's case were of this caliber: Licenciado Lope de Mendoza, a judge who had served in a number of royal courts before joining the tribunal in 1581, and Doctor Pedro de Zárate, a canon lawyer who had been assigned to Toledo after having served as an inquisitor in Zaragoza.[9]

The procedure according to which Lucrecia and her co-conspirators were tried was the "trial of faith," a slow, methodical process modeled on the procedures of the papal inquisition in the Middle Ages. The instructions governing the Spanish Inquisition were originally drafted in 1484 by the first inquisitor general, the notorious Fray Tomás de Torquemada, and subsequently altered and revised. The last revision, published in 1561, stipulated that a trial of faith should contain the following stages:

Denunciation (*denuncia*)
Decision by the judges to pursue the case (*votos*)
Gathering and evaluation of evidence (*testificación*)
Decision of the judges to continue (*votos en sumaria*)
Hearings with the accused (*audiencias*)
Accusations against the accused (*acusaciones*)
Defense by the accused (*defensas*)
Decision by the judges (*votos en definitiva*)
Sentence (*sentencia*).[10]

Superficially similar to the protocol used in criminal courts, this procedure was unique in several important respects. Although royal tribunals conducted their trials in public, inquisitorial trials took place in total secrecy in order to prevent defendants from using the dock as a pulpit for emotional appeals to people gathered in the courtroom. And unlike a criminal trial conducted to establish innocence or guilt, the trial of faith was premised on the guilt of the accused. Once the inquisitors had voted to pursue the case (votos), the guilt of the accused was assumed and the purpose of the trial was to extract a confession. Initially, therefore, the accused was not informed of the charges against him but instead confined to prison to search his conscience and determine the extent of his guilt. Since self-incrimination and repentance were the desired outcome, the accused was never provided with the names of those persons whose testimony had led to his arrest.

To expedite the process, the Holy Office instituted a specific type of judicial proceeding, the *inquisitio.* Modeled after the practices of certain late Roman courts, the inquisitio empowered the judge to control the nature and extent of the questioning as well as the pace at which the trial proceeded. The inquisitors could also order a *sentencia de tormento* (torture) to hasten a confession from a recalcitrant offender. Torture did not figure in every trial of faith, however. Inquisitorial rules instructed that torture be employed with "discretion" and that confessions obtained under duress had later to be ratified by the accused.[11] In practice, the Inquisition was probably more sparing in ordering the torture of prisoners than many secular courts of the time.

At the end of the trial the judges would decide upon an appropriate punishment: a fine, imprisonment, banishment, public flogging, or, in cases of obdurate heretics who refused to recant, death by immolation. The sentence was announced publicly at an auto da fe—except in sensitive cases, for which the auto could be held in private.

Lucrecia made her first appearance before the Inquisition of Toledo at an *audiencia* (hearing) on 4 June 1590, the same day the tribunal had decided to proceed with her case. Several divergent transcripts of this audiencia exist, but all show that it began with the standard questions about Lucrecia's age, place of residence, and civil status. The tribunal did not, however, inquire about her religious knowledge, which was typically measured by a defendant's ability to recite such basic prayers as the Ave Maria and Credo. Lope de Mendoza presided alone because Zárate, his colleague, was ill, and it was he who posed to Lucrecia the question asked of every offender brought to a trial of faith: "Why have you been arrested?" Without hesitation, Lucrecia replied, "because of the dreams that are written." But she quickly added a qualifier: "I have not done anything that would explain why they had brought me here." And another: "I did not think there was anything in my dreams to offend God or anyone else." Her confessors, she asserted, had told her that "it was right for the things in the dreams to be known." Allende, she claimed, told her this "many times," whereas Mendoza had instructed her that "it was good for these things to be known in order to determine whether they are absurdities or things that would be useful for His Majesty to know about." Lucrecia concluded her remarks by acknowledging her responsibility for the dreams attributed to her, but she denied having believed in them: "I was very careful," she said, "not to give them any credit."[12]

From the outset, thus, Lucrecia portrayed herself as a young innocent victimized by the two theologians to whom she had unwittingly revealed her dreams. She also hoped to convince her inquisitors that she was an unlettered woman who had failed to grasp the significance of her dreams, that her female mind was unable to comprehend the complexities of abstract theological thought. At the hearing held on 13 June, Lucrecia complained to her judges: "It is the men who transcribed the dreams who are at fault, because they are men and I am only a woman whom they should have warned." During other sessions she uttered similar disparaging remarks about her intellectual abilities, once referring to herself as a chatterbox ("mujer muy charla") incapable of evaluating her dreams let alone understanding if they contained images or ideas contrary to the faith.[13]

Lucrecia also testified that Allende and Mendoza had deliberately misled her about the dreams' potential significance. The two theologians, she said, had repeatedly assured her that the dreams could not possibly get her into trouble with the Inquisition, and "with this security" she told them her dreams. She herself had done nothing more than "dream and sleep."[14]

Lucrecia's codefendants, however, presented substantially different versions of these events. Guillén de Casaos avowed that he had always dismissed Lucrecia's dreams as an absurd pack of "notable lies." While he admitted to having transcribed a number of dreams, he claimed to have advised Mendoza to abandon "his chimera and deceit."[15] Diego de Vitores said much the same, claiming that he was merely an amanuensis, a "mute instrument" who wrote down the dreams only after receiving assurances from Allende that the project was "approved by specialists in Holy Scripture." His conscience, he said, was clear since he had never given the dreams much credence. Whereas Allende, Vitores pointed out, had once told him that Lucrecia was "the most prodigious woman Spain ever had."[16]

Allende's own defense was decidedly different. While Casaos and Vitores attempted to appear innocent of any wrongdoing, Allende threw himself on the mercy of the tribunal and confessed that if he had erred in transcribing the dreams, he had done so out of ignorance. Mendoza, Allende said, had pressured him, almost forced him, to transcribe Lucrecia's dreams ("casi me forzó la voluntad hacerlo"), and he complied out of theological "curiosity" and in order to see how many "contradictions" the dreams contained. But as for the content of the dreams, he stood by what he had once told Vitores: that if the dreams "[are] not the illusion of the devil, they are her own invention." He also reminded the tribunal that he had destroyed some transcriptions of Lucrecia's earliest dreams because he believed that the three figures who spoke to her represented "an evil spirit and one of sedition and disturbance." The inquisitors, challenging the sincerity of Allende's testimony, asked why he wore a scapular fashioned after the one depicted in Lucrecia's dreams. The friar tried to explain away the cloth by claiming to have worn it solely out of his "devotion to the cross."[17]

Alonso de Mendoza's defense was bolder. He challenged the legality of his arrest, questioned the right of the Holy Office to preside over his case, and argued that his judges should disqualify themselves as prejudiced. He also instituted a *recusación*, a legal plea that he submitted to the Suprema in March 1591, accusing inquisitors Zárate and Mendoza together with several members of the Suprema of prejudice and bias. Recusancies were commonplace in secular tribunals, but the Inquisition rarely had to contend with this particular type of legal maneuvre. But the recusación gave don Alonso the time he needed to appeal the case to the papacy. With the help of his Toledan friend Gerónima Doria, he smuggled out of prison and forwarded to Rome a document stating that he and his friends had been arrested for purely political, as opposed to religious, reasons, specifically for their opposition to Philip's policy of taxing the clergy. In the letter he also cited the Fifth Lateran Council as the source of his authority to transcribe Lucrecia's dreams.[18]

Mendoza's legal maneuverings would ultimately prove fruitless, but they did succeed in bringing his trial and those of Lucrecia and the others to a virtual standstill for a little over a year, that is, from July 1590 until September 1591. A small victory, perhaps, but few other defendants had ever succeeded in bringing the machinery of inquisitorial justice to a halt. While Mendoza took the lead in effecting this procedural turnabout, the scheme was the result of careful planning by every member of the brotherhood, Lucrecia included. According to Juan Ortiz de Salvatierra, the comisario who had investigated the case on Chaves's behalf, Mendoza was already at work on a defense strategy two weeks prior to his arrest. On 22 May, for example, only days before her arrest, Lucrecia, apparently at Mendoza's behest, destroyed various dream transcriptions that happened to be in her possession, a packet said to include copies of dreams as recent as those of 18 May. It was also reported that Lucrecia, after having consulted with Allende and Mendoza, "had the time to prepare her defense," and that the defendants had learned of the charges against them before the trials began.[19] The planning continued even in prison, with Mendoza developing various means of circumventing the rules prohibiting prisoners from communicating. The trials had scarcely begun when the Suprema received reports concerning illicit communications inside the Toledan tribunal's prisons. At the time the council was too busy to investigate, partly because it was following the case against Antonio Pérez in Zaragoza. But reports concerning these communications continued to reach Madrid, and in September 1591 the Suprema launched a full investigation of the Toledan tribunal. The official entrusted to head the *visita* was

Licenciado Pedro Pacheco, a member of the Suprema who had just returned from Zaragoza, where he had sat on the tribunal investigating Pérez. Presumably, in the Suprema's opinion, the two cases were linked.

Inquisitor Pacheco began his visita by interrogating every officer and prisoner who had had contact with Lucrecia and the other members of the brotherhood. By comparing the trial record with the casual, more spontaneous, and ostensibly more truthful comments Lucrecia and her codefendants made to their fellow prisoners, Pacheco hoped to put the Inquisition's case back on its proper track.

Pacheco quickly learned that the confraternity had successfully violated every rule banning communications between prisoners. María de Vega, a *judaizante* (convert who secretly practiced Judaism) with whom Lucrecia shared a cell, admitted that she regularly had served as a go-between for Lucrecia and Vitores, carrying back and forth secret messages since the moment of their arrest.[20] A search of Lucrecia's cell turned up several notes written with ink on scraps of burned paper ("papel quemado"). Primarily love letters, the notes also contained information relevant to their defense. In a note of July 1590, for instance, Vitores informed Lucrecia about the number of interrogations to which he had been subjected and gave her instructions for making an ink out of cotton and dirt. Another note suggested that the brotherhood's hopes for a general uprising against the monarch had not diminished. This particular note indicated that Philip's general in Flanders, the duke of Parma, had "rebelled against His Majesty," possibly a misinterpretation of the duke's increasing dissatisfaction with Philip's Flemish policy in the years following the Armada's defeat.[21]

Pacheco also discovered that inquisitors Zárate and Mendoza, together with Licenciado Andrés de Alava, the tribunal's third oidor, had extended various favors to members of the brotherhood, especially to Lucrecia and don Alonso. The canon, for example, had a private cell and the help of several servants, among them a cook who brought in fresh supplies of food and maintained a small stock of live chickens and other birds in a corner of the prison patio. When Pacheco cut off this privileged supply of delicacies, don Alonso angrily made do with the meager rations provided by the inquisition's *dispensero.*

The trafficking in foodstuffs, however, was only one aspect of the prison's poor security procedures. According to several witnesses, don Alonso's servants freely entered and left the prisons, delivering messages and serving as their master's link with friends and agents in Toledo and Madrid. Pacheco also learned of various instances of fraternization between the jailers and their prisoners. Mendoza had invited the prison warden, Franco Méndez de Luna, into his cell for "banquets" that lasted well into the night, and, according to testimony by Casaos, "the warden, and his assistant, Miguel de Xea, ate and drank in his [Mendoza's] cell; ordinarily there were many birds and capons, blancmange, cakes and pastries, and other foods; the cell was more like a *bodegón* [tavern] than anything else, because of the noise at mealtimes during the day, and at night they stayed on drinking, eating, and talking until 9 or 10 P.M."[22] Even more serious were allegations that inquisitors Zárate and Mendoza had attended these prison parties, accompanied by Lucrecia as well as some other women, including the warden's mistress.

Other illicit contacts between the inquisitors and the confraternity were described by Pedro Ibáñez de Ochandiano, a Basque army captain imprisoned on charges of bigamy.[23] In exchange for what he hoped would be a light sentence, Ibáñez testified that Lucrecia regularly received various presents and gifts of food, including "beef and chicken stews, *empanadas* of fish and of rabbit and hare," which he understood were prepared by Mendoza's cook and delivered to Lucrecia's cell by one of the warden's assistants.[24] Ibáñez also claimed that the warden and his assistants extended numerous favors to Lucrecia, helping, for instance, to carry her chamber pot down to the patio below and allowing her to leave her cell so that she could talk with Mendoza, Vitores, and Casaos. There were also hints of "false keys," the warden's affection for Lucrecia, and even the suggestion that one of his assistants once spent a night in her cell.[25]

As more information about these scandalous events came to light, Pacheco concluded that the responsibility for them largely rested with the inquisitors themselves. Captain Ibáñez's testimony indicated that inquisitors Zárate and Mendoza met with Lucrecia and don Alonso outside their scheduled sessions. Furthermore, the two judges had done little to extract a confession from Lucrecia; she had not even appeared at a hearing since July 1590, a lapse of just over a year. Doubtless, Lucrecia's pregnancy and the birth of her daughter in September or October 1590 was good cause for some delay, but Pacheco suspected Zárate and Mendoza of dragging their feet, and for reasons that had nothing to do with Lucrecia's complaints of poor health.

According to Captain Ibáñez, Lope de Mendoza was so captivated by Lucrecia's physical charms that he arranged clandestine meetings with her in the house of the prison warden. There, the judge once remarked to her, partly in jest, "You are so beautiful that even a dead man could make you pregnant."[26] Inquisitor Mendoza also openly discussed with Lucrecia the nature of her case and even went so far as to say that he did not understand why she had been arrested.[27] Pacheco now thought he understood the slow pace of Lucrecia's trial, and why she boasted to a fellow prisoner that, at worst, she would receive a punishment no more serious than "a sanbenito and lashes."[28] The proceedings so far, Pacheco concluded, had been little more than a sham. At his recommendation, the Suprema suspended inquisitors Alava, Zárate, and Mendoza for "irregularities," "lack of secrecy," and unspecified "abuses." Suspended too was Méndez de Luna, the prison warden; his sentence also included one hundred lashes and imprisonment for various "abuses and crimes." Also removed from office were Miguel de Xea, the warden's assistant, and Benito de Saavedra, the prison's dispensero, who was charged with having allowed don Alonso to use his house for the passing of secret messages.[29]

Pacheco next moved to dismantle don Alonso's elaborate communications network. He arrested several of don Alonso's servants, including Francisca Rodríguez, the wife of the canon's cook, and charged her with having "brought and carried notes and secret messages" in and out of the prison. Her punishment was exile from Toledo.[30] Gerónima Doria received a similar punishment for having smuggled out of the prison the letter don Alonso had addressed to the pope.[31] Pacheco also removed don Alonso from his comfortable cell and, for a time at least, had the canon placed in chains. Finally, at Pacheco's direction, the Suprema allocated funds to construct a new, more secure prison for the Toledan tribunal.[32]

The departure of inquisitors Zárate and Mendoza signified an abrupt change in Lucrecia's fortunes. Pacheco had concluded that much of her previous testimony was not only patently false but intentionally deceptive, a scheme to convince the judges that she was a "loca," a madwoman who could not be held responsible for the content of her dreams.[33] The discovery of the notes exchanged with Vitores proved that Lucrecia was not as "unlettered" as she previously maintained, and the reference in these notes to Parma indicated that she was vitally interested in current events, contrary to her assertions about her inability to understand complex matters. Though Lucrecia was attempting to portray herself as a simple-minded woman who had been manipulated by a group of conniving men, Ibáñez de Ochandiano and other prisoners had told Pacheco that Lucrecia continually boasted of her prophetic powers, comparing herself to the "sun in the window" that enlightens those in darkness and claiming that "everything I have said, in word and in writing, will soon come true."[34]

On 4 November 1591 Pacheco summoned Lucrecia to a new hearing. The session began with questions about her involvement in the many "excesses" his visita had unearthed. Initially, she attempted to divert Pacheco by directing her answers back to what she referred to as the "principal case." She also pleaded for mercy and tearfully stated that Allende and Mendoza had betrayed her: "I told them the dreams in confession, and they divulged them." Pacheco, unmoved by her tears, repeated his question about the illicit communications. When Lucrecia denied ever having conspired with Mendoza and claimed that she had never received any message from Vitores, an angry Pacheco ordered that she be tortured.[35]

On 7 December 1591 Lucrecia was brought to the torture chamber. The trial record does not indicate the method used on

Lucrecia, but a transcript was made of what said in the torture chamber:

> Because the accused is negative about the accusations relating to the "communications," she was tortured, during which she confessed to many things. While in the torture chamber she also asked for a further hearing. Visitor Pacheco came to see her . . . and among other things she confessed that she had been very bad and that she wished to discharge her conscience about everything. She also said that in addition to the torture already administered, the prosecuting attorney had requested that she should be tortured in the principal case, and she begged that for the love of God she not be tortured again because if she dreamed those cursed black dreams and told them as she dreamed them to don Alonso de Mendoza, he made them worse, for which she is not to blame.[36]

This statement was not substantially different from what Lucrecia had previously admitted. But to Pacheco it represented a first step toward a confession that the dreams had been put to political ends. At this point, however, Pacheco's assignment in Toledo was nearing its end, and it was left to another group of judges to persuade Lucrecia to make a full confession of her guilt.

*

When Pacheco left Toledo in April 1592, Lucrecia's case was already in the hands of a newly appointed inquisitor, Licenciado Antonio Morejón, who, like Pacheco, had served on the tribunal assembled to try Antonio Pérez. Later that year a second new inquisitor joined the Toledo panel, Licenciado Gaspar de Quiroga, the nephew of the aging inquisitor general.[37] Neither of these new judges displayed the least sympathy toward Lucrecia. Nor did they allow themselves to be moved by don Alonso's increasingly frequent and often quite violent outbursts against the ongoing miscarriage of justice. Indeed, the more don Alonso protested, the more they considered him, rather than

Lucrecia, the principal culprit in the case. They became convinced that don Alonso's unruly behavior was a sign of madness and certified that he was a "loco furioso."[38]

Lucrecia's trial resumed, with the court naming Licenciado Pedro de Sotocameño, a veteran who had served the Inquisition for over thirty years, to compile the official list of crimes against her. Outside the tribunal Sotocameño was known for his love of painting and sculpture; his small private art collection included works by El Greco.[39] Inside the tribunal Sotocameño was known as a hard-liner who showed no tolerance for religious deviance of any sort. He was also scrupulously honest and one of the few officials attached to the Toledan tribunal who escaped punishment in the wake of Pacheco's investigation.

Sotocameño based the accusations on the transcripts of Lucrecia's hearings as well as the *calificaciones* prepared by Chaves and García de Loaysa at the beginning of her trial and subsequently revised by Fray Juan de Orellana in 1593.[40] The list of seventy-eight charges was headed by several general accusations:

I. She has already testified to having had visions in certain dreams that she claims to have dreamed and which were transcribed. The said dreams contain many errors and heresies, many falsities and pernicious, schismatic, and scandalous lies, impudent slanders, many false testimonies, and blasphemous remarks about the saints mentioned in them.

II. The said dreams and false prophecies attempted to dishonor the King Our Majesty and his ministers and government and announced unfortunate deaths and infamous happenings along with the total end and extinction of all the King's progeny in the near future.

The remaining articles cited specific passages in the dreams and statements made at the hearings that Sotocameño deemed heretical. These included such phrases as "prophets do not necessarily understand what God reveals to them" and "God through his prophets sends falsehoods."

But Sotocameño added a new dimension to Lucrecia's case

with the charge that the dreams were the result of some form of pact—either tacit or express, he could not decide which—with the devil. His reasoning followed the beliefs of the day: Prophecies came either from God or the devil; since the dreams contained falsehoods, lies, and scandalous propositions, their source must be the devil; but the devil could not have orchestrated these dreams without Lucrecia's consent. She was not, therefore, the innocent victim of diabolical illusion, he argued; rather "these things appear to have been thought up while she was awake, and to do this she asked for the devil's help." In sum, Sotocameño charged the so-called dreams were daydreams invented by Lucrecia with diabolical assistance and for seditious intent.[41]

Once the accusations were announced, the accused was given an opportunity to prepare a series of written *defensas*, generally with the assistance of a lawyer (*letrado*). Lucrecia, perhaps with the aid of Dr. Tello Maldonado, the lawyer who assisted don Alonso in his defense, elected to answer the charges one by one, instead of submitting a single statement of innocence or guilt. This time-consuming process actually began during Pacheco's visita, in December 1591, when Lucrecia responded to the first two charges:

> I. It is true that I dreamed many dreams, but I did not want them written, and if they contain heresies or errors it is the fault of those who wrote them.
>
> II. I did not do anything the charge says. . . . and while it is true that I dreamed about some things relating to His Majesty and the end of the House of Austria and other things I cannot now remember, I did relate them to Fray Lucas de Allende and don Alonso de Mendoza, who wrote them down, but I have not defamed our Majesty the King nor did I speak about these matters to anyone else.[42]

In the following months Lucrecia responded to each of the remaining charges, usually by repeating her earlier statements. Once again, she attributed all blame for the texts of the dreams to her copyists, whom she portrayed as either having failed to transcribe the dreams correctly or having deliberately altered them without her knowledge. Article V, for example, accused her of referring to two of the men who appeared in the dreams as Moses and Elijah. Sotocameño claimed this proposition was "scandalous and sacrilegious," but Lucrecia defended herself:

> It wasn't that way; all I said is that I once saw two men holding some wriggly creatures in their hands, I wasn't sure if they were snakes or lizards; upon asking who they were, I was told one was a portrait [retrato] of Moses and the other of Elijah, but I was not told they were actually Moses and Elijah. That is what I told don Alonso and Fray Lucas, and if they wrote anything else, it is their affair, not mine.[43]

Roughly similar was her response to article X, which charged her with identifying the Three Men as the apostles John, Peter, and Luke. In this instance she admitted only to having described these men by their physical appearance—it was Mendoza and Allende who identified them as apostles. Other charges she answered by claiming forgetfulness. Article XXXII stated that the men who appeared in the dreams told her that prophecies never occur according to the "letter" and with "certainty" because "the most sublime things of God are that way."[44] Sotocameño condemned this statement as "manifest heresy," but Lucrecia said that she could not remember the dream in question.

On another occasion the inquisitors asked her to verify the contents of a particular dream. Lucrecia told the judges to question either Mendoza or Allende about the dream "because, as men, they will remember these things better than [I] . . . a woman."[45] As for the charge that she invented a new religious order, la Restuaración, whose adherents were to wear a black scapular with a white cross, she admitted that men wearing such crosses had appeared in her dreams, but she pointed out that she herself had never worn such a garment. The inquisitors showed her one of these scapulars, which she identified as similar to those worn by Allende and Mendoza. But she had never made such a scapular, she explained, nor did she know anything about a new religious order.[46]

On it went. Slowly but systematically, Lucrecia refuted each of the charges on Sotocameño's list. But no sooner had she finished than Sotocameño drew up a new list of accusations based on the testimony of Lucrecia's codefendants. This procedural step necessitated yet another set of defensas, and the acusación-defensa stage of Lucrecia's trial dragged on for over two years. Not until February 1594 did the next stage—her response to the testimony provided by various witnesses—begin. These responses continued through the spring of 1595, but they failed to produce a confession of her guilt. Lucrecia's answers remained evasive—"I never believed in these dreams. . . . I did not understand what I dreamed"—and she regularly denied ever having claimed to be a seer.[47] In one audiencia inquisitors Morejón and Quiroga confronted her with the testimony of a witness who alleged that Lucrecia once boasted that "the topics raised in my dreams can be seen more clearly in the prophecies of Esdras, St. Isidore, St. Epiphanius, and St. Bridgit." Was this not, the inquisitors asked her, an admission that she considered herself a prophet? Attempting to sidestep the issue of her knowledge of prophecy, Lucrecia told them that whenever Mendoza attempted to instruct her, "I didn't want to listen, pleading that I had a headache."[48]

Finally, in June 1595, five years after her trial had begun, the Suprema intervened. Irked by the failure of the Toledan tribunal to obtain a confession, the council asked Morejón and Quiroga for a full report. On 15 June the judges informed Madrid that Lucrecia's case could be reduced to two basic questions: Were the dreams really dreams? Were they diabolical illusions? A week later the Suprema instructed the inquisitors to hasten the trial by torturing Lucrecia once again and then to determine "if what she calls dreams were truly dreams, and if she really dreamed them as she related them and had them copied, or if they were diabolical illusions." If the latter proved to be true, the Suprema directed the inquisitors to ask: "Did she have any tacit or express pact with the devil, or were the dreams simply fictions and deceits and not really dreams at all? And if they were fictions, what motivated her to invent and to fake such frauds? Who advised and helped her to invent and recite them?"[49]

On 23 June, under the Suprema's orders, Lucrecia was again taken to the tribunal's torture chamber. For a second time she listened to a statement urging her, for the good of her body and soul, to tell the truth. The records do not indicate whether Lucrecia was tortured on this occasion, but she did make some surprising, if somewhat contradictory, revelations. At first she maintained that "the dreams were her own." But then she was asked, "Which were the things you invented, and who was it that advised you to create and invent these dreams and for what purpose?" She replied that some of her dreams about the loss of Spain were "her invention and she invented them without having dreamed them." Lucrecia then explained that while no one had ever advised her to invent the dreams about the loss of Spain, she recognized that others wanted to know about this topic and so "to satisfy them she told them the dreams without any other purpose in mind and also because it seemed to her that these things were good for the king to know."[50]

The inquisitors now accused Lucrecia of deliberately trying to mislead them, claiming that her testimony bore little relation to the truth ("poca semejanza de verdad"). She was lying, they said, when she spoke about wanting to warn the king and her desire to work for the good of the kingdom. She was lying and she would be tortured. But just as the *verdugo* began to remove her underskirt (*faldellín*), she whispered that "she had found a way to stop the torture." Freeing herself from his grip, she shouted across the room to the inquisitors that she wanted to tell them something in private. The trial transcript continues:

> The truth is that don Alonso and Fray Lucas persuaded me to relate the dreams so that they could write them and so that they could say that I dreamed them when I really had not. Therefore, I do not know what the papers contain . . . since it was they who wrote them. However, it is true that they copied some dreams that actually occurred, but these were only childish fantasies and even then they

> changed them, adding what they wanted. Because of this I cannot remember the details.

If the dreams contained anything "against his Majesty," she swore, the blame belonged wholly to don Alonso.

The inquisitors again accused Lucrecia of lying. Her testimony contained "many contradictions," they noted. Earlier she had testified that her dreams were in fact dreams; why should they now believe that the dreams were her inventions "for the service of His Majesty the King"? And who could believe that Fray Lucas and don Alonso were wholly responsible for the dreams about the loss of Spain? "For the love of God," they implored her to tell them the truth, otherwise the torture would begin.

No, Mendoza and Allende were not wholly responsible, she admitted. Certain dreams, such as the "childish fantasy" about Piedrola spewing milk and wheat from his mouth, were her own. But the texts of other dreams had been substantially altered by the two churchmen—she knew that but had remained silent on the advice of her mother. Furthermore, she alleged, Allende and Mendoza had "compose[d]" certain dreams, made her memorize them, and then had her recite them to others. Asked why she had agreed to this, Lucrecia responded that "in her heart she [did] not know," but that Mendoza and Allende led her to believe that the purpose of these faked dreams was "to offer a lesson to His Majesty, to help the Republic, and to stop the king from appointing to office people who did not merit it, such as the offices awarded to don Pedro Puertocarrero, bishop of Calahorra; García de Loaysa, a canon of the cathedral of Toledo who was once married; and many others." Finally, she swore that she had never had any contact with the devil. With this admission, the session in the torture chamber came to an end.

Three days later, when asked to ratify the confessions she had made in the torture chamber, Lucrecia changed her story yet again. Now she admitted to having dreamed more of the dreams, including those announcing the death of the marquis of Santa Cruz and the defeat of the Armada, but claimed that it was Mendoza who initially interpreted these dreams as omens pointing to the loss of Spain. When she had claimed "to have dreamed some things and fabricated others without having dreamed," she had done so in order to avoid being tortured and because she did not know how to respond to specific questions about Mendoza and Allende's interpretations of the dreams. But, she asserted, "it is not true that I faked or invented anything, and all the rest is the truth."[51]

Taking this new testimony as a sign that Lucrecia was prepared to assume partial responsibility for the dreams, the inquisitors now sought to establish whether or not Allende and Mendoza had composed any of the dreams. Lucrecia accused Allende and Mendoza of having invented dreams for her during her fourteen months of illness after her arrest by the vicar. The only real dream she had during that period pertained to the Nun of Lisbon, she said. "If there are more dreams from this period," the record continues, "it is certain that they are not hers because she did not dream nor did she ever say she had dreams."[52] Further questioning, however, only revealed new contradictions in her testimony.

Q: Did you ever say that you dreamed something when you actually only "invented" it in your head?
A: No, except for the dreams about the loss of Spain.
Q: Did don Alonso and Fray Lucas talk to you about the loss of Spain?
A: Yes, but not about the things that would occur during the loss.
Q: Did they talk to you about the restoration of Spain, the change in the papal see, the captain-king who would direct this restoration, and the coming Golden Age?
A: All that I dreamed is that there was a war and men with white crosses, but I did not dream about where the army was to gather for the restoration nor about the change in the papal see. Nor do I remember much about it, except that Fray Lucas did tell me that his brother had a cave which could house ten thousand men. But I did not dream about the cave, although I heard about

the provisions stored there. Nor do I remember anything about a king coming to restore Spain, and I am sure that I did not dream that Piedrola was to become king. And when I dreamed about the crosses, I dreamed that it would be wise if the king's soldiers in the Armada and elsewhere wore them, but not specifically about the restoration of Spain.

"The main contradiction" in her argument still vexed the inquisitors: Lucrecia claimed to have forgotten her dreams after relating them, yet during the trial she had provided countless details about them. This important question was put to her:

Q: Please explain the difference between those that were dreams and those which you invented while awake.

A: As I have previously said, I cannot really remember the dreams because I forgot them after they were copied, although I do remember very well some odd things and details, as I have said here in this trial, but not in the order in which they were dreamed. But I do not know how to discover the difference between what I truly dreamed and what they added to the dreams, as I have already said.

With this statement, the hearing—the last at which Lucrecia was asked to appear—came to an end.

In January 1594 a third inquisitor, Dr. Messia de Lasarte, had been appointed to the panel hearing Lucrecia's case. In the weeks after her final testimony, Messia de Lasarte, Morejón, and Quiroga, assisted by two calificadores, struggled to reach a decision about the extent of Lucrecia's guilt.[53] They reviewed the testimony provided by Allende, Mendoza, Casaos, and Vitores, each of whom contended that the dreams recorded in the registers were literal transcriptions of what Lucrecia had told them. The trial record does not indicate the judges' reasoning, but their opinions about Lucrecia were sharply divided. One judge believed Lucrecia was guilty of having invented dreams for seditious purposes, possibly with the devil's assistance. But the two other judges followed the advice of the tribunal's secretary, Juan de Pantoja, described as the person "who best understands this case." Pantoja had concluded that "she is not to blame nor did she ever want her dreams transcribed, and indeed it had pained her to dream them." Lucrecia could not be held responsible for what she had seen in her dreams, Pantoja felt, because she was "weak-minded and extremely timid," like "the ass of Balaam," the humble beast who took fright when it first saw the angel of the Lord (Numbers 22:21–31).[54] It was Allende and Mendoza, Pantoja implied, who were truly at fault.

Deliberations did not resolve these differences in opinion, and on 14 July 1595 the tribunal voted Lucrecia's case *en diferencias.*[55] The judges were agreed that the dreams did contain some false and heretical statements, but they could not reach a unanimous verdict on charges that Lucrecia had consciously invented the dreams for purposes of sedition. It required another month for them to decide upon the extent to which Lucrecia was to be held responsible for the dreams' content. There was, of course, no question of allowing Lucrecia to go unpunished, but the judges chose to sentence her to *abjuración de levi,* the Inquisition's most lenient penalty. The complete list of her crimes was compiled, along with a censored public version that omitted mention of "anything that might cause a scandal, particularly with respect to the King Our Lord, the Prince Our Lord, the Infanta, the loss of the Spanish kingdoms, and the movement of the Apostolic See to this city of Toledo."[56] Also to avoid scandal, the auto da fe would be private.

The conclusion of the trial finally came on 20 August 1595 in an auto da fe staged in the courtyard of the Dominican monastery of San Pedro Martyr. Lucrecia appeared, dressed as a penitent—wearing a sanbenito and a rope around her neck, holding a lighted candle—flanked by two other penitents, both moriscos. The watered-down text of the sentencia was read aloud—the first time Lucrecia was officially informed of all the various crimes she had committed. "That ever since she was young," it was announced, "she began to dream, and had many dreams in which she claimed that the Holy Trinity appeared, along with God himself, our Lord Jesus Christ, Moses and

Ezekiel, and the celestial virgins." The official reading the sentencia then proclaimed that Lucrecia had confessed to having been transported in her dreams by three holy figures—identified as St. John the Baptist, St. Paul, and St. Luke—to "different parts of the earth and sea, to different kingdoms and provinces," where she had witnessed "visions of war and peace, of pleasure and terror, together with others of good and bad things to come."

Following these general accusations Lucrecia learned that she was guilty of, among other crimes, blasphemy, falsehood, and sacrilege, as well as sedition. She was also charged with having made a pact with the devil, relating her dreams to others, and allowing them to be transcribed. The Inquisition also branded her a "mother of prophets" who had encouraged others to foretell the future. Once these charges were read, Lucrecia also learned, as she had suspected, that her punishment would be relatively light: one hundred lashes, banishment from Madrid, and two years' seclusion in a religious house.[57]

The final irony in Lucrecia's case was the inability of the Inquisition to carry out the sentence it had ordered. In the absence of an executioner, the administration of the one hundred lashes had to be postponed for almost a week.[58] Arranging for her seclusion in a religious house proved more difficult still. The only institution willing to accept Lucrecia and her five-year-old daughter was Toledo's Beatas de la Reina, a small Jeronymite convent, and then on the condition that she pay the cost of her food and lodging. Negotiations between the Holy Office and the convent ended, however, when Lucrecia's father, pleading poverty, refused to provide financial support for his daughter and granddaughter.[59] So Lucrecia was placed temporarily in Toledo's San Lázaro Hospital, an institution for beggars and individuals suffering from contagious skin diseases. Two months later, on 27 October, she requested a transfer to the Hospital of St. John the Baptist, a large charitable institution that specialized in the treatment of noncontagious diseases. When the hospital's administrator, Pedro Salazar de Mendoza, refused to admit her, the inquisitors once again wrote to Alonso Franco, soliciting money for Lucrecia and some clothes for her daughter.[60] We do not know how Alonso Franco took this request, but by this point he had evidently broken off relations with Lucrecia.

In the meanwhile, the tribunal in Toledo struggled to bring to a close the trials of the other members of the brotherhood. Two of the defendants, Sacamanchas and Domingo López Navarro, had by now died, but the cases of Casaos, Vitores, Allende, and Mendoza lingered on. Casaos continued to profess innocence, insisting that he had never believed in the dreams, but Sotocameño steadfastly maintained that Casaos should be punished for various crimes, among them heresy, sedition, and perjury. In September 1595, just as the inquisitors were preparing to decide his case, Casaos became gravely ill. He died the following month, without ever having been formally sentenced.

The tribunal voted Vitores's case *en diferencias* on 5 September 1595, with some of the judges recommending a light penalty and urging that Vitores "be absolved of further punishment in consideration of the long time he has already spent in prison." Two weeks later the Suprema ordered that Vitores "be gravely reprimanded in court, warned not to get involved in similar things, and exiled from Madrid and Toledo for the period of two years."[61] Vitores abandoned Toledo in November 1595 and the following year turned up in his native city of Zamora, apparently working once again as a secretary.

The cases of Allende and Mendoza took longer to resolve. The tribunal reached a preliminary decision on Allende in March 1596, handing down the relatively light sentence of one year's seclusion in a religious house and a warning to avoid future encounters with dreams, prophecies, and related phenomena. The verdict drew two appeals to the Suprema: Allende's appeal that the sentence was too harsh and Sotocameño's appeal that the tribunal's decision was little more than a "joke" in light of the "serious crimes with which he [Allende] had been accused and charged."[62] Four months later the Suprema confirmed the tribunal's decision.

To serve his term of seclusion, Allende took up residence in San Juan de los Reyes, an important Franciscan community only a few hundred yards from the prison. But the head of the convent, Fray Juan de Ovando, soon reported Allende to the Holy Office, saying that he "spoke critically about the Holy Office and his inquisitors and, with little respect for the pledge of secrecy to which he was charged, talked about everything that went on in the prisons." Ovando also testified that Allende continued to maintain his innocence and complained about the "many injustices" the Holy Office had committed against him.[63] By October 1597 Allende had moved to a Franciscan house in Ciudad Real, a small town fifty miles south of Toledo. The friars, no doubt impressed by Allende's outspokenness as well as his experience at court, elected him their representative to the order's provincial assembly.[64] We have no further information about Allende. Apparently, he lived out the remainder of his life—he turned fifty-two in 1597—in Ciudad Real.

Mendoza's case proved even more intractable. Comparing himself to the churchmen who had transcribed the revelations of Catherine of Siena and Bridgit of Sweden, he remained firm on his right as a theologian to transcribe Lucrecia's dreams. And he repeatedly challenged the authority of the Inquisition to keep him in prison, alleging that the case against him was essentially political and motivated primarily by personal enmity on the part of the king and his ministers. Sotocameño, however, evidently considered Mendoza the author of Lucrecia's dreams. In his view the canon was guilty not only of various errors of faith in matters of prophecy but also of believing in dreams that were patently "scandalous, seditious, and prejudicial to the Catholic Church and which gave rise to great dissensions and riots" and to "libels against the ministers of the king."[65]

Mendoza's erratic, occasionally violent (and possibly contrived) behavior had also led to questions about his sanity. In January 1594, after a lengthy investigation, the Suprema declared that Mendoza was suffering from a "lack of judgment" and ordered that he be moved out of his prison cell into a monastery.[66] In April he took up residence in Toledo's Augustinian monastery and began preparing a new set of recusancies and other written challenges to the Inquisition's authority. As one of his weary judges put it, "over each word and thing he writes a very long book."[67]

The Toledan tribunal finally managed to decide his case in June 1596, but even then elected not to rule on the charges of sedition.[68] The inquisitors condemned Mendoza to six years of forced seclusion in a monastery. Appeals by Mendoza and by Sotocameño prompted another year of legal wrangling. On 9 September 1597 the council finally decided to reduce the period of enforced seclusion from six years to two in view of the time Mendoza had already spent in prison.[69] A few weeks later Mendoza moved to the Jeronymite monastery of Santa María de la Sisla, on the outskirts of Toledo. His correspondence with the Holy Office now turned to a request for permission to decorate his new cell with "tapestries and paintings . . . to satisfy his eyes," a new bed and windows, as well as permission to read a newly printed book on the history of Nuestra Señora de Loreto, a famous shrine in northern Italy.[70] From these relatively comfortable quarters Mendoza entertained a host of relatives and friends, which provoked the prior to complain in October 1598 that the monastery had become more like "a lunatic asylum than a religious house."[71] It was also reported that Mendoza possessed an annotated copy of Esteban de Garibay's *History of the Chronicles of Spain* in which he had written "comments critical of His Majesty and the Inquisition."[72] On 16 November 1598, two months after the death of Philip II, Mendoza petitioned for his release from the remainder of his seclusion. Pedro Puertocarrero, the new inquisitor general, granted this request on 31 November. But Mendoza, sixty-one years old and ailing, elected to remain at La Sisla, surrounded by his small art collection and personal library. He died there, in relative obscurity, in late September or early October 1603.[73]

CONCLUSION: UNDERSTANDING LUCRECIA

We do not know what became of Lucrecia after her stay in Toledo's Hospital of St. John the Baptist. One day a revealing document may surface, but for now we can only speculate. The letters and reports included in Mendoza's trial record and the parish books of San Sebastián suggest that Lucrecia never returned to her parents' home in Madrid. Had it not been for the falling-out she had with her father, she might have done what many other exiled women did: "left the city by one door but immediately returned by another."[1] But evidently she did not return to Madrid, and a letter from Vitores to the Inquisition dated 2 February 1596, that is, five months after Lucrecia left the hospital, indicates that she had not joined him in Zamora.[2]

Without an obvious trade and with a small child at her side, Lucrecia could not have found work except as a servant, possibly in the house of one of Alonso de Mendoza's many wealthy relations. Or she might have turned to begging or prostitution, although the former had come under royal laws that prescribed harsh penalties for unlicensed vagabonds. Official begging licenses were given only to disabled men and to women who were old, ill, widowed, or mothers abandoned by their husbands. Officials in Toledo, however, would have been unlikely to grant such a license to anyone who was not a native Toledan, let alone to someone recently released from the prisons of the Inquisition, and Lucrecia's name does not appear among the 102 women who applied for such licenses in Toledo in 1598.[3]

Similar restrictions would have prevented Lucrecia from entering one of the *albergües* (almshouses) that came into existence at the end of the sixteenth century.[4] Madrid's albergüe, which provided food and lodging in exchange for work, opened in 1596. (Other cities, Seville and Toledo, for example, decided they could not afford such institutions without financial assistance from the crown.) But the albergües were intended for native citizens, and Lucrecia could not seek official aid in her native Madrid.

One other charitable alternative for women was the religious houses established for *mujeres arrepentidas,* prostitutes who had been persuaded to give up their profession in exchange for an opportunity to save their souls.[5] Some of these houses also offered asylum to other "lost" or "fallen" women, including former prisoners. The city of Toledo had several such houses, notably that of Santa María de la Blanca, which occupied the site of a building formerly belonging to a synagogue. But the surviving records of these institutions make no reference to Lucrecia.

Lucrecia's other choice would have been to leave the district controlled by the Holy Office of Toledo. Southern Spain—Andalusia and particularly the growing cities of Granada and Seville—was a favored destination for poor emigrants from central and northern Spain, especially for the army of *pícaros* and *pícaras* who eked out a living by their wits. One can almost imagine Lucrecia as one of Seville's many street-corner fortune-tellers and oneiromancers, earning a living by the very talents that, five years earlier, had led to her arrest.

*

Lucrecia's story can at once be read as an intriguing episode in the history of the socially defined roles that determine the course of men's and women's lives. Her argument, expressed repeatedly during the course of her trial, that she was a weak woman manipulated by strong men suggests that she was fully prepared to exploit sixteenth-century conceptions of women as a means of strengthening her defense.

From this perspective, Lucrecia's prophetic career can be viewed as essentially that of a woman who sought to enter the world of politics, an arena reserved almost exclusively for men. In her day women who did participate in the realm of politics usually did so by virtue of spiritual powers. Women's "natural forces" were thought to be weaker than men's, but they were often considered the spiritually stronger of the sexes, in part because God had created Adam from mud but fashioned Eve from a rib located close to the heart. By nature, then, women were thought to be more pious and devout and to have a greater propensity for visions, raptures, and other forms of mystical experiences. These "experiences of the heart"[6] were one of the few channels by which women could gain public authority and recognition, and ultimately a political voice. It was her spiritual gifts, for example, that helped Teresa of Jesus to become one of the most respected and influential individuals of her day.

The limited constellation of roles available to women in sixteenth-century Spain, however, cannot help us understand Lucrecia's personal aspirations and private hopes. Though her life is much better documented than that of almost any other sixteenth-century Spanish woman of humble origin, it is difficult to decide what to make of her as an individual. On the one hand, there is something fragile, even gullible about this doncella. Perhaps she was the innocent victim of Mendoza's crafty schemes. Disappointed first by her real father, then by the realm's royal father, she may have found in Mendoza an authority figure worthy of her respect. And while her father punished her for dreaming, and Philip ignored her prophecies, Mendoza rewarded her for them. To please Mendoza, perhaps, she turned all her imaginative energy to answer his promptings: What did you dream about? Did it involve the loss of Spain? Was the king present? Indeed, the number and thematic similarities of the dreams recorded at Mendoza's behest suggest that Lucrecia continued dreaming—or claimed to have continued dreaming—to please him or to avoid incurring his wrath.

If this interpretation of Lucrecia's behavior is true, and not just a straw of a defense she clung to during the closing days of her trial, her prophetic career may have been an extended exercise in fulfilling Mendoza's expectations. Perhaps the dream registers are largely records of a young woman's effort to satisfy a disgruntled churchman's impressions of what political prophecies should be like.

But such a monochromatic explanation ignores all the evidence about the less-submissive, indeed rebellious aspects of Lucrecia's personality. Although she was timid—or feigned timidity—when confronted by figures of authority such as Vicar Neroni, in other situations, notably in the company of her cellmates, Lucrecia was something of a braggart, a young woman who exuded a self-confidence tinged with conceit. Furthermore, while she may have fallen under Mendoza's sway, she had dreamed about the deaths of monarchs and the loss of Spain well before Mendoza had entered her life. Why then, we must ask, did she agree to collaborate with him in what she knew to be a dangerous enterprise? And why did her arrest by the vicar in February 1588 not dissuade her from further involvement with Mendoza, Allende, and the other members of the Brotherhood of the Holy Cross?

The easy answer, and the one Lucrecia wanted the Inquisition to believe, is that she was an ignorant doncella victimized by the clerics in whom she had placed her trust. Her accusations that Mendoza doctored the texts of at least some of the dreams is plausible, but even if she was unaware of these alterations, she fully understood the political purposes to which the dreams were being put. Perhaps, then, it was the strength of her political beliefs that moved her to continue serving as a seer of the confraternity that developed around her. Still, one can imagine that the nineteen-year-old Lucrecia did not fully understand the implications of her actions when she first presented herself to Mendoza as a clairvoyant with dreams pertaining to the loss of Spain.

Whatever her initial motivations, once the dreams were publicized the humble, anonymous Lucrecia quickly attained a select status. As a divinely inspired seer, she held what sociologists describe as a "special deviant position."[7] Such liminal positions always entail certain dangers, but also certain benefits. The risks were all too obvious at a time when neither Catholics nor Protestants were prepared to treat deviants leniently. But Lucrecia and her mother clearly relished the attention the dreams brought, not to mention the alms provided by Mendoza, the duchess of Feria, and other sympathizers. In the role of prophet Lucrecia gained entrée to a social network of powerful churchmen, wealthy noblemen, and scholars—a life she had glimpsed while serving at the royal court, but one that a woman of her modest background could never hope to enter.

Doubtless, some of her adherents and supporters viewed her as a mere curiosity, one of "the ignorant and rustic who dream marvelous things, including predictions about future events."[8] In contrast, Lucrecia seems to have viewed herself as a celebrity. From an early age, she had learned that dreams brought attention, both her father's punishments and her neighbors' regard. Recognition and identity could be earned by dreaming as long as she continued to dream dreams that attracted the interest of family, neighbors, and, ultimately, Mendoza and his friends. How Lucrecia was able to discipline her mind to this task, we do not know; perhaps she discovered or was taught a method from Loyola's *Spiritual Exercises.*[9]

The dreams also offered Lucrecia new opportunities to make a new family for herself: first, to select Mendoza as a surrogate father, and then to find a good husband. The dreams, she must have suspected, would bring to her doorstep at least a few suitors. We do not know how she first met Diego de Vitores, although he later informed the Inquisition that before meeting her he had heard her described as "a pretty, virtuous woman of good habits."[10] In his testimony he did not mention the dreams, but it is difficult to imagine that he had not heard about them.

A desire for power is yet another possible motive for Lucrecia's willingness to go along with Mendoza. As an uneducated daughter of a solicitor, Lucrecia could observe, come into contact with, and even possess direct knowledge of affairs at court, yet never have any influence on them. In many of her dreams, however, Lucrecia is cast in the role of the king's spiritual advisor, counseling Philip on the need to institute fiscal reforms as well as on personal matters such as the marriage of the infanta. In dreams dating from the period of Lucrecia's illness, Philip appears as a supplicant visiting Lucrecia's bedside to seek her counsel. In the dream of 19 March 1588, Philip is seated at the head of Lucrecia's bed:

P: Fray Lucas told me that you were very sick in bed, so I came to see you.

L: He exaggerates.

P: [*Asking for more attention*] Look, I am the king speaking.

L: I'd be happier with the sight of Piedrola.

P: But don't you realize, I am the king.

L: But probably only for this year.

P: What will happen to my son [Philip] who is now ill?

L: Make note that he is like the son of David, and you should thank God for not having taken him already; in time, your policies would have harmed him. [*Then, realizing that Philip is barefoot, she asks*] How did you get here?

P: In a litter.

L: Be sure to return on foot.

P: I don't like you, but please don't give me away.

L: Oh, Philip, if you only knew in whose hands the tambourine is!

This last reference is to a popular proverb, "En buenos manos está el pandero" (The tambourine is in good hands), meaning that whoever plays the instrument embodies life, vitality, and worldly experience.[11]

In the dreams, then, Lucrecia had the satisfaction of putting the king in his place. In real life, of course, there was no question of her even speaking to the king after she had left her maidservant's post. That she understood the prerogatives of authority and influence, however, is clear from an offhand comment she made to one of her cellmates. She had the power to ruin both Allende and Mendoza, she said: "if I told [the tribunal] the truth, it would destroy them."[12]

Learned astrologer, divine prophet, royal confidant, amazon-like warrior, national savior, and queen—in the imaginary landscapes of her dreams Lucrecia could summon and command men. Glory and renown may be the stuff most dreams are made of, yet Lucrecia seems to have gone one step further, becoming something of the standard-bearer she dreamed herself to be. Nowadays, a woman like Lucrecia might be labeled a psychoneurotic whose dreams are riddled with unresolved Oedipal impulses, among them, efforts to please her mother's desire for social advancement and a displaced hostility toward Alonso Franco. But in sixteenth-century Spain Lucrecia's dreams were perceived as a threat to the foundations of secular authority, vested in the monarch; of spiritual authority, vested in the church; and of social power and privilege, vested in the hands of well-born and well-educated men. Her supporters claimed that her dreams were divinely inspired, but the inverted legal and moral order depicted in the dreams convinced others she was dim-witted or insane.[13] Lucrecia was among those Fray Pedro Navarro criticized as "those unstable, illuminated evil women who go from house to house, recounting visions and every morning describing as revelations the absurdities they dream at night."[14]

After the trial, Lucrecia's dreams were locked away, hidden from view, in the Inquisition's archives for hundreds of years. Today, what her dreams have to say about the injustices in Philip's Spain remains vitally important. In her way, Lucrecia represents the social and political conscience of sixteenth-century Spain, and her attacks on Philip, her criticisms of his rule, and her dreams of a new, more equitable monarchy constitute a *cri de coeur,* the voice of those Spaniards for whom Philip's military adventures abroad meant higher taxes and a lower standard of living at home. A message similar to Lucrecia's could be heard in Zaragoza in 1591, when the townspeople, provoked by the Inquisition's arrest of Antonio Pérez, protested the loss of their provincial liberties and shouted "Viva la libertad!" (Long live liberty!).[15] The same message was repeated later that year when street placards denouncing the new *millones* tax appeared in Avila—"And you, Philip, be happy with what is yours, and don't take away someone else's"[16]—and again in Madrid, where more than five hundred artisans rioted in protest of the new tax.[17]

Lucrecia's dreams also anticipated by more than a decade the biting denunciation of Philip's rule by Iñigo Ibáñez de Santa Cruz, the arbitrista who claimed that Philip bequeathed to his heir a Spain "consumed by blind government." Had Philip lived four years longer, wrote Santa Cruz, with a candor rarely found among political writers of his day, "he would have destroyed everything."[18] Lucrecia's criticisms of Philip were further vindicated by Juan de Mariana, Francisco Suárez, Mateo Lisón y Viedma, and other writers of the late sixteenth and early seventeenth century.[19] Philip and his heirs, Philip III (1598–1621) and Philip IV (1621–1665), all these commentators concurred, had neglected the principal duties of a monarch: to administer justice with equity, to respect vassals' traditional privileges and rights, and to rule by virtue of a contract that limited the crown's ability to govern without the kingdom's consent.

Some thirty years after Lucrecia's trial, Quevedo published his *Sueños y discursos,* that masterpiece of Golden Age literature in which dreams are used to paint a satirical portrait of Spanish society. Against this literary conceit, there was the more popular view of dreams articulated by Quevedo's contemporary, Calderón de la Barca: "dreams are only dreams," passing phantasma that vanish with the night. As with the dreams, so too the dreamers: Lucrecia is all but forgotten, unmentioned in any of the many histories of King Philip's reign. Nonetheless, Lucrecia's dreams were shared by others of her era and almost certainly by those later generations of Spaniards for whom the wisest and safest moment to criticize their rulers occurred during sleep.

CALENDAR OF LUCRECIA'S DREAMS

The dream registers are in the collection of the Archivo Histórico Nacional, Sección de Inquisición, in Madrid. Locations are given here by legajo (leg.), expediente (exp.), and folio (fol.); variant texts are indicated in brackets. Notations enclosed in quotation marks are those that appear in the registers.

	1587	*leg./exp.*	*fol.*
1.	? Nov	3712/2	13
2.	9 Nov	3712/2	14
3.	10? Nov	3712/2	14
4.	11 Nov	3712/2	16
5.	12 Nov	3712/2	16
6.	13 Nov	3712/2	17
7.	15 Nov	3712/2	18
8.	15 Nov	3712/2	19
9.	16 Nov	3712/2	19
10.	17 Nov	3712/2	21
11.	19 Nov	3712/2	22–23
12.	20 Nov	3712/2	24
13.	21 Nov	3712/2	26
14.	22 Nov	3712/2	27
15.	23 Nov	3712/2	29
16.	24 Nov	3712/2	31
17.	25 Nov	3712/2	33
18.	26 Nov	3712/2	35
19.	27 Nov	3712/2	36–37
20.	28 Nov	3712/2	37
21.	29 Nov	3712/2	38
22.	30 Nov	3712/2	38
23.	1 Dec	3712/2	1
24.	2 Dec	3712/2	2
25.	3 Dec	3712/2	2v–3
26.	4 Dec	3712/2	6–11
27.	5 Dec	3712/2	11–12
28.	6 Dec	3712/2	12–19
29.	7 Dec	3712/2	19–22
30.	8 Dec	3712/2	22–26
31.	9 Dec	3712/2	26–30
32.	10 Dec	3712/2	30–32
33.	11 Dec	3712/2	32–34
34.	12 Dec	3712/2	34–36
35.	13 Dec	3712/2	36–39
36.	14 Dec	3712/2	39–41
37.	15 Dec	3712/2	41–45
38.	16 Dec	3712/2	45–50
39.	17 Dec	3712/2	50–54
40.	18 Dec	3712/2	54–57
41.	19 Dec	3712/2	58–63
42.	20 Dec	3712/2	63–66
43.	20 Dec	3712/2	66–67 ["at 5 P.M."]
44.	21 Dec	3712/2	67–72
45.	22 Dec	3712/2	72–75
46.	23 Dec	3712/2	75–79
47.	24 Dec	3712/2	79–81
48.	25 Dec	3712/2	81–83
49.	26 Dec	3712/2	83–86

	1587	*leg./exp.*	*fol.*
50.	27 Dec	3712/2	86–87
51.	28 Dec	3712/2	87–90
52.	28 Dec	3712/2	90–92
53.	29 Dec	3712/2	92–93
54.	29 Dec	3712/2	93–96
55.	30 Dec	3712/2	96–99
56.	31 Dec	3712/2	99–102
	1588	*leg./exp.*	*fol.*
57.	1 Jan	3712/2	102–3
58.	1 Jan	3712/2	103–6
59.	2 Jan	3712/2	103
60.	3 Jan	3712/2	104–7
61.	4 Jan	3712/2	107–11
62.	5 Jan	3712/2	111–14
63.	6 Jan	3712/2	114–16
64.	7 Jan	3712/2	116–19
65.	8 Jan	3712/2	119–23
66.	8 Jan	3712/2	123
67.	9 Jan	3712/2	123–27
68.	10 Jan	3712/2	127–30
69.	11 Jan	3712/2	131–32
70.	12 Jan	3712/2	132–36
71.	12 Jan	3712/2	136–38
		["in the morning"]	
72.	13 Jan	3712/2	138–41
73.	14 Jan	3712/2	141–43
74.	15 Jan	3712/2	143–45
75.	16 Jan	3712/2	145–48
76.	17 Jan	3712/2	148–51
77.	18 Jan	3712/2	151–52
78.	19 Jan	3712/2	152–55
79.	19 Jan	3712/2	155–57
80.	20 Jan	3712/2	157–60
81.	21 Jan	3712/2	160–63
82.	22 Jan	3712/2	163–68
83.	23 Jan	3712/2	168–72
84.	24 Jan	3712/2	172–75
85.	25 Jan	3712/2	175–78
86.	25 Jan	3712/2	178–80
		["before I awoke"]	
87.	26 Jan	3712/2	180–84
88.	27 Jan	3712/2	184–87

	1588	*leg./exp.*	*fol.*
89.	28 Jan	3712/2	187–90
90.	29 Jan	3712/2	190–93
91.	30 Jan	3712/2	193–98
92.	31 Jan	3712/2	198–204
93.	1 Feb	3712/2	204–10
94.	2 Feb	3712/2	210–14
95.	3 Feb	3712/2	214–18
96.	4 Feb	3712/2	218–22
97.	4 Feb	3712/2	222–23
			["at 5 A.M."]
98.	5 Feb	3712/2	223–27
99.	6 Feb	3712/2	227–31
100.	6 Feb	3712/2	231–32
			["at 5 A.M."]
101.	7 Feb	3712/2	232–39
102.	8 Feb	3712/2	239–42
103.	9 Feb	3712/2	242–49
104.	10 Feb	3712/2	249–53
105.	11 Feb	3712/2	253–57
106.	12 Feb	3712/2	257–61
107.	13 Feb	3712/2	261–63
108.	14 Feb	3712/2	263–65
109.	15 Feb	3712/2	266–68
110.	16 Feb	3712/2	268–71
111.	17 Feb	3712/2	271–73
112.	18 Feb	3712/2	273–76
113.	18 Feb	3712/2	276
		["in the afternoon during a nap on a rug"]	
114.	19 Feb	3712/2	276–79
115.	19 Feb	3712/2	279–81
		["in the morning"]	
116.	20 Feb	3712/2	281–87
117.	21 Feb	3712/2	278–95
118.	22 Feb	3712/2	295–99
119.	23 Feb	3712/2	299–303
120.	24 Feb	3712/2	303–8
121.	24 Feb	3712/2	308–10
			["after lunch"]
122.	25 Feb	3712/2	310–13
123.	26 Feb	3712/2	313–17
124.	27 Feb	3712/2	317–21
125.	28 Feb	3712/2	321–24

	1588	*leg./exp.*	*fol.*
126.	29 Feb	3712/2	324–27
127.	1 Mar	3712/2	327–30
128.	1 Mar	3712/2	330–31
	["after finishing lunch"]		
129.	1 Mar	3712/2	331–33
	["at 4 P.M."]		
130.	2 Mar	3712/2	333–34
131.	3 Mar	3712/2	334–36
132.	4 Mar	3703/1	52v
133.	5 Mar	3712/2	336–39
134.	6 Mar	3712/2	339–42
135.	6 Mar	3712/2	342–44
	["at 6 A.M."]		
136.	7 Mar	3712/2	344–47
137.	8 Mar	3712/2	347–51
138.	8 Mar	3712/2	351
139.	9 Mar	3712/2	351–58
140.	9 Mar	3712/2	358–61
141.	10 Mar	3712/2	361–64
142.	10 Mar	3712/2	364–65
	["just before waking"]		
143.	11 Mar	3712/2	365–68
144.	12 Mar	3712/2	368–70
145.	13 Mar	3712/2	370
146.	14 Mar	3712/2	371–72
147.	15 Mar	3712/2	372–75
148.	16 Mar	3712/2	375–79
149.	16 Mar	3712/2	379–81
	["between 6 and 7 P.M."]		
150.	17 Mar	3712/2	381–86
151.	17 Mar	3712/2	386–92
	["after falling back to sleep"]		
152.	19 Mar	3712/2	392–94
	["at 6 A.M. after being up all night with a high fever"]		
153.	19 Mar	3712/2	396–401
	["after finishing lunch"]		
154.	20 Mar	3712/2	401–3
155.	21 Mar	3712/2	403–5
	["at midnight"]		
156.	21 Mar	3712/2	405–7
	["at 6 A.M."]		

	1588	*leg./exp.*	*fol.*
157.	22 Mar	3712/2	407–10
158.	22 Mar	3712/2	410–14
	["at 6:30 A.M."]		
159.	23 Mar	3712/4	1
	["there was no dream because she was sick"]		
160.	24 Mar	3712/4	1
		[3703/1	72]
161.	25 Mar	3712/4	2v
		[3703/1	72–73]
162.	26 Mar	3712/4	4
		[3703/1	73v]
163.	27 Mar	3712/4	5
		[3703/1	74]
164.	28 Mar	3712/4	6
	["at 5 A.M."]		
		[3703/1	74]
165.	29 Mar	3712/4	6
		[3703/1	74]
166.	30 Mar	3712/4	7
		[3703/1	74v]
167.	1 Apr	3712/4	9
		[3703/1	75v]
168.	1 Apr	3712/4	10
		[3703/1	75v]
169.	1 Apr	3712/4	11
		[3703/1	75]
170.	2 Apr	3712/4	11
171.	3 Apr	3712/4	11
		[3703/1	76]
172.	3 Apr	3712/4	12
		[3703/1	76]
173.	8 Apr	3712/4	13
	["at 8 A.M."]		
		[3703/1	76v]
174.	13 Apr	3712/4	13
		[3703/1	76]
175.	14 Apr	3703	77v
176.	15 Apr	3712/4	14
		[3703/1	77v]
177.	16 Apr	3703	77v–78
178.	17 Apr	3712/4	15
		[3703/1	77v–78]

	1588	*leg./exp.*	*fol.*
179.	17 Apr	3712/4	15
		["after lunch"]	
		[3703/1	78]
180.	18 Apr	3712/4	15–17
		[3703/1	79–81]
181.	18 Apr	3712/4	18
		[3703/1	78]
182.	22 Apr	3712/4	18
		[3703/1	78v]
183.	29 Apr	3712/4	19
		[3703/1	82]
184.	30 Apr	3712/4	19
		[3703/1	82]
185.	1 May	3712/4	19
		[3703/1	82]
186.	2 May	3712/4	19
		[3703/1	82v]
187.	5 May	3712/4	20
		[3703/1	82v]
188.	9 May	3712/4	21
		[3703/1	74]
189.	10 May	3712/4	21
		[3703/1	43]
190.	15 May	3712/4	21
		[3703/1	46]
191.	5 Jun	3712/4	24
		[3703/1	48]
192.	7 Jun	3712/4	24
		[3703/1	43v]
193.	12 Jun	3712/4	25
		[3703/1	44]
194.	15 Jun	3712/4	25
		[3703/1	50v]
195.	15 Jun	3712/4	25
196.	17 Jun	3712/4	25
		[3703/1	51]
197.	21 Jun	3712/4	25
		[3703/1	52]
198.	27 Jun	3712/4	26
		[3703/1	54]
199.	28 Jun	3712/4	26–30
		["at 3 A.M."]	
		[3703/1	54]

	1588	*leg./exp.*	*fol.*
200.	29 Jun	3712/4	30
		[3703/1	57v]
201.	3 Jul	3703/1	57v
202.	5 Jul	3712/4	30
		[3703/1	57v]
203.	8 Jul	3712/4	31
		[3703/1	66]
204.	13 Jul	3712/4	32
		[3703/1	68]
205.	15 Jul	3712/4	33
		[3703/1	68v–69]
206.	17 Jul	3712/4	34
		[3703/1	70]
207.	18 Jul	3712/4	35–36
		[3703/1	62]
208.	21 Jul	3712/4	36–37
		[3703/1	60]
209.	22 Jul	3712/4	38
		[3703/1	61]
210.	27 Jul	3712/4	39
		[3703/1	68v]
211.	28 Jul	3712/4	39
		[3703/1	65v]
212.	29 Jul	3712/4	40
		[3703/1	64]
213.	2 Aug	3712/4	41
		[3703/1	85v]
214.	4 Aug	3712/4	44
215.	5 Aug	3712/4	44
216.	6 Aug	3712/4	44
		[3703/1	266v]
217.	12 Aug	3712/4	46–47
		[3703/1	62]
218.	15 Aug	3712/4	42
219.	15 Aug	3703/1	58v
		["in the afternoon"]	
220.	19 Aug	3712/4	42
		[3703/1	58v]
221.	23 Aug	3712/4	50
		[3703/1	74]
222.	26 Aug	3712/4	50
		[3703/1	75]
223.	28 Aug	3712/4	51

	1588	*leg./exp.*	*fol.*
224.	29 Aug	3712/4	54
225.	1 Sep	3712/4	55
226.	1 Sep	3712/4	57
227.	2 Sep	3712/4	59
228.	9 Sep	3712/4	61
229.	16 Sep	3712/4	63
			["at 3 A.M."]
230.	16 Sep	3712/4	64
			["at 8 A.M."]
231.	23 Sep	3712/4	66
232.	30 Sep	3712/4	67
		[3703/1	13]
233.	7 Oct	3712/4	70
234.	7 Oct	3712/4	72
235.	14 Oct	3712/4	74
		[3703/1	15]
236.	21 Oct	3712/4	76
237.	22 Oct	3712/4	77
238.	24 Oct	3712/4	80
239.	25 Oct	3712/4	80
240.	26 Oct	3712/4	81
241.	27? Oct	3712/4	82
242.	? Oct	3712/4	83
243.	30 Oct	3712/4	84
		[3703/1	24–24v]
244.	1 Nov	3712/4	86
		[3703/1	24v–25]
245.	3 Nov	3712/4	87
		[3703/1	28]
246.	4 Nov	3712/4	88
		[3703/1	11]
247.	6 Nov	3712/4	90
		[3703/1	34]
248.	9 Nov	3703/1	5
249.	? Nov	3703/1	5v
250.	11 Nov	3712/4	91
		[3703/1	3]
251.	14 Nov	3712/4	92
252.	19 Nov	3712/4	94
253.	20 Nov	3712/4	95
		[3703/1	9]
254.	25 Nov	3712/4	96
		[3703/1	22–23]

	1588	*leg./exp.*	*fol.*
255.	26 Nov	3703/1	26
256.	2 Dec	3712/4	98
		[3703/1	18]
257.	23 Dec	3712/4	99
		[3703/1	36]
258.	? Dec	3703/3	40
259.	? Dec	3712/4	104
260.	25 Dec	3712/4	106
261.	29 Dec	3712/4	104
		[3703/1	217]
262.	30 Dec	3712/4	104
		[3703/1	7]

	1589	*leg./exp.*	*fol.*
263.	13 Jan	3712/4	106
264.	21 Jan	3712/4	107
265.	10 Feb	3712/4	108
266.	17 Feb	3712/4	109
267.	24 Feb	3712/4	111
268.	3 Mar	3712/4	112
269.	10 Mar	3712/4	112
270.	17 Mar	3712/4	114
271.	24 Mar	3712/4	116
272.	5 Apr	3712/4	117
273.	7 Apr	3712/4	118
274.	13 Apr	3712/4	118
275.	16 Apr	3712/4	118
276.	20 Apr	3712/4	119
277.	30 Apr	3712/4	120
278.	1 May	3712/4	120
			["during afternoon nap, at 5 P.M."]
279.	5 May	3712/4	121
280.	12 May	3712/4	121
281.	18 May	3712/4	126
282.	24 May	3712/4	123
283.	26 May	3712/4	124
284.	? May	3712/4	127
285.	? May	3712/4	128
286.	2 Jun	3712/4	128
		[3703/1	281]
287.	? Jun	3712/4	130

	1589	*leg./exp.*	*fol.*
288.	17 Jun	3712/4	132
		[3703/1	132]
289.	20 Jun	3712/4	133
290.	21 Jun	3712/4	134
		[3703/1	271]
291.	27 Jun	3712/4	135
		[3703/1	271]
292.	28 Jun	3712/4	136
		[3703/1	271v]
293.	23 Jun	3712/4	137
		["víspera de san juan"]	
294.	24 Jun	3712/4	138–39
		["in the afternoon"]	
		[3703/1	284]
295.	2? Jun	3712/4	140
296.	23 Jun	3712/4	139
		[3703/1	282v]
297.	30 Jun	3712/4	141
		[3703/1	265]
298.	4 Jul	3712/4	143
299.	7 Jul	3712/4	144
300.	14 Jul	3712/4	146
301.	17 Jul	3712/4	146
		[3703/1	290]
302.	? Jul	3712/4	148
		[3703/1	290]
303.	? Jul	3712/4	150
304.	? Jul	3712/4	151
305.	? Jul	3712/4	151
		["in the afternoon"]	
306.	? Jul	3712/4	152
307.	28 Jul	3712/4	153
308.	2 Aug	3703/1	42
309.	4 Aug	3712/4	155
310.	11 Aug	3712/4	156
311.	18 Aug	3712/4	157
312.	25 Aug	3712/4	158
313.	1 Sep	3712/4	160
314.	8 Sep	3712/4	160
315.	15 Sep	3712/4	162
		[3703/1	278]
316.	22 Sep	3712/4	163
		[3703/1	277v]

	1589	*leg./exp.*	*fol.*
317.	24 Sep	3712/4	165
		[3703/1	249]
318.	25 Sep	3712/4	166
319.	6 Oct	3712/4	167
	[Mendoza comments, "here a dream is missing; it is the one Fray Lucas gave to the Prior don Hernando (de Toledo) because he asked for it"]		
		[3703/1	281]
320.	13 Oct	3712/4	169
321.	20 Oct	3712/4	170
322.	27 Oct	3712/4	171
323.	3 Nov	3712/4	173
		[3703/1	37]
324.	10 Nov	3712/4	179
		[3703/1	287]
325.	11 Nov	3712/4	180
		[3703/1	279]
326.	13 Nov	3712/4	181
		[3703/1	279]
327.	15 Nov	3712/4	181
		[3703/1	277]
328.	17 Nov	3712/4	182
		[3703/1	277]
329.	18 Nov	3712/4	181
		[3703/1	279]
330.	24 Nov	3712/4	183
		[3703/1	285]
331.	28 Nov	3712/4	184
		[3703/1	312]
332.	1 Dec	3712/4	186
333.	3 Dec	3712/4	188
		[3703/1	304]
334.	5 Dec	3712/4	188
		[3703/1	304]
335.	9 Dec	3712/4	190
		[3703/1	302]
336.	15 Dec	3712/4	191
		[3703/1	301]
337.	22 Dec	3712/4	193
		[3703/1	310]

	1589	*leg./exp.*	*fol.*
338.	27 Dec	3712/4	194
		[3703/1	306v]
339.	29 Dec	3712/4	195
		[3703/1	308]

	1590	*leg./exp.*	*fol.*
340.	5 Jan	3712/4	196
		[3703/1	306]
341.	7 Jan	3703/1	307
342.	12 Jan	3712/4	197
		[3703/1	314]
343.	13 Jan	3712/4	198
		[3703/1	318v]
344.	14 Jan	3712/4	199
	["at 6 P.M., I was tired, lay down in bed"]		
		[3703/1	319]
345.	16 Jan	3712/4	200
		[3703/1	319v–320]
346.	19 Jan	3712/4	201
		[3703/1	320]
347.	21 Jan	3712/4	204
	["at 6 P.M."]		
		[3703/1	321]
348.	26 Jan	3712/4	204
		[3703/1	321v]
349.	1 Feb	3712/4	207
		[3703/1	308]
350.	1 Feb	3703/1	322
351.	2 Feb	3712/4	209
		[3703/1	322v]
352.	2 Feb	3712/4	212
	["at 6 P.M."]		
353.	9 Feb	3712/4	213
354.	11 Feb	3712/4	221
355.	16 Feb	3712/4	217
356.	19 Feb	3712/4	223
357.	20 Feb	3712/4	223–29
358.	23 Feb	3712/4	229–34
359.	23 Feb	3712/4	234–36
	["the dream after 1 P.M."]		
360.	24 Feb	3712/4	236

	1590	*leg./exp.*	*fol.*
361.	2 Mar	3712/4	236–46
362.	3 Mar	3712/4	246–52
363.	3 Mar	3712/4	249
	[first dream copied by Vitores]		
364.	4 Mar	3712/4	253
365.	5 Mar	3712/4	254
366.	6 Mar	3712/4	256
367.	7 Mar	3712/4	260–63
368.	9 Mar	3712/4	263–68
369.	10 Mar	3712/4	268–72
370.	11 Mar	3712/4	272–75
371.	12 Mar	3712/4	276–83
372.	13 Mar	3712/4	283–88
373.	14 Mar	3712/4	288–93
374.	15 Mar	3712/4	298
375.	15 Mar	3712/4	298–302
376.	17 Mar	3712/4	302–4
377.	19 Mar	3712/4	304–8
378.	20 Mar	3712/4	308–14
379.	21 Mar	3712/4	314–19
380.	22 Mar	3712/4	319
381.	23 Mar	3712/4	319
382.	24 Mar	3712/4	325
383.	25 Mar	3712/4	326
384.	26 Mar	3712/4	329
385.	27 Mar	3712/4	332
386.	28 Mar	3712/4	336
387.	29 Mar	3712/4	336
388.	30 Mar	3712/4	342
389.	1 Apr	3712/4	349
		[3712/2	129]
390.	2 Apr	3712/4	353–56
	["in the afternoon, when I normally fall asleep"]		
391.	3 Apr	3712/4	356
392.	5 Apr	3712/4	360–65
393.	6 Apr	3712/4	365–70
		[3712/2	132–33]
394.	8 Apr	3712/4	370
		[3712/2	133–34]
395.	10 Apr	3712/4	374
396.	12 Apr	3712/4	380

	1590	*leg./exp.*	*fol.*
397.	13 Apr	3712/4	384–88
398.	15 Apr	3712/4	388–94
399.	17 Apr	3712/4	394–98
400.	18 Apr	3712/4	411–13
401.	18 Apr	3712/4	62
		["after eating"]	
402.	19 Apr	3712/4	398
403.	20 Apr	3712/4	402
404.	21 Apr	3712/4	68
405.	24 Apr	3712/4	69
406.	26 Apr	3712/4	71
		["after 3 A.M."]	
407.	26 Apr	3712/4	73
408.	27 Apr	3712/4	73
409.	30 Apr	3712/4	75
410.	1 May	3712/4	76v
411.	2 May	3712/4	78
412.	4 May	3712/4	79v–81v
413.	8 May	3712/4	86
	["sleeping in the afternoon"]		
414.	11 May	3712/4	82
415.	13 May	3712/4	84

ABBREVIATIONS

Archives and Libraries

ABHS	Archivo y Biblioteca Heredía Spínola, Madrid (also known as Archivo Zabalburrú).
ACT	Archivo de la Catedral de Toledo.
AGS	Archivo General de Simanças.
AHN Inq	Archivo Histórico Nacional, Madrid, Sección de Inquisición. References are to legajo/expediente/pieza.
AHPT	Archivo Histórico Provincial de Toledo.
APR	Archivo del Palacio Real, Madrid.
ASF	Archivio di Stato, Florence.
ASV NS	Archivio Segreto Vaticano, Rome, Nunziatura di Spagna.
BAV	Biblioteca Apostolica Vaticana, Rome.
BL	British Library, London.
BL Add.	British Library, Additional manuscripts.
BL Eg.	British Library, Egerton manuscripts.
BN	Biblioteca Nacional, Madrid.
IVDJ	Instituto de Valencia de Don Juan, Madrid.
RAH	Real Academia de Historia, Madrid.

Other Abbreviations

ACC	*Las actas de las cortes de Castilla,* 60 vols. Madrid 1877–1974.
AIEM	*Anuario del instituto de estudios madrileños.*
BAE	Biblioteca de autores españoles.
CSPV	Great Britain. Public Record Office. *Calendar of State Papers and Manuscripts relating to English affairs existing in the archives and collections of Venice,* ed. Rawdon Brown and others. London, 1864–.

exp. expediente (file).
fol. folio.
leg. legajo (bundle).
lib. libro (book).
no. número (number).

NOTES

Introduction

1. Sigmund Freud, "Family Romances," in *The Standard Edition of the Complete Psychological Works,* ed. and trans. James Strachey (1909; London, 1959) 9:235–41.

2. Sigmund Freud, *The Interpretation of Dreams,* ed. and trans. James Strachey (1900; Harmondsworth, England, 1982), p. 769.

3. For this prophecy, see Alfonso X, el Sabio, *Primera crónica general de España,* ed. Ramón Menéndez Pidal (Madrid, 1955), 1:277.

4. Moses Gaster, "The Letter of Toledo," *Folk-lore* 13 (1902): 115–32. See also Robert E. Lerner, *The Powers of Prophecy: The Cedar of Lebanon Vision from the Mongol Onslaught to the Dawn of the Enlightenment* (Berkeley, 1983).

5. José Tarré, "Las profecías del sabio Merlín y sus imitaciones," *Analecta sacra tarraconensia* 16 (1943): 135–71.

6. See Joaquín Gimeno Casalduero, "La profecía medieval en la literatura castellana y su relación con las corrientes proféticas europeas," *Nueva Revista de Filología Hispánica* 20 (1971): 64–89.

7. This tradition is outlined in Ronald Cueto Ruiz, "La tradición profética en la monarquía católica en los siglos 15, 16 y 17," *Arquivos do Centro Cultural Português* 17 (1982): 411–44.

8. Keith Thomas, *Religion and the Decline of Magic* (London, 1971), p. 171.

9. Jean Gerson, cited in Paschal Boland, *The Concept of Discretio Spirituum in Johannes Gerson's "De Probatione Spirituum" and "De Distinctione Verarum Visionum A Falsis* (Washington, D.C., 1959), p. 30.

10. See Caroline Bynum, *Jesus as Mother: Studies in the Spirituality of the High Middle Ages* (Berkeley and Los Angeles, 1982), chap. 5; *Holy Feast and Holy Fast: The Religious Significance of Food to Medieval Women* (Berkeley and Los Angeles, 1987), chap. 1. Also useful is her "Women Mystics and Eucharistic Devotion in the Thirteenth Century," *Women's Studies* 11 (1984): 179–214.

11. The thirteenth-century German visionary Hildegard of Bingen, for example, had a series of heavenly visions that advocated the importance of clerical chastity as well as the necessity of church reform. See Barbara Newman, "Hildegard of Bingen: Visions and Validation," *Church History* 54

(1985): 163–78; *Sister of Wisdom: St. Hildegard's Theology of the Feminine* (Berkeley and Los Angeles, 1987).

12. Sor María de la Antigua, *Desengaño de religiosos y de almas,* ed. Pedro de Valbuena (Seville, 1678), p. 777. Sor Caterina Paluzzi, a Dominican tertiary in Rome, also had a vision of a new convent and insisted that the institution be built in her native town of Morlupo. Sor Caterina's spiritual reputation was such that she was invited to preach at various nunneries in Rome, and with the support of several cardinals the new convent was built; see Romana Guarnieri, "'Nec domina nec ancilla, sed socia.' Tre casi di direzione spirituale tra cinque e seicento," in *Women and Men in Spiritual Culture,* ed. Elisja Schulte von Kessel (The Hague, 1986), pp. 111–32.

13. See Adriano Prosperi, "Dalle 'divini madri' ai 'padri spirituali,'" in Schulte von Kessel, *Women and Men in Spiritual Culture,* pp. 71–91, and Gabriella Zarri, "Pietà e profezia alle corti padane: Le pie consigliere dei principi," in *Il Rinascimento nelle corti padane* (Bari, 1977), pp. 201–39.

14. Sor María's letters to Philip IV are published in Francisco Silvela, *Cartas de la venerable madre Sor María de Agreda y del señor rey don Felipe IV,* 2 vols. (Madrid, 1885–1886). See also Joaquín Pérez Villanueva, "Sor María de Agreda y Felipe IV, un epistolario en su tiempo," in *Historia de la iglesia de España,* ed. R. García-Villoslada (Madrid, 1979), 4:359–417; and Thomas D. Kendrick, *Mary of Agreda: The Life and Legend of a Spanish Nun* (London, 1967). For another of Philip IV's "spiritual mothers," see Joaquín Pérez Villanueva, *Felipe IV y Luisa Enríquez Manrique de Lara, Condesa de Paredes de Nava* (Salamanca, 1986).

Sor María de Santo Domingo, known as the Beata de Piedrahita (b. 1485), is a somewhat earlier example of a Spanish spiritual mother. A Dominican tertiary, she followed the example of Franciscan reformers such as Catherine of Siena and Cardinal Jiménez de Cisneros in championing the reform of her own order by advocating increased austerity and a more intensely devotional routine. Sor María's spiritual authority derived from a series of raptures, visions, prophecies, and stigmata. Despite the enmity of Cajetan, the head of the Dominican order, who attempted to silence her, Sor María earned the respect of King Ferdinand as well as the Duke of Alba, who made her the abbess of the new reformed Dominican convent he had founded in the village of Aldeanueva. According to Ferdinand's chronicler, Pedro Martyr d' Anghiera, Sor María's prophecies about the future of the church were instrumental in Cisneros's decision to lead a crusade to Oran in 1509. See Vicente Beltrán de Heredía, *Historia de la reforma de la provincia española* (Rome, 1938), pp. 71–142; Ramón Alba, *Acerca de algunas particularidades de las comunidades de Castilla* (Madrid, 1975), pp. 86–88; Bernardino Llorca, *La inquisición española y los alumbrados (1508–1667)* (Salamanca, 1980), pp. 42–53; and Jodi Bilinkoff, "The Beata de Piedrahita," unpublished paper delivered at the 1988 Annual Meeting of the Society of Spanish and Portuguese Historical Studies, Nashville, Tenn. For the beata's own writings, see Sor María de Santo Domingo, *Libro de la oración,* ed. José Manuel Blecua (Madrid, 1948).

15. *Les revelations celestes et divines de St. Brigitte de Suede,* trans. Jacques Ferraige (Paris, 1624). See especially bk. 6, chap. 9; bk. 7, chaps. 11, 18, 19, and 27. On Brigit's reputation, see Auke Jelsma, "The Appreciation of Brigit of Sweden (1303–1373) in the 15th Century," in Schulte von Kessel, *Women and Men in Spiritual Culture,* pp. 163–75.

16. Alfred D. Cheney, "The Holy Maid of Kent," *Transactions of the Royal Historical Society* 18 (1904): 108–29; and Alan Neame, *The Holy Maid of Kent: The Life of Elizabeth Barton, 1506–1534* (London, 1971). Another early-sixteenth-century politically minded visionary is Catarina de Raconsi. In addition to "acceptable" visions concerning the reform of the church, she had others depicting Pope Julius II in Hell, the captivity and eventual release of the King of France—a reference to the capture of Francis I by the Spanish in 1525—and the conversion of the Turks to Christianity during the 1530s; Guillaume Postel, *Le thresoir des propheties de l'univers,* ed. François Secret (1564; The Hague, 1969), p. 22.

17. Sor María's stigmata were publicized throughout Europe by her famous confessor, Fray Luis de Granada, who described her as "another St. Catherine of Siena" and wrote a short hagiographic treatise about her: *Relación de la vida y milagros de la priora de la Anunciata* (Paris, 1586). Reports of Sor María's miracles were also included in the correspondence of the Fuggers, the famous German banking house. It is said that no visitor to Lisbon failed to visit the Dominican convent of the Annunziata in order to catch a glimpse of the nun and her wounds.

18. Daniel A. Mortier, *Histoire de maîtres généraux de l'ordre des frères prêcheurs* (Paris, 1911), 5:646. Sor María's political interests are confirmed by Guillén de Casaus, the astrologer who also befriended Lucrecia: "it is certain that all was faked [by Sor María] and designed to favor the party of don Antonio"; AHN Inq 3712/2/5, letter to Alonso de Mendoza, Madrid, 19 Nov. 1588.

19. The site of her exile was later changed to Abrantes, a small town north of Lisbon. For Sor María, see Ramón Robres Lluch and José Ramón Ortolá, "La monja de Lisboa. Sus fingidos estigmas. Fray Luis de Granada y el Patriarca Ribera," *Boletín de la Sociedad Castellonense de Cultura* 23 (1947): 182–214, 230–78. See also Alvaro Huerga, "La vida seudomística y el proceso inquisitorial de Sor María de la Visitación," *Hispania Sacra* 12 (1959): 35–96, and his "La Monja de Lisboa y Fray Luis de Granada," *Hispania Sacra* 12 (1959): 333–56; and *The Fugger News Letters: A Selection, 1566–1605,* ed. Victor von Klarwill, trans. Pauline de Chary (London, 1924), p. 265. The account of Sor María's miracles and the woodcut illustrating her *llagas* that appeared in part 3 of Villegas's *Flos sanctorum* (Toledo, 1588) were censored by the Inquisition in 1589; AHN Inq lib. 1, fol. 212, letter of 27 June 1589 ordering a recall of all copies of this work, and leg. 4436, no. 12.

20. Saints' attributes are discussed in Donald Weinstein and Rudolf M. Bell, *Saints and Society: Two Worlds of Western Christendom, 1000–1700* (Chicago, 1982). For Spain, see Isabelle Poutrin, "Souvenirs d'enfance: L'appren-

tissage de la sainteté dans l'Espagne moderne," *Mélanges de la Casa de Velázquez* 23 (1987): 331–54.

21. The term *street* or *marketplace prophet* is that of Ottavia Niccoli, "Profezie in piazza: Note sul profetismo populare nell'Italia del primo cinquecento," *Quaderni Storici* 41 (1979): 500–539. See also her *Profeti e populo nell'Italia del Rinascimento* (Bari, 1987).

22. See Paul J. Alexander, "The Medieval Legend of the Last Roman Emperor and Its Messianic Origin," *Journal of the Warburg and Courtauld Institutes* 41 (1978): 1–15.

Chapter 1

1. AHN Inq 4492/27.

2. On Magdalena de la Cruz, see Henry C. Lea, *Chapters from the Religious History of Spain* (Philadelphia, 1890), pp. 330–38, and Jesús de Imirizaldu, *Monjas y beatas embaucadoras* (Madrid, 1977), pp. 31–62.

3. For Francisca's trial, see AHN Inq 113/5. Both Francisca and Lucrecia were prosecuted by the same *fiscal,* Pedro Sotocameño, and both received sentences of exile and lashes.

4. For criticisms of Teresa, see Vicente Beltrán de Heredía, "Un grupo de visionarios y pseudoprofetas durante los últimos años de Felipe II y repercusión de ello sobre la memoria de Santa Teresa," *Revista Española de Teología* 7 (1947): 506–30, and Enrique Llamas Martínez, *Santa Teresa de Jesús y la inquisición española* (Madrid, 1972), pp. 486–88.

5. *The Letters of St. Teresa of Jesus,* trans. E. Allison Peers (London, 1980), 2:409.

6. AHN Inq 2105, testimony of Guillén de Casaos, 17 June 1592.

7. ASF Mediceo 4920, fol. 515v (copy 535v), Cammillo Guidi to the Grand Duke of Tuscany, 30 May 1590.

8. AHN Inq 234/24.

9. For the lineage of Lucrecia's father, see AHN Inq 2105, fol. 5v.

10. On *solicitadores,* see Richard L. Kagan, *Lawsuits and Litigants in Castile, 1500–1700* (Chapel Hill, N.C., 1981), pp. 52–57.

11. For information on Lucrecia's siblings, see AHN Inq 115/23, fols. 152–55. María was born in 1573, Ana in 1576, María Magdalena in 1574, and Alonso in 1575.

12. According to a (probably incomplete) listing of San Sebastián's residents in 1597, the parish contained 1,150 houses and 5,781 "personas de confesión," that is, persons over the age of six or seven; AGS Expedientes de Hacienda, leg. 121. For more information on San Sebastián, see Claude Larquié, "Barrios y parroquias urbanas: El ejemplo de Madrid en el siglo xvii," *AIEM* 12 (1976): 54; Matias Fernández García, "Pintores de los siglos xvi y xvii, que fueron feligreses de la parroquia de San Sebastián," *AIEM* 17 (1980): 109–35.

13. According to one witness, the León house was a "casa accesoria" of the duchess of Feria. The duchess herself lived in a palace located on the calle de la Concepción Gerónima, near the Plaza Mayor; AHN Inq 3712/2/2, fol. 174v, testimony of Mayor Méndez de Soto, 20 June 1592. Lucrecia's dream of 26 Jan. 1590 also suggests that her father rented the house from the duchess.

14. Cristóbal Pérez de Herrera, cited in Cefano Caro López, "Casas y alquileres en el antiguo Madrid," *AIEM* 20 (1983): 107.

15. For these estimates, see Claudia Sieber, "The Invention of a Capital: Philip II and the First Reform of Madrid" (Ph.D. dissertation, Johns Hopkins University, 1985), chap. 4, and David Ringrose, *Madrid and the Spanish Economy, 1560–1850* (Berkeley and Los Angeles, 1983), pp. 20–28.

16. On the Genoese banking community, see Ruggiero Romano, "Banchieri genovesi alla corte di Filippo II," *Revista Storica Italiana* 61 (1949): 241–47.

17. In this dream she sells "telas de gorgüeras," material used for the fancy ruff collars then in fashion. In the dream of 23 Aug. 1588, she purchases *lino* (linen) in the Plaza Mayor.

18. Mayor Méndez de Soto, a servant of the duchess of Feria, specifically noted that Lucrecia and her mother "buscaban entre señores limosnas, y esta testiga lo pedió en su nombre a la duquesa de Feria, la cual dió algunas limosnas"; AHN Inq 3703, fol. 600, testimony of 11 Apr. 1595. The Prior Hernando de Toledo also offered alms to the León family.

19. AHN Inq 3703, fols. 609–610v. The original of Carrasco's testimony reads: "gente muy honrada y que vivían honestamente y recogidamente aunque pasaban necesidad."

20. In her testimony of 24 July 1590 Lucrecia suggests that Puebla knew about her dreams; AHN Inq 3712/2, fol. 50.

21. Dream of 22 Mar. 1588. On this convent, see Gerónimo de Quintana, *A la muy antigua . . . villa de Madrid. Historia de su antigüedad, nobleza, y grandeza* (Madrid, 1629), pp. 416–18; Antonio Rodríguez León Pinelo, *Anales de Madrid,* ed. Pedro Fernández Martín (Madrid, 1971), p. 100; and Carmen Rubio Pardos, "La calle de Atocha," *AIEM* 9 (1973): 87.

22. The dreams that mention the sermons are those of 18 Apr. 1588; 2 Oct. 1588; 11 Feb. 1590; and 3 Mar. 1590. The visit to the hospital appears in the dream of 21 Jan. 1588. Visits to other churches are described in the dreams of 23 Dec. 1587; 14 Jan. 1588; 10 Feb. 1588; 30 Sept. 1588; 16 and 24 Apr. 1589; and 16 Jan. 1590. The romería to San Blas occurs in the dream of 13 July 1588; others are in the dreams of 7 Dec. 1587; 26 Oct. 1588; and 21 Apr. 1590.

23. Vives's *De institutione feminae cristianiae* (Louvain, 1524), originally written for Catherine of Aragon, was translated into Castilian as *De la instrucción de mujeres cristianas* (Valencia, 1528). For a modern edition, see Juan Luis Vives, *Formación de la mujer cristiana,* in *Obras completas,* ed. Lorenzo Riber (Madrid, 1947), 1:987–1185. The first English translation of this important work appeared in 1540.

24. Juan de Obregon, a resident of the nearby plazuela de Angel, stated that "vivían honesta y recogidamente y eran tenidas por mujeres y personas honradas, buenos cristianos, y temorosos de Dios"; AHN Inq 3703, fol. 610v.

25. Beltrán de Heredía, "Un grupo de visionarios." The alumbrados first surfaced in Spain between 1500 and 1520. Among the extensive literature on the sect, see especially Bernardino Llorca, *La inquisición española y los alumbrados (1508–1667)* (Salamanca, 1980); Alvaro Huerga, *Historia de los alumbrados* (Madrid, 1980); and Ricardo García-Villoslada, ed., *Historia de la iglesia de España* (Madrid, 1980), vol. 3, pt. 2, pp. 146–59.

26. According to Sebastián de Covarrubias, *Tesoro de la lengua castellana* (Madrid, 1611), p. 202, beata refers to "a woman in religious habit who, outside of a [religious] community and residing in her own house, professes celibacy and leads a retiring life, praying and doing works of charity." For a discussion of the term and its origins, see Francisco Avellá Chafer, "Beatas y beaterios en la ciudad y arzobispado de Sevilla," *Archivo Hispalense* 65 (1982): 101–2.

27. See Ernest W. McDonnell, *Beguines and Beghards in Medieval Culture* (New Brunswick, N.J., 1954).

28. William A. Christian, *Local Religion in Sixteenth-Century Spain* (Princeton, 1981), p. 17.

29. See Juan López, *Historia general de Santo Domingo,* pt. 5 (Madrid, 1621), pp. 296–308.

30. AHN Inq. 3712/2/2, no folio, testimony of 10 Feb. 1588.

31. The original reads: "frío, vomitas, cámaras"; AHN Inq 3712/2, fol. 11, note attached to dream of 5 Dec. 1587.

32. AHN Inq 3712/2/2, no folio.

33. For the age of marriage in sixteenth-century Castile, see Bartolomé Bennassar, *Valladolid au siècle d'or* (Paris, 1967), p. 197, and Angel Rodríguez Sánchez, *Cáceres: Población y comportamientos demográficos en el siglo xvi* (Cáceres, 1977), pp. 195–98.

34. AHN Inq 3712/2/2, fol. 199, note attached to dream of 7 Feb. 1588, in which Alonso de Mendoza compares Ana Ordoñez to the mother in Maccabees 6:20–29, who urges her seven sons to be courageous in the face of death. On another occasion, Ana was heard to remark, "it seems to me that it is St. Peter who speaks to her"; AHN Inq 3703, fol. 358, testimony of Fray Lucas de Allende, 5 June 1593.

35. Lucrecia reports discussing marriage with a friar attached to the Monastery of La Victoria; AHN Inq 3712/2/2, no folio.

36. For the dream of 28 Dec. 1587, the original reads: "quiero ser casada"; AHN Inq 3712/2, fols. 93–96. In the second dream, that of 6 Mar. 1588, the original reads: "ya era vieja." Lucrecia also mentions marriage—and children—in her dream of 2 May 1590.

37. Vitores was previously in the service of don Antonio de Toledo, an influential courtier who served as one of the king's *gentilhombres de cámara* as well as his *cazador mayor* (chief hunter). It is not clear when Vitores met Fray

Lucas, but the latter was a close friend of don Antonio. The autobiographical statement Vitores gave the Inquisition is found in AHN Inq 115/23.

38. An example of Vitores's poetry is the sonnet dedicated to Diego Pérez de Mesa, one of Spain's leading humanists, and published in the introduction to Julio Falcó, *Libro de los maravillosos efectos de la limosna* . . . , trans. Diego Pérez de Mesa (Alcalá de Henares, 1589). A copy of this extremely rare volume is in the library of El Escorial. The copy of Petrarch's works is mentioned in AHN Inq 2105/1, fol. 106.

39. AHN Inq 3077, no. 78.

40. Lucrecia's awareness of her predicament is evident in the dream of 28 July 1588, in which an angel informs Alonso Franco that his daughter's task is "to sound the alarm, and if she were married she would lose the grace that until now has given her these visions."

41. AHN Inq 3077, no. 78, "Relación del proceso de Lucrezia de León," 4 June 1590.

42. AHN Inq 3079, no. 204, letter of 27 Oct. 1595 from the director of the San Lázaro hospital requesting some clothes for "the girl to whom [Lucrecia] gave birth while in the prisons of the Inquisition."

43. AHN Inq 115/23, three unfoliated *billetes* included after fol. 167.

44. AHN Inq 3712/2, fol. 53v, testimony of 22 Sept. 1591, and fol. 68, testimony of 26 Feb. 1594, in which Lucrecia said "I am an ignorant woman."

45. On 23 May 1590 the agent who gathered information from Lucrecia noted: "no lo firmó porque dijo no saber escribir"; AHN Inq 3712/2, fol. 38. On 26 June 1595, the record notes "lo firmó Lucrecia de León, ante Secretario Pantoja"; AHN Inq 3712/2, fol. 84.

46. AHN Inq 115/23, fol. 114v. Vitores's impression of Lucrecia's reading ability is consistent with details in the dream registers. In the dream of 16 Feb. 1590 Lucrecia deciphers various inscriptions, although in an earlier dream, of 16 Nov. 1587, when she is asked to read a (Latin?) inscription the transcription states: "She became angry and said that she did not know how to read."

47. AHN Inq 3712/3, fol. 1v.

48. Lucrecia's inquisitors learned from her fellow prisoners of her attempt to disguise the extent of her learning. Pedro Ibáñez de Ochandiano testified that "although she has admitted to this tribunal that she cannot write . . . the truth is that she can"; AHN Inq 115/23, fol. 19v.

49. Juan Luis Vives, *Socorro de los pobres* [1523] in *Obras completas* 1:1398, and *Formación de la mujer cristiana* in *Obras completas* 1:1001 and 1026–28. See also Gaspar de Astete, *Tratado del gobierno de la familia y estado de las viudas y donzellas* (Valladolid, 1597), bk. 2, "De las donzellas."

50. Juan de la Cerda, *Libro intitulado vida política de todos los estados de mujeres* (Alcalá de Henares, 1599), pp. 6–10. We may note that Teresa of Jesus did not encourage the nuns in her order to learn Latin or, as she put it, "I would rather have them parade their simplicity, which is very proper to saints, than be such rhetoricians"; *Letters of St. Teresa,* 1:137. Teresa was herself literate, but not in Latin.

51. AHN Inq 115/23, fol. 114v. Most Spanish women of the period were unable to read. Claude Larquié calculates that only 25 percent of women who drafted testaments, as compared to 68 percent of men, could sign their names: "L'alphabetisation à Madrid en 1650," *Revue de Histoire Moderne et Contemporaine* 28 (1981): 132–57. But Larquié's sample is limited to women who prepared testaments—presumably the wealthiest and best educated. For a critical overview of literacy in Castile, see Sara T. Nalle, "Literacy and Culture in Early Modern Castile," *Past & Present* 125 (Nov. 1989): 65–96.

52. AHN Inq 115/23, fol. 108.

53. On 15 Sept. 1593 Ana Ordoñez claimed that she was unable to sign the testimony she had delivered to the Inquisition "por no saber escribir"; AHN Inq 3703, fol. 9.

54. AHN Inq 3712/2, fol. 24. In this dream Lucrecia visits the royal palace and sees the infanta Isabella in tears. When Lucrecia asks the infanta why she has not yet married, Isabella responds that it is the king's fault, since he is "as careless about this as your father" (tan descuidado como el tuyo es su padre). In the dream of 28 July 1588 Alonso Franco chastises Lucrecia for telling her dreams to others. In her dream of 21 Apr. 1589, however, Lucrecia offers a mass for her father's health and the salvation of his soul.

55. AHN Inq 3712/2/2, fol. 194v.

56. Astete, *Tratado del gobierno de la familia,* p. 149.

57. For a brief discussion of Juan de Dios, see Juan Blázquez Miguel, *La inquisición en Castilla–La Mancha* (Madrid, 1986), pp. 114–15.

58. AHN Inq 2085, fol. 195. According to one witness, Lucrecia knew Juan de Dios personally and even claimed that he visited her on Mendoza's orders. She also said that the prophet received money from Mendoza; ibid., fol. 197.

59. Navarro claims to have blessed Lucrecia in this manner during her protracted illness in the spring and summer of 1588; AHN Inq 2105/1, fol. 37, testimony of 29 May 1590.

60. "What she knows about dreams and divination, these men [Allende and Mendoza] taught her"; AHN Inq 3712/2/2, fol. 189. A similar statement appears in AHN Inq 2085/1, fol. 200v. Another witness noted that Mendoza gave Lucrecia "many lessons and advice on how to understand if her dreams come from a good or a bad spirit"; AHN Inq 115/23, fol. 110.

61. AHN Inq 2085, fol. 189.

62. The original reads "no tenían buena voluntad al Rey"; AHN Inq 2105/1, fol. 172v.

63. Ann E. Wiltrout, *A Patron and a Playwright in Renaissance Spain: The House of Feria and Diego Sánchez de Badajoz* (London, 1987), p. 11. Isabel de Mendoza, daughter of the duke of Infantado, was the second wife of Lorenzo Suárez de Figueroa (d. 1606), son of Lady Jane Dormer, wife of the first duke of Feria.

64. APR leg. 113, "Capítulo de las etiquetas establecidas para el servicio del Príncipe, Infantes y Infantas, hijos de Felipe II." These protocols were

originally written for the infante don Diego, who died in 1582 at the age of seven.

65. These images appear in the dreams of 18 July 1588, and those of 17, 21, and 25 Mar. 1590.

66. AHN Inq 115/23, fol. 108. See also 2085/1, fol. 193.

67. AHN Inq 115/23, fol. 108, testimony of Diego de Vitores, 28 Jan. 1593. But the only royal document that refers to Lucrecia is an undated memorandum in which Philip, alluding to her prophetic dreams, obliquely describes her as "that woman" ("esta mujer"); ABHS carpeta 143, fol. 212, consulta of 26 July 1589.

68. The text reads: "Lucrecia se holgaba cuando contara cosas contra su Majestad"; AHN Inq 2105/1, fols. 192v–193. The same witness also reported that whenever the conversation turned to Philip II, "Lucrecia de León decía mal de Su Majestad."

69. Dream of 6 Dec. 1587. In Spain, as elsewhere, the *noche de San Juan* was traditionally associated with witchcraft and magical cures. See Juan Blázquez Miguel, *Hechicería y superstición en Castilla–La Mancha* (Toledo, 1985), p. 62.

70. These images appear in the dreams of 1 Apr. 1588; 22 Mar. 1588; and 21 Feb. 1588.

71. AHN Inq 3712/2/2, fol. 48v.

72. For this discussion, see AHN Inq 2105/1, fol. 205. After listening to her cellmate describe such an object made out of sheepskin, Lucrecia noted that she preferred to make "the member out of a special kind of wood, with hinges and nails, and a cover of satin or velvet" and claimed that she had a friend in Madrid who possessed one.

73. AHN Inq 2085, fol. 199.

74. AHN Inq 2085, fol. 192v; 3712/2/2, fol. 189.

75. AHN Inq 3712/2/5, Lucrecia to Mendoza, 8 May 1590, no folio.

76. AHN Inq 3712/2/6, fol. 192, no. 26, Mendoza to Ana Ordoñez, 12 Feb. 1589; no. 56, Mendoza to Lucrecia, Feb. 1588?

Chapter 2

1. Juan de Pineda, *Diálogos familiares de la agricultura cristiana* [1589], BAE (Madrid, 1963), 161:241.

2. Hippocrates, *De insomnium,* translated in *Works,* ed. William H. S. Jones (New York, 1931), 4:420–27. Those dreams, Hippocrates wrote, that "repeat in the night a man's actions or thoughts in the daytime . . . are good for a man," a sign of physical well-being. In contrast, "dreams contrary to the acts of the day and that include some struggle" are signs of bodily disturbance and indicate the need for emetics, physical exercise, a light diet, or some other form of treatment.

3. See Galen, *Opera omnia,* ed. Carolus G. Kühn (Hildesheim, 1964–1965), 6:832–835, and 16:219–26 and 524–27.

4. The Hellenistic tradition of oneiromancy is examined in S. R. F. Price, "The Future of Dreams: From Freud to Artemidorus," *Past & Present* 113 (Nov. 1986): 3–37.

5. The best modern English edition of this important work is Artemidorus Daldianus, *The Interpretation of Dreams,* trans. Robert J. White (Park Ridge, N.J., 1975). For the treatise's history, see Simone Collen-Roset, "Le *Liber Theasuri Oculti* de Pascalis Romanus," *Archives d'Histoire Doctrinale et Littéraire du Moyen Age* 30 (1963): 112–98; Steven R. Fischer, "Dreambooks and the Interpretation of Medieval Literary Dreams," *Archiv für Kulturgeschichte* 65 (1983): 3–20; and Alice Browne, "Girolamo Cardano's *Somniorum Synesiorum Libri IIII,*" *Bibliothèque d'Humanisme et de Renaissance* 41 (1979): 130.

6. Fischer, "Dreambooks," p. 3. The *Oneirocritica* was not available in Spanish until 1918, and so Alonso de Mendoza had to send to Paris to obtain a copy of this important work.

7. References to discussions of dreams, however, are relatively few. One appears in a letter of the seventeenth-century French jurist Nicolas Pasquier, in which he informs his brother how he had related to his wife a particularly disturbing dream concerning the death of their father; Olivier Lefèvre d'Ormesson, *Journal,* ed. Adolphe Chéruel (Paris, 1860–1861), 1:lvii. Another example occurs in the memoirs of Gervase Holles, a seventeenth-century English gentleman, who noted that two days prior to his wife's death in childbirth, he dreamed that his wife and new daughter were dead. He proceeded to recount the dream to his parents-in-law, but "they being rigid Puritans, made slight of it"; Alfred C. Wood, ed., *Memoires of the Holles Family, 1493–1656* (London, 1937), p. 231. Yet another reference to the domestic discussion of dreams occurs in the seventeenth-century memoirs of Lucy Hutchinson, who, like Holles, was a Puritan. She records how her mother spoke about a dream she had experienced and then how her father attempted to interpret it. Lucy herself referred to the dream as "vain prophecy"; Lucy Hutchinson, *Memoirs of the Life of Colonel Hutchinson* (London, 1863), p. 16.

8. Juan Luis Vives, "Sueño de Escipion," in *Obras completas,* ed. Lorenzo Riber (Madrid, 1947), 1:609.

9. The estimate is that of the astrologer Amador de Velasco y Muñeco, who was himself arrested by the Inquisition in 1578; AHN Inq 97/8. Regarding inquisition trials of *conjuros,* Sebastián Cirac Estopañan notes that in 1494 the Holy Office in Cuenca arrested a Jewish fortune-teller, Alonso Gil, whose possessions included a book of oneiromancy, *Experimentos o solturas de sueños;* Sebastián Cirac Estopañan, *Los procesos de hechicería en la inquisición de Castilla la Nueva* (Madrid, 1942), p. 30.

10. AHN Inq 82, n. 24.

11. Aristotle explains his theories about dreams in the essays "De somnia et vigilia" (On Dreams) and "De divinatione per somnium" (Divination in

Sleep), in Aristotle, *The Complete Works,* vol. 3, *The Parva Naturala,* trans. J. J. Beare (Oxford, 1963), pp. 453b–464b.

12. The translation is that of Browne, "Girolamo Cardano's *Somniorum Synesiorum,*" p. 126. The standard edition of Macrobius's *Commentary on the Dream of Scipio* is that edited by William H. Stahl (New York, 1952).

13. Scipion Duplaix, *Les causes de la veille et du sommeil des songes et de la vie et de la mort* (Lyon, 1620), pp. 74–75. For earlier typologies based on Macrobius, see the dream theories of Synesius (370?–413), translated as "Le traite des songes" in Christan Lacombrade, *Synesius de Cyrène* (Paris, 1951), 150–69; and for Tertulian's theories, see Jacques Le Goff, "Le christianisme et les rêves (IIe–VIIe siècle)," in *L'imaginaire médiéval* (Paris, 1985), p. 286.

14. The biblical justification for Augustine's suspicion of dreams rests in part upon Deuteronomy 13:3 ("You shall not listen to the words of the prophet or to that of the dreamer of dreams"). See also Martine Dulaey, *La rêve dans la vie et la pensée de Saint Augustine* (Paris, 1973).

15. On dream theory in late antiquity and the Middle Ages, in addition to Dulaey, *La rêve,* and Le Goff, "Christainisme et les rêves," see Francis X. Neuman, "Somnium: Medieval Theories of Dreaming and the Form of Vision Poetry" (Ph.D. dissertation, Princeton University, 1972); and A. C. Spearing, *Medieval Dream Poetry* (Cambridge, 1976). Note that St. Jerome was even more skeptical about dreams than Augustine. Following Aristotle, he attributed most dreams to purely natural causes such as food, yet his sixfold classification of dreams made allowance for "revelation." Similarly, Gregory the Great admitted that prophetic dreams were difficult to decipher but refused to discount them entirely inasmuch as the Bible contained numerous instances in which dreams served as a method of divine communication; Gregoire le Grand, *Dialogues,* ed. Adalbert de Vogüé, trans. Paul Antin (Paris, 1980), bk. 4, chap. 50, p. 173.

16. Thomas Aquinas, *Summa theologica,* ed. Blackfriars (London, 1964), vol. 40, question 95. Aquinas's suspicion of divination was echoed in such "popular" works as the *Speculum laicorum,* vernacular translations of which had appeared by the late thirteenth century. For the Castilian version, see *Speculum laicorum: El espéculo de los legos,* ed. José María Mohedano Hernández (Madrid, 1951), especially chap. 74, "De las adevinaciones."

17. Gerson's position on dreams is examined by Paschal Boland, *The Concept of Discretio Spirituum in Johannes Gerson's "De Probatione Spirituum" and "De Distinctione Verarum Visionum A Falsis"* (Washington, D.C., 1959).

18. Ibid., p. 30.

19. Karl-Joseph Hefele, *Histoire des counciles,* trans. H. Leclerq (Paris, 1917), 8:526.

20. AHN Inq lib. 1226, fols. 787–812v.

21. No single work summarizes Renaissance thinking on dreams, but the subject may be approached through Lynn Thorndike, *A History of Magic and Experimental Science,* 6 vols. (New York, 1923–1958). See also Manfred Weid-

horn, *Dreams in Seventeenth-Century English Literature* (The Hague, 1970), especially pp. 28–48, and Browne, "Girolamo Cardano's *Somniorum Synesiorum*" and her "Descartes' Dreams," *Journal of the Warburg and Courtauld Institutes* 40 (1977): 256–73.

22. See Kaspar Peucer, *Commentarius de pruecipuis divinationum generibus* (Wittenburg, 1553), bk. 10; I have consulted the French edition, *Les devins ou commentaire des principales sortes de divinations,* trans. Simon Coulart Senlisen (Antwerp, 1584). For Argenterio, see his *De somno et de vigilia* (Florence, 1556), chaps. 1 and 2. For Bodin's theories, see his *Colloquium of the Seven about Secrets of the Sublime,* trans. Marion Kuntz (Princeton, 1975). "Certain dreams are true," Bodin wrote, "yet many are false," and "when there are many dreams, there are many deceptions." Bodin also recognized the power of what he described as "true dreams and nocturnal visions." "Dreams," he wrote, "often come after a heavy meal. Yet when a sober man whose soul is free from business, lust, idle cares and greed sleeps soberly he often has true dreams and excellent visions. He is taught to avoid base things, to preserve honest ones, and to know the future, and these can generally be called prophecies. Indeed, prophecy is a divine power granted by a gift of God for seeing and announcing the future, and this gift has been bestowed not only to men of old but also to men of our time" (p. 181). Similar ideas are found in Alessandro Carriero, *De somnis deque divinatione per somnia brevis consideratio* (Padua, 1575). Carriero, a lawyer by training and later a priest, believed, like Aristotle, that most dreams had natural causes but admitted to "revelations divinaeque visiones" (fol. 7v).

23. Though Scott advocated that those who prophesy through dreams be punished, even he could not refute the possibility of "divine" dreams; see his *The Discoverie of Witchcraft* [1584], ed. Montague Summers (New York, 1930), bk. 10, pp. 101–5.

24. San Isidoro de Sevilla, *Etimologías,* ed. José Oroz Reta and Manuel A. Marcos Casquero (Madrid, 1982–1983), p. 671. Alfonso X, el Sabio, *Setenario,* ed. Kenneth H. Vanderford (Buenos Aires, 1945), p. 48: "Que cosa es ssuenno."

25. BN MS. 8113, especially fols. 24–37.

26. See Vives, "Tratado del Alma," bk. 2, chap. 14, in *Obras Completas* 2:1222–26. Vives's dream theories are discussed in Louis J. Swift, "'Somnium Vivis' y el 'Sueño de Escipión,'" in *Homenaje a Luis Vives* (Madrid, 1977), pp. 89–112, and Julian Palley, *The Ambiguous Mirror: Dreams in Spanish Literature* (Chapel Hill, N.C., 1983), pp. 67–70.

27. Pedro Ciruelo, *Treatise Reproving All Superstitions and Forms of Witchcraft,* trans. Eugene A. Maio and D'Orsay W. Pearson (Rutherford, N.J., 1977), p. 160. The original work was published in Barcelona in 1528 as *Tratado en el qual se repruevan en todas las supersticiones y hechizerías.*

28. One of the divinely inspired dreams cited by Ciruelo is that in which God spoke to Balaam the Diviner, Numbers 22:20. He also notes that in

which an angel of the Lord advised Joseph to marry Mary, informing him their child, to be named Jesus, would be conceived by the Holy Spirit, Matthew 1:20.

29. See, for example, Sebastián Fox Morcillo, *De naturae philosophia* (Louvain, 1554), bk. 5, chap. 16, fol. 208v. Similarly, Juan Baptista Fernández, *Primera parte de las demonstraciones católicas* (Logroño, 1593), p. 222v, believed that the majority of dreams had natural causes but admitted that "I cannot deny that dreams can also proceed from God."

30. AHN Inq 3712/2/2, fols. 79v, 202.

31. "Niñerías y disparates de los niños"; AHN Inq 3712/2/6, n. 25, Mendoza, paraphrasing Ana Ordoñez, in a letter to Alonso Franco de León, 18 Mar. 1588.

32. AHN Inq 3713, fol. 503.

33. See Benedictus Pererius, S.J., *De magia, de observatione somniorum et de divinatione astrologica*. . . (Venice, 1591). Pererius, however, advocated that repetitive dreams be carefully investigated as they might prove diabolical.

34. AHN Inq 3712/2/2, fol. 122, report of Juan Ortiz de Salvatierra, 3 May 1590.

35. AHN Inq 3712/2/2, no folio, testimony of María Diaz.

36. AHN Inq 115/23, fol. 4; 3712/2, fol. 40, audiencia of 4 June 1590; fol. 63v, audiencia of 24 Oct. 1592; fol. 66, audiencia of 7 Nov. 1592.

37. AHN Inq 3712/2/2, fol. 165v.

38. AHN Inq 3713/3/11, fol. 149, testimony of Alonso Franco, Jan. 1596.

39. The original reads: "desde pequeña comenzó ésta a entender estos sueños y la azotaban sus padres hartas veces porque los decía"; AHN Inq 3712/2/2, fol. 40v.

40. The original reads: "unos desvaríos diabólicos"; AHN Inq 3712/2/2, fol. 48, audiencia of 24 July 1590.

41. This interview reportedly took place in the Capilla de San Luis de Francia in Madrid's Trinitarian monastery; AHN Inq 3712/2/2, fol. 48v.

42. AHN Inq 3703, vol. 217.

43. AHN Inq 3712/2/3, fol. 1.

44. The original reads: "aunque no fuese más de como unos libros de caballerías." Lucrecia stated that this same friar, accompanied by the *cura* of San Sebastián, Alonso Puebla, told her exactly the same thing; AHN Inq 3712/2/2, fols. 49v–50.

45. AHN Inq 3712/2/2, fol. 47. On this particular morning Alonso found Lucrecia "in bed with a fever."

46. The original reads: "en confesión le decía los dichos sueños"; AHN Inq 3712/2/2, fol. 49.

47. The original reads: "la inquisición no tenía que ver en aquellos sueños, no creyéndoles pues no era contra la fe"; AHN Inq 3712/2/2, fol. 45.

48. The original reads: "si en los dichos sueños hubiera cosa de la inquisición, el trajera a ésta por las orejas a la inquisición"; AHN Inq 3712/2/2, fol. 49.

49. AHN Inq 2085/1, fol. 197.

50. AHN Inq 3712/2/2, fol. 191, note attached to dream of 7 Feb. 1588.

51. The original reads: "tengo por de mucho misterio y digna de mucha consideración y ponderación es que sí despues de haber tenido alguno sueño está día o dos o más, sin escribirle, demás que no puede tener en si sosiego por el grande deseo que dice le viene de decirlo para que se escribiera"; AHN Inq 3712/2/3, fol. 4v.

52. The original reads: "tiene la memoria tan fija, no sólo de las cosas que ve en general pero de las palabras que le dicen y particularidades que ella nota en las personas que ve ansí en las faciones de los rostros, trajes y colores de los vestidos, figuras de los animales y aves, traza de los edificios, disposición de los ríos, montes, valles, arboles, [illegible word], ciudades, castillos, iglesias, caminos y costas de las mares, islas y tierras firmes por donde la llevan en imaginación y de los nombres que le dicen que tienen con no ser las mas de ellos cosas que ella las ha visto, ni oído antes de ahora nombrar, por que ni su estado ni su profesión ni la conversación de las personas con quienes se ha criado le han dado ocasión de saberlo, que como si lo fuese leyendo por un papel y fuese muy buena lectora lo podría leer, con ser verdad que cuando empezó a tener estas visiones sabía leer muy poco y escribir nada con aquella facildad y presteza lo va refiriendo y una vez referido y escrítolo, así se lleva de la memoria como si nunca lo hubiese visto y soñado de lo cual yo soy buen testigo"; AHN Inq 3712/2/3, fols. 4v–7.

53. AHN Inq 3712/2/6, no. 33. Four days previously, Allende had reported that Lucrecia was "very ill; no visions; I have nothing to write"; ibid., no. 35.

54. Ibid., no. 64, Juan de Trijueque to Bartolomé Martínez (Mendoza's secretary).

55. Ibid., no. 34.

56. His memo continues: "She is honorable; I will examine her and do what is necessary so she is not deceived. If the deception is mine, I pray that the Lord give me strength to remain in his divine service; I remain obedient to the inquisitors." The original reads: "una mujer de quien tengo satisfacción es honrada con intento de examinar lo que conviene para su desengaño y si es mío el engaño supplico a Nro. Dios da claridad para que la tenga en su divino servicio y estoy sujeto a los Sres. Inquisidores"; AHN Inq 3703/2, fol. 87.

57. The original reads: "desde este sueño en adelante se han escrito con más cuidado y así van más seguidas las cosas y no trastocadas."

58. Lucrecia told the inquisitors that Sacamanchas was fired "because he did not copy the dreams faithfully; he mixed them up. The Ordinary Man and the other two men [the Three Men] spoke to me about this in my dreams and got angry with me for allowing it to happen. I then told Fray Lucas [de Allende] to advise Sacamanchas to stop doing what he was doing and return to his trade"; AHN Inq 3712/2/2, fol. 43.

59. Note attached to dream of 3 Nov. 1589. Mendoza was also prone to error. "I spend so many hours praying during the day and working at night,"

he wrote to Vitores, "that it is easy to make a mistake"; AHN Inq 3712/2/6, no. 16, letter of 28 Apr. 1590.

60. Note attached to dream of 16 Mar. 1588.

61. AHN Inq 3712/2/6, no. 13, letter of 15 Apr. 1590. I have not been able to determine the artist(s) engaged by Mendoza or even if the paintings in question were ever executed, although it was reported that Mendoza "hired a painter and had some frames made." Among the subjects commissioned was a representation of Lucrecia's dream of a flock of emaciated lambs tended by a pastor who had fallen asleep, another in which she saw an angel standing on a rock, and a third depicting a small boy whom Lucrecia carried on her back to Toledo; AHN: Inq. 3712/2/2, fols. 71v–73.

62. On the morning of 11 Dec. 1587, for example, Mendoza visited Lucrecia to review the dreams he himself did not write "por saber si estaban bien o los faltaba algo" (to see if they were correct or if something was missing); note attached to dream of that day. Other dreams, such as that of 1 Mar. 1588, are accompanied by the note, "Esto escribió Fray Luis y recorríle con ella yo" (Fray Luis wrote this and I went over it with her).

63. AHN Inq 3712/2/2, fol. 143.

64. Ibid., fol. 25.

65. See Alice Browne, "Girolamo Cardano's *Somniorum Synesiorum*." Cardano also discusses his dreams in his autobiography, *De vita propria liber;* see Jerome Cardan, *The Book of My Life*, trans. Jean Stoner (New York, 1962), pp. 156–62.

66. *The Diary of William Laud*, in *Works* (Oxford, 1853), 3:144–249, dreams of 8 Mar. 1627 and 21 Aug. 1625. Laud's dream life is briefly examined in Charles Carlton, "The Dream Life of Archbishop Laud," *History Today* 36 (Dec. 1986): 9–14.

67. See *The Diary of Ralph Josselin, 1616–1683*, ed. Alan Macfarlane (London, 1976). Josselin recorded only thirteen dreams between 1644 and 1658.

68. See Alice Thornton, *Autobiography*, ed. C. Jackson (London, 1875), pp. 169 and 213. Similarly, in his autobiography the seventeenth-century Italian rabbi Leon Modena recorded those dreams he considered extraordinary; *Autobiography of a Seventeenth-Century Venetian Rabbi*, ed. and trans. Mark R. Cohen (Princeton, 1988), pp. 89–90, 99.

69. On the difficulty of putting dreams into words, see Donald F. Spence, *Narrative Truth and Historical Truth* (New York, 1961), especially chap. 3.

70. AHN Inq 3712/2/6, no. 13, Mendoza to Vitores, 15 Apr. 1590.

71. For this genre in Spain, see Miguel Avilés, *Sueños ficticios y lucha ideológica en el Siglo de Oro* (Madrid, 1978).

Chapter 3

1. AHN Inq 3712/2/6, no. 13, Mendoza to Vitores, 15 Apr. 1590. The chapter title is from AHN Inq 3712/2/2, fol. 193, a statement attributed to Lucrecia by Mendoza.

2. AHN Inq 3703, fol. 118, testimony of 26 June 1590.

3. Comment attached to dream of 2 Mar. 1590.

4. Both quotations in this paragraph are from AHN Inq 3712/2/2, fol. 141, note attached to dream of 20 Jan. 1588.

5. AHN Inq 2105/1, testimony of 22 May 1592.

6. Following Hippocrates, Juan Huarte de San Juan, one of the most influential Spanish writers on the subject of wit and imagination, noted that adolescents were neither "hot, cold, humid, or dry, but in the middle of these qualities, temperate"; *Examen de ingenios para las ciencas* [1575], ed. Esteban Torre (Madrid, 1976), p. 433.

7. Ibid.

8. Comment to the dream of 14 Mar. 1590.

9. AHN Inq 3712/2/2, fol. 122, note attached to dream of 11 Jan. 1588.

10. AHN Inq 3712/2, fol. 50v.

11. For Mendoza's identifications, see AHN Inq 3712/2, fol. 57. The Old Fisherman first appears with a lion in the dream of 10 Dec. 1587. The Young Fisherman paints in the dreams of 12 and 18 Dec. 1587.

12. Dream of 9 Oct. 1588. Similarly, in the dream of 16 Feb. 1588 the Ordinary Man, asking if there is anyone wishing to serve God, gathers a crowd in Madrid and urges them "to talk about what my companions and I show you." The implication is that he speaks with divine authority.

13. Dreams of 25 Dec. 1588 and 17 Mar. 1589.

14. Dreams of 2 June, 24 Aug., and 22 Dec. 1589.

15. AHN Inq 3712/2/5, no folio.

16. Miguel's appearances in the dreams are as follows: masked man (4 Dec. 1587); anonymous prophet (12 Dec. 1587, 27 Mar. 1588); as Piedrola (31 Dec. 1587; 1, 7 Feb. 1588; 8, 15, 16 Mar. 1588; 14 Oct. 1588; 14 Nov. 1588); shepherd (30 Jan. 1588); a New David (21 July 1588); king (10 Mar. 1589; 5, 12 Apr. 1590); commander of an army wearing white crosses (20 Oct. 1589; 21 Jan. 1590; 1 Feb. 1590); a monarch (26 Jan. 1590, 20 Mar. 1590); a crusader (7 Mar. 1590); and Lucrecia's husband (26 Apr. 1590).

17. Lucrecia could have learned about Joan of Arc, known in sixteenth-century Spain as "la Ponzella de Francia," from Alonso de Villegas, *Flos sanctorum, adiciones a la tercera parte* (Toledo, 1588), vida 198. The image of the *doncella guerrera* is a standard Renaissance motif and appears in such popular Spanish works as Jorge de Montemayor, *Los siete libros de la Diana* (Valencia, 1559?) as well as in numerous *romances*. See Ramón Menéndez Pidal, *Flor nueva de romances* (Madrid, 1959), pp. 242–46; Estelle Irizarry, "Echoes of the Amazon Myth in Medieval Spanish Literature," in Beth Miller, ed., *Women in Hispanic Literature* (Berkeley, 1983), pp. 53–66; and Malveena Mackendrick, *Women and Society in Golden Age Spanish Drama* (Cambridge, 1974), especially pp. 61–62.

18. AHN Inq 3712/4, fol. 152.

19. For the dreams in which Miguel reconquers Spain, is elected king, and marries Lucrecia, see note 16. Lucrecia gives birth to Miguel's child in the

dream of 18 Apr. 1590. Miguel's crusade and the transfer of the Holy See are variously outlined in dreams of 11 Feb. 1588, 1 Oct. 1589, and 2 Feb. 1590. The terrestrial paradise is described in the dreams of 7 and 26 Jan. 1590. The original reads: "vuestras Indias deseadas, que será el siglo dorado, y tiempo de Dios."

20. Specific references to the Apocalypse as well as to other biblical prophecies occur in the dreams of 2 and 20 Mar. 1590.

21. El Encubierto makes an appearance in the dream of 17 Feb. 1588.

22. For these romances, see Ramón Menéndez Pidal, *Romancero tradicional* (Madrid, 1977), 1:53–55, 104, 120–31, and his *Flor nueva*, pp. 59–61. See also Antonio Rodríguez Moniño, ed., *La silva de romances de Barcelona, 1561*, (Salamanca, 1969), pp. 308, 327, 332.

23. See especially *Crónica del rey don Rodrigo con la destrucción de España y como los moros la ganaron* (Alcalá de Henares, 1587). The earliest printed versions of this chronicle date from 1527.

24. The description of Idiáquez and Moura appears in the dream of 9 Feb. 1590. Auñón is criticized in the dreams of 10 Nov. and 21 Dec. 1587; 5 Jan. and 23 Dec. 1588; and 28 June 1589. For Auñón's reputation as a gambler, see ABHS carpeta 132, fol. 194, Presidente Barajas to the king, 18 Feb. 1589.

25. Santa Cruz is attacked for being concerned only for his ambitions rather than "the good of the Republic"; dream of 8 Jan. 1588. Parma is variously accused of lending money to Queen Elizabeth, congratulating her for having taken an Indies fleet, and doing little to help Philip recover from the defeat of the Armada; dreams of 23 Dec. 1588; 17 July and 10 Nov. 1589. The dream of 8 Jan. 1588 refers to Quiroga as one who "is so unlettered that he is scarcely qualified to be a village priest"; that of 22 Jan. 1588 states that "he has frequently corrupted God's church." Criticisms of Quiroga's "greed" and "lack of charity" appear in the dream of 15 Feb. 1590.

26. These criticisms are contained in the dreams of 15 and 22 Jan. 1588.

27. Dream of 1 Apr. 1588. Once again, there are obvious parallels between Philip and Lucrecia's father, who also failed to listen to his daughter's dreams.

28. The alcabala is criticized in dreams of 25 Nov. 1587, 19 and 21 Jan. 1588, and 4 Nov. 1588; the sale of tierras baldías in those of 7 Feb. 1588 and 5 Mar. 1590.

29. Dream from Oct. 1587 destroyed by Allende in Nov. 1587; AHN Inq 3712/2/3, fol. 7.

30. By 1587 Isabella's unmarried status had become a source of worry and concern at the royal court, and the Cortes twice petitioned the king to request that he arrange for an early match; *ACC* 10:158, petitions of 25 Sept. and 2 Oct. 1587. See also *CSPV* 8:339. Isabella eventually married Archduke Albert of Austria in 1599, when she was thirty-three.

31. Dreams of 16 Mar. 1588 and 14 July 1588. In a dream from July 1589, during another quarrel Isabella criticizes Philip for not marrying her sister Clara Eugenia to the duke of Parma and giving her Portugal as a dowry.

32. For Castilian law on sedition and treason, see *Nueva recopilación de todas las leyes* . . . (Alcalá de Henares, 1569), libro 8, título 18, ley 1, and libro 8, título 26, ley 11.

Chapter 4

1. This discussion of prophecy follows that of Keith Thomas, *Religion and the Decline of Magic* (London, 1971), pp. 451–514; Thomas A. Kselman, *Miracles and Prophecies in Nineteenth-Century France* (New Brunswick, N.J., 1983); and Michael Adas, *Prophets of Rebellion* (Cambridge, 1979), pp. xvii–xxvii, 92–121.

2. For Philip II as a New David, see Alain Milhou, *Colón y su mentalidad mesiánica en el ambiente franciscanista español* (Valladolid, 1983), p. 245. Philip was also referred to as a "New Constantine"; see Antonius Ruvio, *Assertionum catholicarum adversus Erasmi* (Salamanca, 1568), cited in Bruce Mansfield, *Phoenix of His Age: Interpretations of Erasmus* (Toronto, 1979), p. 72. The prophecies that accompanied the birth of Philip IV's children, Carlos and Fernando, are reported by Cristóbal López de Cañete, *Compendio de los pronósticos y baticinios antiguos y modernos que publicavan la declinacion general de la secta de Mohama, y libertad de Hierusalem y Palestina* (Madrid, 1623).

3. Ottavia Niccoli, *Profeti e populo nell'Italia del Rinascimento* (Bari, 1987).

4. Vicente Ferrer, "Tratado del cismo moderno," in *Biografía y escritos de San Vicente Ferrer*, ed. José M. de Garganta and Vicente Forcada (Madrid, 1956), p. 448.

5. Nicolas B. Round, "La rebelión toledana de 1449," *Archivium* 16 (1966): 385–446.

6. Another was Fray Polanco, also a Franciscan, who preached against the Flemings in the court of Charles V and prognosticated disaster unless the new monarch reformed his government; Joseph Pérez, "Moines frondeurs et sermons subversifs en Castille pendant le premier séjour de Charles-Quint en Espagne," *Bulletin Hispanique* 67 (1965): 5–24; Ramón Alba, *Acerca de algunas particularidades de las comunidades de Castilla* (Madrid, 1975).

7. See Gaspar Escolano, *Decada primera de la historia de la insigne y coronada ciudad y reyno de Valencia. Segunda parte* (Valencia, 1611), pp. 1610–21. The incident is also discussed in Ricardo García Carcel, *Las germanías de Valencia* (Barcelona, 1981), pp. 132–38. According to Escolano, a second rey encubierto caused a riot in the city of Valencia in 1523 when his followers sacked parts of the city on Holy Thursday. For another version of these same incidents, see Martin de Viciniana, *Libro quarto de la crónica de la inclita y coronada ciudad de Valencia* (Barcelona, 1566), pp. 201–4, 221.

8. The vision also warned that if this condition were not met, Philip would die before reaching Portugal. The Franciscan friar called in to investigate the

widow asserted these visions were not "God's work" but rather "diabolical illusions." At his suggestion the widow—who had reportedly had a vision in 1568 that presaged the imprisonment of don Carlos, Philip's disturbed son—was ordered into seclusion, never to be heard from again; Gregorio de Andrés, "Las revelaciones de una visionaria de Albuquerque sobre Felipe II," in *Homenaje a Luis Morales Oliver* (Madrid, 1986), pp. 419–27.

9. According to one witness, Lucrecia knew Juan de Dios personally and even claimed that he had visited her on Mendoza's orders. She also said that the prophet received money from Mendoza; AHN Inq 2085, fol. 197.

10. ASF Mediceo, filza 5037, fols. 520–21, Avvisi di Madrid, 9 Feb. 1585.

11. The Pérez affair is summarized in Joaquín Pérez Villanueva, "Un proceso resonante: Antonio Pérez," in *Historia de la inquisición en España y América* (Madrid, 1984), 1:842–76. For Pérez's own version of his arrest and trial, see Alfredo Alvar Ezquerra, ed., *Antonio Pérez, relaciones y cartas* (Madrid, 1986), 1:99–212.

12. See especially Gregorio Marañon's *Antonio Pérez* (Madrid, 1947), and *Los procesos de Castilla contra Antonio Pérez* (Madrid, 1947).

13. For the *desengaño* of the 1590s, see Colin Martin and Geoffrey Parker, *The Spanish Armada* (London, 1988), p. 260. The political and social unrest of this decade are examined in Antonio Domínguez Ortiz, "Un testimonio de protesta social a fines del reinado de Felipe II," in *Homenaje a Pedro Sainz Rodríguez* (Madrid, 1986), 3:219–26; Charles Jago, "Habsburg Absolutism and the Cortes of Castile," *American Historical Review* 86 (1981): 307–26; and Albert W. Lovett, "The Vote of the Millones, 1590," *Historical Journal* 30 (1987): 1–20.

14. The best brief biography of Philip is Geoffrey Parker's *Philip II* (Boston, 1979; rev. ed., London, 1988)

15. Albert Mousset, *Dépêches diplomatiques de M. de Longlée, résident de France en Espagne (1582–1590)* (Paris, 1912), p. 227, dispatch of 15 Feb. 1586.

16. On 11 May 1587, for example, Guido Battiglino, secretary of the Florentine ambassador in Madrid, noted that "the first news [of Drake's attack] sparked rumors and greatly disturbed the spirit of this court"; ASF Mediceo, filza 5103, fol. 243. On Philip's health at the time of Drake's raid, see Martin and Parker, *Spanish Armada,* pp. 135–36. The king's health began to fail as early as 1584, according to Ambassador Longlée. See Albert Mousset, *Un résident de France en Espagne au temps de la Ligue (1583–1590)* (Paris, 1908), p. 48.

17. *ACC* 8:465, letter of 27 May 1587.

18. Cited in Mousset, *Un résident de France en Espagne,* p. 48.

19. Dispatch of 21 May 1587; *CSPV* 8:277.

20. ASF Mediceo, filza 5037, fol. 99, Nov. 1562.

21. BN MS. 3826, "Sobre la entrada de los grandes en palacio," fol. 95. The duke's complaints may also reflect a change in court etiquette instituted in Oct. 1586.

22. ASF Mediceo, filza 5037, fol. 579.

23. Alonso de Orozco, *Obras* (Madrid, 1756), vol. 3, chap. 63, p. 47.

24. ASF Mediceo, filza 5037, fols. 594–595v. See also Carlos Alonso, *Los apócrifos del Sacramonte de Granada* (Valladolid, 1979).

25. For these astronomical phenomena see Robin B. Barnes, *Prophecy and Gnosis: Apocalypticism in the Wake of the Lutheran Reformation* (Stanford, Calif., 1988), pp. 120–21, 158–60, 163–64. See also Duff Hart-Davis, *The Armada* (London, 1988), pp. 11–14.

26. AHN Inq 3712/2/6, letter of Miguel Gaztelu to Luis Quijada, 1 Jan. 1570.

27. Even Philip was relatively tolerant of Piedrola. In a *consulta* of 1 June 1577, the king wrote: "I know about him; I do not regard him as very trustworthy although he appears to be well-intentioned." At the time, Piedrola seems to have been in Naples, although he was soon to return to Madrid; BL Eg. 1506, fols. 59–60.

28. On 19 Nov. 1578 Diego de Chaves, the royal confessor, met with Piedrola, discussed his prophecies, and hoped to arrange for him to see the king just after Christmas; BL Eg. 1506, fol. 94. It is not known whether the meeting ever occurred.

29. This material is drawn from the *traza de la vida* Piedrola prepared for the Inquisition; cf. BN MS. 10,470, "Vida y sucesos estranissimos del profeta, ni falso, ni santo Miguel Piedrola en tiempo de Phelipe segundo," fols. 1–117. Further details of Piedrola's biography appear in AHN Inq 3712/2/6, no. 8. Secondary literature on Piedrola is sparse. See Vicente Beltrán de Heredía, "Un grupo de visionarios . . . ," *Revista Española de Teología* 7 (1947): 373–97; and María Zambrano, Edison Simons, and Juan Blázquez Miguel, *Sueños y procesos de Lucrecia de León* (Madrid, 1987), pp. 44–46.

30. AHN Inq 3712/2/6, Juan de Zúñiga to Cardinal Quiroga, 4 Jan. 1580. Piedrola's activities in Naples are not well documented, but according to this letter he had been barred, for reasons unknown, from entering the house of the Spanish viceroy.

31. ASV NS, filza 34, fols. 352–54, dispatch of 20 May 1588.

32. BN MS. 10,470, fols. 96v–97.

33. AHN Inq 3712/2/6, no. 8, letter of Mendoza to Gerónimo de Mendoza Manrique, 19 Sept. 1587, in which he refers to Piedrola as a "true prophet."

34. Orozco, *Obras* 3 : 47–48. On Piedrola's ties with Herrera and Quiroga, see AHN Inq 3712/2/5, Agustín Parra to Juan de Herrera, 22 June 1588. Referring to Herrera's inquiry about Piedrola, Parra reports that Piedrola, at least prior to his arrest in Sept. 1587, was Quiroga's *familiar,* a term which connotes that he had received financial and possibly political support from the cardinal.

35. Jerónimo de Sepúlveda, "Historia de varios sucesos del reino de Felipe II, 1584–1603" *Ciudad de Dios* 115 (1918): 304. See also IVDJ, envío 189, fol. 176, which contains a series of letters pertaining to his case. AGS Estado, leg. 165, fol. 340 contains a copy of the Inquisition's *sentencia* of 10

Dec. 1588 against Piedrola. Further references to Piedrola occur in BL Eg. 1506, fols. 59–60, 93–95v; BL Eg. 2058, fols. 205–6v.

36. Also in this group were Dr. Mantilla, a court physician, and the alchemist Agustín Parra, a friend of both Juan de Herrera and Alonso de Mendoza.

37. ASV NS, filza 33, fol. 33, letter of Juan Baptista de Pesaro, 5 June 1587.

38. *ACC* 9:119.

39. For Orozco's comments, see his *Obras* 3:48; it is reported that Piedrola and Orozco had an "odio mortal" for one another. About Juan Baptista little is known except that he had studied theology in Spain at the University of Alcalá de Henares. His campaign against Piedrola apparently began in Barcelona during the spring of 1587; AHN Inq 3712/2/6, no. 8.

40. AHN Inq 3712/2/6, papel contra García de Loaysa por Alonso de Mendoza, 7 Aug. 1587. According to Piedrola, Fray Juan's sermons began on 11 June 1587 and prompted what he described as an "alboroto" (uproar, riot) in Madrid.

41. IVDJ, envío 89, no. 176, report of the vicar of Madrid, 9 Aug. 1587. Fray Luis's testimony reads: "que no se podría poner en duda sin que el tenía espíritu de profecía." For Fray Luis on prophecy, see Colin P. Thompson, *The Strife of Tongues: Fray Luis de León and the Golden Age of Spain* (Cambridge, 1988), pp. 94–101.

42. ASF Mediceo, filza 5103, fol. 430.

43. AHN Inq 3712/2/6, no. 8. Mendoza had also written to Cardinal Colonna the previous August, complaining about a letter in which García de Loaysa had attacked Piedrola.

44. Piedrola's *sentencia* is noted in Gerónimo Roman de la Higuera, "Historia eclesiástica de Toledo," BN MS. 1293, vol. 7, fol. 239. Higuera refers to him as a "false prophet."

45. AHN Inq 3712/2/5, no. 5, letter of Agustín Parra to Juan de Herrera, 22 June 1588. Parra also noted that the underlying reason for Piedrola's arrest was Quiroga's decision to distance himself from the soldier-prophet.

46. AHN Inq 3712/2/6, no. 25, Mendoza to Alonso Franco de León, 18 Mar. 1588.

47. AHN Inq 2105/1, fol. 205v.

48. Alberto García Caraffa and Arturo García Caraffa, *Diccionario heráldico y genealógico de apellidos españoles* (Madrid, 1919–1968), 56:43.

49. On Bernardino de Mendoza, see De Lamar Jensen, *Diplomacy and Dogmatism* (Cambridge, Mass., 1964), p. 59. Bernardino's *Comentarios sobre las guerras de los Paises Bajos* was first published in 1592. While in England, he is said to have earned Elizabeth's ire for having announced, "Bernardino de Mendoza was not born to disturb countries but to conquer them."

50. Also at court were Alonso's brothers Juan and Antonio and two cousins: Iñigo, archpriest of Madrid and a royal chaplain, and Rodrigo, duke of Pastrana and a member of the king's household. For more on this family, see AHN Inq 3713/2/11, fol. 153v, testimony of Diego de Vargas Manrique.

51. Mendoza's appointment to the university is mentioned by Vicente Beltrán de Heredía, "La teología en la universidad de Alcalá," in *Miscelánea Beltrán de Heredía* (Salamanca, 1973), 4:138; Bartolomé Alcaraz, *Chrono-historia de la Compañía de Jesús en la provincia de Toledo* (Madrid, 1710), 2:201. Alvar Gómez de Castro's praise of Mendoza originally appeared in *De rebus gestis a Francesco Ximeno Cisnerio* (Alcalá de Henares, 1569); *De las hazañas de Francisco Jiménez de Cisneros,* ed. José Oroz Reta (Madrid, 1984), p. 352. Mendoza delivered his sermon honoring the queen on 5 Nov. 1568, praising her for her fight against heresy; for extracts, see AHN Inq 3713/2/11, fol. 134. Mendoza's appointment as magistral canon is dated 3 Feb. 1578; ACT Libros Capitulares, vol. 16, fol. 172. Information on his income—3,000 ducats a year from canonry and another 2,500 from his dignity—is derived from "La Santa Iglesia de Toledo," BAV MS. Barbarini 3560, fols. 10–70; see also Inocente López Celada, *Evolución de las rentas del cabildo de la catedral de Toledo durante el último cuarto del siglo xvi* (Toledo, 1980), p. 102.

52. AHN Inq 3713/4/11, fol. 181v, testimony of Francisco Monsalve.

53. AHN Inq 3713/4/11, fol. 179v, testimony of Antonio Cordoves.

54. AHN Inq 4436/18. Mendoza discovered an error in this breviary which referred to Mary as an "innupta virgo" (unmarried virgin) instead of "intacto virgo" (chaste virgin).

55. AHN Inq 3713/4/11, fol. 179, testimony of don Pedro de Ribera, señor of Malpica.

56. AHN Inq 3713/2/8, fol. 312v, testimony of Lic. Alonso Serrano, a member of the Consejo del Arzobispado de Toledo. AHN Inq 3713, pieza 8, fol. 297, testimony of Dr. Tello Maldonado, 3 Nov. 1593. Maldonado, a law professor at the University of Toledo, also served the Inquisition as an attorney who oversaw financial matters (*juez de bienes confiscados*).

57. On 8 Jan. 1582 the cathedral chapter, referring to an "exceso" Mendoza committed while delivering the sermon of the Epiphany, suspended him from his activities in the cathedral for four months and deprived him of the right to deliver this sermon for ten years; ACT Libros Capitulares 17, entry for 8 Jan. 1582. Five days later, however, Archbishop Quiroga annulled this penalty; ibid., entry for 13 Jan. 1582. On Mendoza's relationship with the Doria, see AHN Inq 3713/4/8, fol. 299, testimony of Pedro Salazar de Mendoza, 4 Nov. 1593.

58. AHN Inq 3712/2/5, no. 5, Agustín Parra to Mendoza, letters of 21 and 26 Oct. 1588 and 6 Nov. 1588. See also AHN Inq 3712/2, fol. 186, testimony of Juan Ocio de Salazar, 22 Sept. 1591.

59. On 19 Dec. 1516 the Lateran Council decreed that preachers were to refrain from prophecy and that the teachings of anyone who claimed to have experienced divine revelations had first to be examined by theologians and approved by the pope or a bishop; *Conciliorum oecumenicorum decreta* (Basel, 1962), pp. 610–14. For Mendoza's interpretation of this decree, see AHN Inq 3712/2/6, papel contra García de Loaysa, 7 Aug. 1587.

60. AHN Inq 3712/2/2, fol. 205v.

61. AHN Inq 3703, fol. 118.

62. AHN Inq 3712/2/2, fol. 143.

63. AHN Inq 3712/2/2, fols. 20, 141; 3712/2/6, nos. 16 and 17, Mendoza to Vitores, 6 and 28 April 1590. "Divine prophet" appears in AHN Inq 3712/2/2, fol. 141.

64. AHN Inq 3712/2/2, fol. 149. Two years later Mendoza reiterated his view of the monastery when, comparing the Escorial to other Jeronymite houses where visitors ("caminantes") are readily "received and entertained," he wrote that at the Escorial "few are admitted and fewer permitted to stay, not even religious belonging to other orders"; note attached to dream of 2 Apr. 1590. See also note attached to dream of 6 Apr. 1590.

65. Note attached to dream of 19 Jan. 1588.

66. On this meeting see the pamphlet *Congregación de las iglesias metropolitanas y catedrales de los reinos de Castilla y León,* BN Varios especiales 3/18355.

67. AHN Inq 2085, fol. 193v, as reported by Pedro Ibáñez de Ochandiano.

68. According to Lucrecia, Mendoza faulted Loaysa for having accepted the position of *limosnero mayor* in Madrid without having resigned his canonry in Toledo, a violation of the Council of Trent's decrees on clerical residence; AHN Inq 2085, fol. 192v.

69. Note attached to dream of 17 Jan. 1588. For the so-called morisco scare, see Albert W. Lovett, *Philip II and Mateo Vázquez de Leca: The Government of Spain (1572–1592)* (Geneva, 1977), pp. 181–87.

70. AHN Inq 3712/2/6, no. 12, Mendoza to Casaos, 21 Feb. 1589.

71. AHN Inq 3712/2/6, no. 52, Mendoza to Casaos, no date. Five days after the secretary's escape, Vitores described Pérez to Mendoza as another "count Julian," a reference to the ruler of Ceuta who, to avenge King Roderic's rape of his daughter, helped the Muslim army gathered in North Africa to invade Spain; AHN Inq 3712/2/5, Vitores to Mendoza, 24 Apr. 1590.

72. AHN Inq 2085, fol. 195. Lucrecia told a fellow prisoner that "don Alonso had a great rancor against the king and that he felt aggrieved at not having been appointed bishop." She also told a cellmate that "don Alonso desired to be pope"; AHN Inq 2085, fol. 195.

73. Luis Cabrera de Córdoba, *Felipe segundo, rey de España* (1619; Madrid, 1877), bk. 2, chap. 8, p. 230.

74. Allende's biography appears in AHN Inq 3073, fols. 230–31. Quotations are from this same legajo, fol. 611v.

75. Mendoza described Trijueque in a note attached to the dream of 8 Jan. 1588 as "a court constable; a well-intentioned, virtuous man; a friend of Beaumont and someone who has had a few visions." Two days later Lucrecia told Fray Lucas that Trijueque "had made many miracles with his hands"; AHN Inq 3712/2/2, fol. 115. Trijueque was among those arrested in May 1590, but he died soon thereafter (a consulta of 26 Dec. 1590 indicates that his *vara* of alguacil was vacant); ABHS carpeta 143, fol. 275.

76. Allende's account of the looting appears in AHN Inq 3703, fol. 365.

77. Documents cited in Marañon, *Antonio Pérez,* vol. 2, appendix 14.

78. AHN Inq 3712/2/5, billete dated 10 Jan. 1588. In this same pieza, in a billete of 23 Jan. 1588, Allende states that Lucrecia "is good and with such a spirit that one has the security she speaks truthfully."

79. AHN Inq 3712/2/5, billete of Allende to Mendoza, 31 Nov. 1588; AHN Inq 3703, fol. 214.

80. AHN Inq 3712/2/6, no. 43.

81. Casaos's biography appears in AHN Inq 2105/1, "discurso de la vida," 24 July 1590.

82. AHN Inq 2105/1, audiencia of 20 May 1592.

83. AHN Inq 2105/1, audiencia of 4 July 1592. The Spanish text reads: "que la defensa de estados no consiste en los soldados sino en justicia y bondad y vasallos bien tratados."

84. On Casaos as an astrologer, see AHN Inq 97/8, the trial of Lic. Amador de Velasco.

85. Casaos comments on his various dreams and visions in his defensas of 20 May 1592; AHN Inq 2105/1, after fol. 90. Casaos may have harbored a grudge against royal authority since 1580, when the Royal Council of the Indies prevented him, as governor of Yucatan, from appointing subordinate judges in the provinces of Campeche, Tabasco, and Valladolid. See Peter Gerhard, *The Southeast Frontier of New Spain* (Princeton, 1979), pp. 38, 59, 100, 121, 138. Gerhard mistakenly refers to Casaos as Las Casas, as does David Henige, *Colonial Governors* (Madison, Wis., 1970), p. 346.

86. AHN Inq 3712/2/2, testimony of Lucrecia, 28 Sept. 1594. The original reads: "era plática entre los dichos don Alonso y don Guillén y fray Lucas que ellos entre si decían y afirmaban que hasta tres relojes que tenían Su Magestad no decían verdad."

87. AHN Inq 2105/1, fol. 172v, audiencia of 5 Feb. 1594; fol. 176, audiencia of 7 July 1594.

88. AHN Inq 3712/2/5, Casaos to Mendoza, 2 Mar. 1590.

Chapter 5

1. Cited in Paschal Boland, *The Concept of Discretio Spirituum in Johannes Gerson's "De Probatione Spirituum" and "De Distinctione Verarum Visionum A Falsis"* (Washington, D.C., 1959), p. 30.

2. Clemente Sánchez de Vercial, *Libro de los exemplos por A.B.C.,* ed. John Easton Keller (Madrid, 1986), pp. 235, 329. The Spanish texts read: "Del engaño de mujer tú debes bien guardar" and "Tú debes de saber a todas visiones non es de creer."

3. Fray Martín de Castañega, *Tratado de las supersticiones y hechicerías* [1529] (Madrid, 1946), chap. 5, pp. 37–39.

4. Diego de Simancas, *Institutiones catholicae* (Valladolid, 1552), chap. 20,

fols. 69–72, recommends that claims of divine revelation by "simple [unlettered] men and weak women" require thorough investigation.

5. Cited in Teresa of Jesus, *Life,* trans. David Lewis (London, 1911), p. xxvii. Bañes's censorship of Teresa's autobiography is dated 6 July 1575.

6. Juan de Horozco y Covarrubias, *Tratado de la verdadera y falsa prophecía* (Segovia, 1588), pp. 57–61v.

7. For Magdalena de la Cruz, see AHN Inq 4442/27. For Francisca de Avila, AHN Inq 113/5.

8. Pedro de Rivadeneyra, "Tratado de la Tribulación," in *Obras* (BAE, Madrid, 1868) 60:439.

9. Pedro Navarro, *Favores del rey del cielo* (Madrid, 1622), p. 72.

10. AHN Inq lib. 1226, fol. 811. On contemporary attitudes toward women, see Ian MaClean, *The Renaissance Notion of Woman* (Cambridge, 1980), pp. 42–43.

11. Teresa of Jesus, *Complete Works,* ed. and trans. E. Allison Peers, (London, 1946), 3:43.

12. AHN Inq lib. 1226, fol. 811.

13. The Nun of Lisbon had several Spanish imitators. In 1588 the Inquisition of Valencia condemned a Negro freedwoman, Catalina Ferrara, for false and demonic visions. According to her trial record, Catalina's visions "raised considerable commotion in the entire city"; AHN Inq lib. 937, fols. 100v–106v; lib. 938, fol. 170v. I am grateful to Professor William Monter for these references to Catalina Ferrara. Isabel de Jesús, a Dominican nun in Huete who claimed to have stigmata and who prophesied about events related to "the war with England" was yet another of Sor María's Spanish imitators. She was investigated by the Holy Office in 1590; AHN Inq 496/1.

14. Rivadeneyra, "Tratado," p. 443.

15. AHN Inq 3712/2/5, Allende to Mendoza, 29 May 1588.

16. AHN Inq 2085/1, fol. 200v. The original reads: "con este camino pensaba disculparse."

17. Bridgit of Sweden, *Les revelations celestes et divines,* trans. Jacques Ferraige (Paris, 1624), bk. 6, chap. 9; bk. 7, chaps. 11, 18, 19, and 27.

18. Navarro, *Favores del rey del cielo,* p. 72.

19. Teresa's correspondence illustrates her noninterference in secular politics. One can point to little beyond her letter of 22 July 1579, addressed to the bishop of Evora, which touches upon Philip II's claim to the Portuguese throne; *Letters,* trans. E. Allison Peers (London, 1980), 2:676.

20. Casaos later told the Inquisition that the "publicity of these revelations" led to Lucrecia's arrest by the vicar; AHN Inq 2105/1, audiencia of 26 June 1590.

21. Chaves was appointed royal confessor in 1577. For a brief outline of his career, see Vicente Beltrán de Heredía, "La facultad de teología en la universidad de Santiago," *Miscelánea Beltrán de Heredía* (Salamanca, 1973), 4:211.

22. For Juana Correa's testimony, see AHN Inq 3712/2/2, testimony of

10 Feb. 1588. For that of María Núñez, see AHN Inq 3712/2/2, fol. 88–88v, testimony of 13 Feb. 1588.

23. During Lucrecia's confinement in the house of notary Juan García, Allende was allowed to visit her and to copy the new dreams she had. According to Mendoza, however, these dreams were poorly transcribed because Allende was in a hurry and the work was done in a dark confessional; AHN Inq 3712/2/5, billetes of Feb. 1588.

24. AHN Inq 3712/2/2, fol. 119v.

25. AHN Inq 2105/1, testimony of Guillén de Casaos, 26 June 1590.

26. AHN Inq 3077, fol. 66, report of 14 Feb. 1588.

27. AHN Inq 3712/2/6, no. 50.

28. Mendoza to Fray Luis de León, 13 Feb. 1588; AHN Inq 3712/2/6, no. 50.

29. Ibid., no. 92.

30. Ibid., no. 93, Mendoza to Quiroga, 19 Feb. 1588.

31. Quiroga's intervention is described in AHN Inq 3712/2/2, fol. 142, and 3712/2/6, no. 25.

32. ABHS carpeta 142, no. 157, letter of Arcedeano de Toledo to Mateo Vázquez, 4 June 1588. Chaves's antipathy for Quiroga dates from at least 1579; see ASV NS 22, fols. 52–53, letter of papal nuncio, 19 Feb. 1579.

33. AHN Inq 3712/2/5, 22 Feb. 1588.

34. AHN Inq 3712/2/6, no. 25, Mendoza to Alonso Franco, 18 Mar. 1588.

35. AHN Inq 3712/2/2, fol. 51v; 3712/2/6, no. 60, Alonso Franco to Mendoza, 30 Mar. 1588. The original reads: "sin escándalo ni daño de nadie."

36. AHN Inq 3712/2/2, fol. 52. The original reads: "quitar la vida."

37. For evidence of these alms, see AHN Inq 3712/2/2, fol. 141, testimony of Navarro, 28 May 1590; 3712/2/6, no. 25, letter of Mendoza to Alonso Franco, 18 Mar. 1588, in which Mendoza states that he is prepared to help Lucrecia "with the *hacienda* God has given me."

38. AHN Inq 2105, "Apuntamientos de la defensa de don Guillén de Casaos," no folio.

39. The caves may well be those, which can still be seen, carved into the north side of the hill, upon which sits the shrine of Our Lady of Castellar.

40. In a letter of 31 Mar. 1588, Fray Lucas de Allende reports "Juan de Herrera went to Aranjuez and from there, accompanied by Cristóbal de Allende, to inspect that 'nest' [nido] and to draw some plans that will be pleasing to God"; AHN Inq 3712/2/6, no. 31. Herrera also reportedly gave Cristóbal de Allende five hundred reales toward the purchase of supplies for Sopeña; AHN Inq 3712/2/2, fol. 156. The supplies are also mentioned in AHN Inq 3712/2/6, no. 64. Fray Francisco de Murga testified that Herrera, in addition to designing the chapel, prepared "trazas" (plans) for three or four "aposentos" (rooms); AHN Inq 3712/2/2, fol. 180v, testimony of 17 Sept. 1590.

41. AHN Inq 3712/2/6, no. 16, Mendoza to Vitores, 28 April 1590. In the same letter Mendoza suggests that Vitores and Fray Lucas go with him to the caves at the end of May in order to escape the summer heat.

42. The traditional account of this year is Martin Hume, *The Year After the Armada* (London, 1891). See also Colin Martin and Geoffrey Parker, *The Spanish Armada* (London, 1988), pp. 255–64.

43. For these raids, see Edward P. Cheyney, *History of England from the Defeat of the Armada to the Death of Elizabeth* (London, 1974), 1:154–81; Richard B. Wernham, *After the Armada* (Oxford, 1984), pp. 107–30.

44. Dreams of 21 Sept., 1 Oct., 3 Dec. 1589.

45. AHN Inq 3712/2/6, no. 71, letter of 13 June 1589.

46. See Henry Clifford, *The Life of Lady Jane Dormer, Duchess of Feria* (London, 1887); Ann E. Wiltrout, *A Patron and a Playwright in Renaissance Spain: The House of Feria and Diego Sánchez de Badajoz* (London, 1987).

47. Domingo Navarro informed the Inquisition that the duchess had "considerable" contact with Lucrecia; AHN Inq 3712/2/2, fol. 52. Similarly, Allende reported that "she went to the house of the duchess of Feria and other places where she talked about these things [the dreams]"; AHN Inq 3703, fol. 353.

48. AHN Inq 3703, fols. 119–129v.

49. AHN Inq 3712/2/6, Mendoza to Vitores, 24 Apr. 1590.

50. Among this group, Navarro's loyalty to Lucrecia is perhaps the most questionable. On 17 April 1590 Vitores informed Mendoza of his shock upon learning that "a man [Navarro] who has joined the *gremio*" once called the dreams "frauds to deceive the king"; AHN Inq 3712/2/5, no folio.

51. Two other officials who apparently knew about the dreams were Iñigo López de Zárate, the king's secretary for Italian affairs, and Andrés de Prada, a secretary attached to the Council of War; AHN Inq 3713/2/11, fol. 151v, and 3703, fol. 347. In 1596 Herrera testified that he had declined to speak to the king about Lucrecia's dreams "because I was afraid that everyone would consider me crazy"; AHN Inq 3703, fol. 156.

52. AHN Inq 3712/2/5, letter of 26 Mar. 1590, no folio. Incidentally, the letter is signed. In the same pieza, see also her letter of 13 Apr. 1590, in which she asks Mendoza about his interpretations of several of her dreams, and that of 8 May 1590, which describes her visit to the Madrid shrine of Nuestra Señora de Fuencarral and provides Mendoza with some news about the religious wars in France.

53. On the limits of political and religious freedom, see Henry Kamen, "Toleration and Dissent in Sixteenth-Century Spain," *Sixteenth-Century Journal* 19 (1988): 3–23.

54. ASV NS 34, fol. 197, Cesare Speciano to Cardinal Montalto, 5 Mar. 1588. I am grateful to Ignacio Tellechea Idigoras of the Pontifical University of Salamanca for this reference.

55. On the Index, see Virgilio Pinto Crespo, *Inquisición y control ideológico en la España del siglo xvi* (Madrid, 1983), pp. 67–86, 197–204. On Quiroga's

life, see Maurice Boyd, *Cardinal Quiroga, Inquisitor General of Spain* (Dubuque, Iowa, 1954), the only published biography.

56. Piedrola was in touch with Quiroga as early as 1578; AHN Inq 3712/2/6, Piedrola to the Archbishop of Toledo, 28 July and 4 Sept. 1578. In the second of these notes Piedrola warns Quiroga about "plagas" (stains) in the royal blood.

57. ABHS carpeta 143, fol. 212, consulta of 26 July 1589. The original reads: "no os de espantar del que dice sino lo que no dice."

58. For the political situation in Aragon, see Albert W. Lovett, "Philip II, Antonio Pérez, and the Kingdom of Aragon," *European History Quarterly* 18 (Apr. 1988): 131–53.

59. AHN Inq 3712/2/2, fol. 119v, letter to Juan de Zúñiga, a member of the Suprema, 9 May 1590: "por que es mujer simple y de poca edad."

60. AHN Inq 3712/2/2, fol. 120.

61. AHN Inq 3077, no. 26, Lope de Mendoza to the Suprema, 10 May 1590.

62. AHN Inq 3712/2/2, fols. 18 and 170v.

63. Reports of Inquisitor Mendoza, AHN Inq 3077, nos. 29–31; 3712/2/2, fol. 20. JHS for Jesus, MARIA for Mary, and INRJ for Jesus of Nazareth, king of the Jews.

64. On the arrests, see AHN Inq 3077, nos. 33–36; and 3712/2/2, fols. 28–38.

65. AHN Inq 2085/1, fol. 205v, testimony of Captain Ibáñez de Ochandiano. A similar dragon appears in Lucrecia's dream of 12 Mar. 1590.

Chapter 6

1. AHN Inq 3071, no. 28, letter to the Suprema, 3 June 1573.

2. Jean-Pierre Dedieu, "Les inquisiteurs de Tolède et la visite du district," *Mélanges de la Casa de Velázquez* 13 (1977): 235–56.

3. AHN Inq 3068, n. 28. By 1596, however, the number of *familiares* had diminished to thirty-eight; AHN Inq 3080, fol. 69.

4. For the tribunal's personnel in 1595, see AHN Inq 3079, fol. 145, and Jean-Pierre Dedieu, *L'administration de la foi: L'inquisition de Toledo (xvie–xviiie siècle)* (Toledo, 1989), p. 160. For the organization of the Holy Office in general, Roberto López Velaz, "Estructura y funcionamento de la burocracia inquisitorial, 1643–1667," in *La Inquisición española: Nueva visión, nuevos horizontes,* ed. Joaquín Pérez Villanueva (Madrid, 1980), pp. 159–239. Salazar de Mendoza is listed among the calificadores and consultores retained by this tribunal in 1590; see AHN Inq 3077, no. 63. Mariana is first listed as a calificador in 1577; see AHN Inq lib. 1, exp. 2, fol. 74v.

5. AHN Inq 3077, no. 39. The tribunal estimated that its annual expenses were 6,000 ducats, its revenues only 3,700 ducats.

6. See Jaime Contreras and Gustav Henningsen, "Forty-four Thousand

Cases of the Spanish Inquisition (1540–1700): Analysis of a Historical Data Bank," in *The Inquisition in Early Modern Europe,* ed. Gustav Henningsen and John Tedeschi (Dekalb, Ill., 1986), pp. 100–129.

7. For a chronological listing of Toledo's trials of faith, see Jean Pierre Dedieu, "The Archives of the Holy Office of Toledo as a Source for Historical Anthropology," in *The Inquisition in Early Modern Europe,* ed. Henningsen and Tedeschi, pp. 181–82, and his *L'administration de la foi,* pp. 238–39.

8. AHN Inq 3076, n. 11, letter of 14 Apr. 1587. The shortage of penitents was a chronic problem. In 1600, in order to stage an auto for the new king Philip III, Toledo resorted to importing twenty penitents from the tribunals of Llerena, Granada, Valladolid, and Córdoba; see AHN Inq 3082, no. 12, letter of 14 Feb. 1600.

9. Lope de Mendoza was named to Toledo on 17 July 1581; AHN Inq lib 358, fol. 3. His annual salary was officially set at 150,000 maravedís. Zárate joined the tribunal in Jan. 1590; AHN Inq 3077, no. 2. For the careers of Toledo's inquisitors, see Dedieu, *L'administration de la foi,* p. 163.

10. For a detailed explanation of inquisitorial procedures, see Dedieu "Archives of the Holy Office," pp. 177–80.

11. *Copilación de las instrucciones del oficio de la Santa Inquisición* (Toledo 1561), in Gaspar Isidro de Argüello, *Instrucciones del Santo Oficio de la Inquisición* (Madrid, 1630), p. 34.

12. AHN Inq 3712/2, audiencia of 4 June 1590.

13. AHN Inq 3712/2, audiencia of 13 June 1590, fols. 44v–45; audiencia of 22 Sept. 1591, fol. 53v.

14. AHN Inq 3712/2, audiencias of 13 June and 5 July 1590.

15. AHN Inq 2105/1, audiencia of 6 Dec. 1591. Casaos's first audiencia occurred on 21 June 1590.

16. AHN Inq 115/23, fols. 47–54.

17. AHN Inq 3077, no. 78; leg. 3703/2, fols. 216ff. Allende's first audiencia occurred on 16 June 1590.

18. The formal recusación of inquisitors Mendoza and Zárate, together with that of the inquisitor general, two members of the Suprema, and García de Loaysa, was filed on 8 Mar. 1591. However, Mendoza first challenged the authority of the Inquisition's jurisdiction on 20 July 1590, six weeks after his arrest; AHN Inq 3077, nos. 75 and 108.

19. AHN Inq 3712/2, fol. 190v. Allende learned of the sedition charges from one of the carters who transported him from Madrid to Toledo; AHN Inq 3703, fol. 352. Lucrecia's destruction of her papers is noted in AHN Inq 3712/2, fol. 92.

20. AHN Inq 115/23, fol. 21. Vega was initially queried about these billetes on 6 Sept. 1590. A resident of the town of Alcázar de San Juan, María de Vega was "reconciled" to the church along with twenty-four other *judaizantes* at the auto da fe held in Toledo on 9 Sept. 1591. On the mass arrest of this community of Portuguese conversos, see RAH Colección Salazar y Castro, MS. N4, fol. 59.

21. These billetes are included in AHN Inq 115/23, no folio.

22. AHN Inq 2105, testimony of Casaos, 19 June 1591.

23. Despite Ibáñez's willingness to testify, the Inquisition sentenced him to four years in the galleys. He appeared at the auto da fe staged in Toledo on 9 Sept. 1591; RAH Colección Salazar y Castro, MS. N4, fol. 59.

24. AHN Inq 114/10, audiencia of 5 Apr. 1591.

25. AHN Inq 2085, fols. 182–85.

26. AHN Inq 114/10, testimony of 4 Apr. 1591. The original reads: "el cual [Mendoza] la había dado un abrazo y díjole que hermosa estáis a que un muerto la podía empreñar." Ibáñez de Ochandiano further attested: "la quería mucho el dicho inquisidor [Mendoza]"; AHN Inq 2105, fol. 182.

27. AHN Inq 114/10, audiencia of 4 Apr. 1591. The original reads: "que [Mendoza] no entendía aquel negocio suyo; no sabía porque la tenían presa."

28. AHN Inq 2085, fol. 199, testimony of Ibáñez de Ochandiano. This witness also informed Pacheco that Lucrecia and Guzmán, a converso, had conversations at night during which "they spoke badly of the king." Guzmán had apparently attracted Lucrecia's eye, and she supposedly once remarked that he could become her "galán" if he were rich.

29. AHN Inq 6/1, Visita a la inquisición de Toledo, 31 Oct. 1592; also AHN Inq 2105, no. 76.

30. AHN Inq 2105, no. 74.

31. Ibid.

32. Reports on the new prison appear in AHN Inq 3077, no. 133, 25 June 1591; no. 134, 1 July 1591; no. 167, 23 Oct. 1591; no. 168, 6 Nov. 1591.

33. AHN Inq 3712/2/2, fol. 199v, testimony of Juan Ocio de Salazar. Salazar, another prisoner, claimed that Lucrecia had told him that she would be compared to Balaam's ass and would therefore be considered "presa por loco" (arrested for madness). In his audiencia of 15 Oct. 1591, Ibáñez de Ochandiano reported that Lucrecia wanted to be thought of as a "loca"; AHN Inq 2085, fol. 197v.

34. AHN Inq 2085, fols. 204–6.

35. AHN Inq 3712/2/2, fol. 54.

36. AHN Inq 3712/2/2, fol. 55.

37. Morejón's letter of appointment is dated 13 Apr. 1592, Quiroga's 19 Dec. 1592; AHN Inq 3078, no. 21, fol. 103.

38. For reports of Mendoza's "madness" and erratic behavior, see AHN Inq 3078, no. 123, 23 Mar. 1591; 114/10, audiencias of 17 and 30 May 1592; 3713/2/8, passim.

39. Sotocameño's art collection is listed in an *inventario de bienes* made after his death on 18 Aug. 1607; AHPT leg. 2146, fols. 251ff. He had been appointed fiscal in 1565; AHN Inq 3079, no. 145.

40. For the original *calificaciones*, see AHN Inq 3077, no. 51, and 3703, fols. 132–61. The tribunal formally requested Orellana's assistance on 10 March 1593; AHN Inq 3078, no. 112.

41. AHN Inq 3712/2/2, fol. 54v, acusaciones of 7–23 Dec. 1591.

42. AHN Inq 3712/2/2, fol. 55, audiencia of 9 Dec. 1591.

43. AHN Inq 3712/2/2, fol. 56v.

44. AHN Inq 3712/2/2, fol. 58v.

45. AHN Inq 3712/2/2, fol. 65, no. 28, audiencia of 7 Nov. 1592.

46. AHN Inq 3712/2/2, fols. 60v–62v.

47. AHN Inq 3712/2/2, fols. 68v–69v, audiencia of 6 Feb. 1594. The original reads: "nunca creyó estos sueños ni ella entiende ni sabe lo que contienen; no entendía lo que soñaba."

48. AHN Inq 3712/2/2, fol. 72, audiencia of 1 Oct. 1594.

49. AHN Inq 3712/2/2, fol. 77v; 3079, no. 147.

50. The text of this audiencia is recorded in AHN Inq 3712/2/2, fols. 78v–82v.

51. AHN Inq 3712/2/2, fols. 80v–82.

52. The text of this audiencia is recorded in AHN Inq 3712/2, fols. 85–87.

53. The calificadores were two Dominican friars, Juan de Cepeda and Juan de la Fuente.

54. AHN Inq 3079, fol. 147, letter of 15 June 1595.

55. AHN Inq 3079, no. 159.

56. AHN Inq 3079, no. 168, letter of 7 Aug. 1595.

57. AHN Inq 3079, no. 125, letter of 21 Aug. 1595.

58. AHN Inq 3079, no. 175, letter of 21 Aug. 1595. The original reads "no se han executado hoy las azotes porque no hay ministro que está en esa corte"; ibid., no. 179, letter of 25 Aug. 1595, the day on which the lashes were administered.

59. Ibid.

60. AHN Inq 3079, no. 204, letter of 27 Oct. 1595.

61. AHN Inq 115/23, fols. 166–67.

62. AHN Inq 3703, fol. 626.

63. AHN Inq 3703/2, letters of 27 Aug. and 2 Sept. 1596.

64. AHN Inq 3703, letter of 14 Oct. 1597.

65. AHN Inq 3712/2/11, calificaciones of 14 Oct. 1590.

66. For the investigation, see AHN Inq 3712/2/9, fols. 297–325. For the declaration of madness and the transfer, pieza 9, fols. 321 and 332. After having complained about mosquitoes in his cell, the noise made by the nearby river, and other inconveniences, which he compared to the tribulations of Job, Mendoza was removed from the prison on 27 Apr. 1594.

67. AHN Inq 3079, no. 179.

68. AHN Inq 3712/2/11, 28 June 1596. According to the original, the judges ruled "sin tocar en la culpa de la sedición." It was roughly at this point that the Inquisition discovered that Mendoza had written a short poem, which he claimed was inspired by a comedy of Terence:

> What is it to be jailed
> For apostolic heresy and blasphemy
> As a fearless, dangerous traitor

and for other madnesses they say I've done.
And that in six years his case has never
been sentenced, the Council of the Inquisition afraid
of his dignity ? [*mayoral*] and who his brothers are.

69. AHN Inq 3712/2/11, 13 Sept. 1597.

70. AHN Inq 3713/2/11, letters of 1 Sept. and 1 Oct. 1597.

71. AHN Inq 3713/2/11, letter of 5 Oct. 1598.

72. AHN Inq 3080, fol. 147, letter of 8 Oct. 1598.

73. On 12 Oct. 1603 the cathedral chapter of Toledo requested one of its members to assign Mendoza a tomb within the precincts of the church; ACT Libros Capitulares, no. 23.

Conclusion

1. Sor Magdalena de San Gerónimo, *Razón y forma de la galera, y casa real, que el Rey N.S. manda hazer en estos reinos para castigo de las mugeres vagrantes y ladronas, alcahuetas, hechizeras, y otras semejantes* (Salamanca, 1608), p. 30. Sor Magdalena urged that incarceration and workhouses replace exile as a punishment, since female prisoners often violated their sentences and returned to live "with greater liberty and shame than before."

2. AHN Inq 3712/2/11, fol. 176.

3. See Linda Martz, *Poverty and Welfare in Habsburg Spain* (Cambridge, 1983), pp. 153–54.

4. Ibid., pp. 88–90.

5. Francisco de Pisa, *Apuntamientos para la ii parte de la "Descripción de la imperial ciudad de Toledo,"* ed. José Gómez-Menor Fuentes (Toledo, 1976), p. 71.

6. Anne L. Barstow, *Joan of Arc: Heretic, Mystic, Shaman* (Lewiston, N.Y., 1986), p. 35.

7. Kai Erickson, *Wayward Puritans* (New York, 1966), p. 15.

8. Pierre Bouistau, Claude Tesserant, and François Belleforest, *Historias prodigiosas y maravillosas de diversos sucesos acaecidos en el mundo,* trans. Andrea Pescioni (Madrid, 1603), 188v. This history of natural wonders, published originally in French in 1575, was first translated into Castilian in 1585. The rage for human prodigies seems to have led Prior Hernando de Toledo to keep a charismatic vision-prone *doncellita* on display in his Madrid townhouse; AHN Inq 2105/1, testimony of Diego Cavallero Bazan, 4 June 1590.

9. Loyola believed that spiritual discipline resulted from a repetitive cycle of preparatory prayer, meditation, and contemplation. Similarly, Teresa of Jesus believed that visions were the product of prayer, experience, and spiritual direction; *Life,* trans. David Lewis (London, 1911), chap. 40, sections 12–16.

10. AHN Inq 115/23, fol. 46v.

11. For this and other meanings, mostly sexual, attached to this proverb, see George A. Shipley, "A Case of Functional Obscurity: The Master

Tambourine-Painter of *Lazarillo, Tratado VI,*" *Modern Language Notes* 97 (March 1982): 225–53. A variant of this proverb, "En manos está el pandero que lo sabe bien tocar," appears in Sebastián de Covarrubias, *Tesoro de la lengua castellana* (Madrid, 1611), p. 850.

12. AHN Inq 2085, fol. 201, testimony of Ibáñez de Ochandiano. This witness also reported that Lucrecia had said that Mendoza and Casaos would "pay her to keep quiet."

13. Juan Ortiz de Salvatierra, comisario of the Holy Office, described her as "simple-minded"; AHN Inq 3712/2/2, report of 3 May 1590. Agustín Parra described her as dim-witted ("un poco falta de juicio") in a letter to Alonso de Mendoza, 1 Aug. 1588; AHN Inq 3712/2/5.

14. Fray Pedro Navarro, *Favores del rey del cielo,* p. 72.

15. Pedro José Pidal, *Historia de las alteraciones de Aragon en el reinado de Felipe II* (Madrid, 1862), 2:423. The riots began on 24 May 1591; Albert W. Lovett, "Philip II, Antonio Pérez, and the Kingdom of Aragon," *European History Quarterly* 18 (Apr. 1988): 131–53.

16. The placard was discovered on 21 Oct. 1591. The original reads: "Y tú, Felipe, conténtate con lo que es tuyo y no pretendas lo ajeno"; Pidal, *Historia de las alteraciones,* 2:240. For these protests, see Antonio Domínguez Ortiz, "Un testimonio de protesta social a fines del reinado de Felipe II," in *Homenaje a Pedro Sainz Rodríguez* (Madrid, 1986).

17. The Madrid riot is reported by Augusto Tito, a Florentine agent, who also claimed that "la mala satisfatione e cosi universale et nella grandi et nelle picoli"; ASF Mediceo, filza 5031, 273v–274. See also Pidal, *Historia de las alteraciones,* 2:240.

18. Iñigo Ibáñez de Santa Cruz, "Las causas de que resultó el ignorante confuso gobierno que hubo en el tiempo del Rey N.S. que sea en gloria," RAH MS. 9/3507, fols. 755 and 760.

19. This subject is briefly discussed in my essay "Olivares and Education," in *La España de Felipe IV,* ed. Antonio García Sanz (Valladolid, 1990), and more fully in the excellent introduction to Francisco Suárez, *De juramento fidelitatus,* ed. L. Pereña (Madrid, 1979). For Juan de Mariana's "contracturalist" ideas, see his *De rege et regis institutione* (Toledo, 1599); Spanish trans. *Del rey y de la dignidad real* (Madrid, 1961). For Lisón y Viedma, see Jean Vilar, "Formes et tendances de l'opposition sous Olivares: Lisón y Viedma, *Defensor Patria,*" *Mélanges de la Casa de Velázquez* 7 (1971): 263–94. See also Gutierre Marques de Careaga, *Por el estado y monarchía española* (Granada, 1620).

SELECT BIBLIOGRAPHY

The basic source material for this study is the voluminous trial record of Lucrecia and her associates. These documents are now preserved in the Sección de Inquisición of Madrid's Archivo Histórico Nacional:

trial of Diego de Vitores, legajo 115/23
trial of Guillén de Casaos, legajo 2105/1
trial of Fray Lucas de Allende, legajo 3703
trials of Lucrecia de León and Alonso de Mendoza, legajos 3712–13.

Relevant material is also to be found in the *proceso* of Pedro Ibáñez de Ochandiano, the prisoner whose testimony shed important light on Lucrecia's personality (legajos 114/10 and 2085). Additional information about these trials is contained in the correspondence of the Toledan tribunal of the Holy Office, especially legajos 3077–82.

Despite this wealth of archival material, the secondary literature on Lucrecia is brief and often misleading. Contemporary references are few, and she did not reenter the historical record until 1890, when she earned a brief reference in Henry C. Lea's *Chapters from the Religious History of Spain* (Philadelphia, 1890), pp. 359–60. She next appeared in Manuel Serrano y Sanz's valuable checklist of female authors in Golden Age Spain. Included in his *Apuntes para una biblioteca de escritoras españolas* (Madrid, 1903) is a brief mention of Lucrecia along with excerpts from two of her dreams and extracts from her *sentencia.*

The next scholar to write about Lucrecia was the Dominican historian Vicente Beltrán de Heredía, who investigated her case prior to World War I but did not publish his findings until 1947. In an article about the visionary tradition in sixteenth-century Spain, he erroneously linked Lucrecia to the *alumbrados;* see his "Un grupo de visionarios y pseudoprofetas . . ." *Revista Española de Teología* 7 (1947): 373–97 and 483–534. Still, Beltrán de Heredía must be thanked for having indicated the precise location of Lucrecia's trial record in the Inquisition archives. The following year Manuel de la Pinta Llorente, a historian of the Spanish Inquisition, used this record to provide what remains the best succinct summary of Lucrecia's story; see his *La inquisición española* (Madrid, 1948), pp. 316–17. Llorente's call for a detailed study of Lucrecia unfortunately went unanswered.

Among the more recent work is Jesús de Imirizaldu's short and rather confusing account of Lucrecia's case in *Monjas y beatas embaucadoras* (Madrid, 1977), pp. 17–20 and 65–69. Though he provides a complete transcription of the sentencia excerpted some years before by Serrano y Sanz, Imirizaldu dismisses Lucrecia as a "crazy dreamer" and does relatively little to advance our knowledge of her. Equally superficial are Julio Caro Baroja's remarks about Lucrecia in *Las formas complejas de la vida religiosa en España* (Madrid, 1978), a well-known study of Spanish religious life in the sixteenth and seventeenth centuries.

In the past five years we have come to know Lucrecia somewhat better through several works of literary history written by Alain Milhou. In his study of the messianism of Christopher Columbus, Milhou relates some of the imagery appearing in Lucrecia's dreams to the medieval tradition of apocalyptic and prophetic literature to which Columbus was heir.* Milhou's search for the literary lineage of Lucrecia's dreams is invaluable for an understanding of the evolution of apocalyptic and millennial ideas in Spain, although references to this lineage cannot explain the overtly political content of her dreams. Finally, we have María Zambrano, Edison Simons, and Juan Blázquez Miguel's *Sueños y procesos de Lucrecia de León* (Madrid, 1987), which presents transcripts of thirty dreams and extracts from the trial. The authors' emphasis on the superstitious aspects of the case, however, diverts their attention from both the dream texts and the historical and political context of Lucrecia's extraordinary career.

Manuscripts

BN MS. 721. "Sentencia de Lucrezia de Leon en el auto de la fee que se hizo en Toledo," fols. 135–136v.

*Alain Milhou, *Colón y su mentalidad mesiánica en el ambiente franciscanista español* (Valladolid, 1983), pp. 245–47, 316–17; see also his "De la destruction de l'Espagne à la destruction des Indes: histoire sacrée et combats idéologiques," *Etudes sur l'impact culturel du nouveau monde* (Paris, 1984), 3:18; and "La chauve-souris, le nouveau David et le roi cache (trois images de l'empereur des derniers temps dans le monde ibérique, xiiie–xviie s.), *Mélanges de la Casa de Velázquez* 18 (1982): 61–78.

MS. 10,470. "Vida y sucesos estranissimos del profeta, ni falso, ni santo Miguel Piedrola en tiempo de Phelipe segundo," fols. 1–117.

RAH MS. 9/3507. Iñigo Ibáñez de Santa Cruz, "Las causas de que resultó el ignorante confuso gobierno que hubo en el tiempo del Rey N.S. que sea en gloria." Coleción Salazar y Castro, MS. N4.

Printed Sources

Adas, Michael. *Prophets of Rebellion.* Cambridge, 1979.

Alba, Ramón. *Acerca de algunas particularidades de las comunidades de Castilla.* Madrid, 1975.

Alcaraz, Bartolomé. *Chrono-historia de la Compañía de Jesús en la provincia de Toledo.* 2 vols. Madrid, 1710.

Alexander, Paul J. "The Medieval Legend of the Last Roman Emperor and Its Messianic Origin." *Journal of the Warburg and Courtauld Institutes* 41 (1978): 1–15.

Alonso, Carlos. *Los apócrifos del Sacramonte de Granada.* Valladolid, 1979.

Alvar Ezquerra, Alfredo, ed. *Antonio Pérez, relaciones y cartas.* 2 vols. Madrid, 1986.

Andrés, Gregorio de. "Las revelaciones de una visionaria de Albuquerque sobre Felipe II." In *Homenaje a Luis Morales Oliver,* pp. 419–27. Madrid, 1986.

Aristotle. *The Complete Works.* Vol. 3, *The Parva Naturala.* Trans. J. J. Beare. Oxford, 1963.

Artemidorus Daldianus. *The Interpretation of Dreams.* Trans. Robert J. White. Park Ridge, N.J., 1975.

Astete, Gaspar de. *Tratado del gobierno de la familia y estado de las viudas y donzellas.* Valladolid, 1597.

Avellá Chafer, Francisco. "Beatas y beaterios en la ciudad y arzobispado de Sevilla." *Archivo Hispalense* 65 (1982): 99–132.

Avilés, Miguel. *Sueños ficticios y lucha ideológica en el Siglo de Oro.* Madrid, 1978.

Barnes, Robin B. *Prophecy and Gnosis: Apocalypticism in the Wake of the Lutheran Reformation.* Stanford, Calif., 1988.

Barstow, Anne L. *Joan of Arc: Heretic, Mystic, Shaman.* Lewiston, N.Y., 1986.

Beltrán de Heredía, Vicente. *Historia de la reforma de la provincia española.* Rome, 1938.

———. "Un grupo de visionarios y pseudoprofetas durante los últimos años de Felipe II y repercusión de ello sobre la memoria de Santa Teresa." *Revista Española de Teología* 7 (1947): 373–97, 483–534.

———. *Miscelánea Beltrán de Heredía.* 4 vols. Salamanca, 1973.

Bennassar, Bartolomé. *Valladolid au siècle d'or.* Paris, 1967.

Blázquez Miguel, Juan. *Hechicería y superstición en Castilla–La Mancha.* Toledo, 1985.

———. *La inquisición en Castilla–La Mancha.* Madrid, 1986.

Bodin, Jean. *Colloquium of the Seven about Secrets of the Sublime.* Trans. Marion Kuntz. Princeton, 1975.

Boland, Paschal. *The Concept of Discretio Spirituum in Johannes Gerson's "De Probatione Spirituum" and "De Distinctione Verarum Visionum A Falsis."* Washington, D.C., 1959.

Bouistau, Pierre, Claude Tesserant, and François Belleforest. *Historias prodigiosas y maravillosas de diversos sucesos acaecidos en el mundo.* Trans. Andrea Pescioni. Madrid, 1603.

Boyd, Maurice. *Cardinal Quiroga, Inquisitor General of Spain.* Dubuque, Iowa, 1954.

Bridgit of Sweden. *Les revelations celestes et divines de St. Brigitte de Suede.* Trans. Jacques Ferraige. Paris, 1624.

Browne, Alice. "Descartes' Dreams." *Journal of the Warburg and Courtauld Institutes* 40 (1977): 256–73.

———. "Girolamo Cardano's *Somniorum Synesiorum Libri IIII.*" *Bibliothèque d'Humanisme et de Renaissance* 41 (1979): 123–35.

Burke, Peter. "L'histoire sociale des rêves." *Annales E.S.C.* 28 (Apr.–May 1973): 329–42.

Bynum, Caroline. *Jesus as Mother: Studies in the Spirituality of the High Middle Ages.* Berkeley and Los Angeles, 1982.

———. *Holy Feast and Holy Fast: The Religious Significance of Food to Medieval Women.* Berkeley and Los Angeles, 1987.

———. "Women Mystics and Eucharistic Devotion in the Thirteenth Century." *Women's Studies* 11 (1984): 179–214.

Cabrera de Córdoba, Luis. *Felipe segundo, rey de España.* 3 vols. Madrid, 1619; Madrid, 1877.

Cardan, Jerome [Girolamo Cardano]. *The Book of My Life.* Trans. Jean Stoner. New York, 1962.

Carlton, Charles. "The Dream Life of Archbishop Laud." *History Today* 36 (Dec. 1986): 9–14.

Caro Baroja, Julio. *Las formas complejas de la vida religiosa en España.* Madrid, 1978.

Caro López, Cefano. "Casas y alquileres en el antiguo Madrid." *AIEM* 20 (1983): 92–154.

Castañega, Martín de. *Tratado de las supersticiones y hechicerías.* Logroño, 1529; Madrid, 1946.

Cerda, Juan de la. *Libro intitulado vida política de todos los estados de mujeres.* Alcalá de Henares, 1599.

Cheney, Alfred D. "The Holy Maid of Kent." *Transactions of the Royal Historical Society* 18 (1904): 108–29.

Cheyney, Edward P. *History of England from the Defeat of the Armada to the Death of Elizabeth.* London, 1974.

Christian, Jr., William A. *Local Religion in Sixteenth-Century Spain.* Princeton, 1981.

Cicero. *De divinatione.* Trans. William A. Falconer. Cambridge, Mass., 1938.

Cirac Estopañan, Sebastián. *Los procesos de hechicería en la inquisición de Castilla la Nueva.* Madrid, 1942.

Ciruelo, Pedro. *Tratado en el qual se reprueuan en todas las supersticiones y hechizerías.* Barcelona, 1528. English translation: *Treatise Reproving All Superstitions and Forms of Witchcraft.* Trans. Eugene A. Maio and D'Orsay W. Pearson. Rutherford, N.J., 1977.

Clifford, Henry. *The Life of Lady Jane Dormer, Duchess of Feria.* London, 1887.

Collen-Roset, Simone. "Le *Liber Theasuri Oculti* de Pascalis Romanus." *Archives d'Histoire Doctrinale et Littéraire du Moyen Age* 30 (1963): 112–98.

Congregación de las iglesias metropolitanas y catedrales de los reinos de Castilla y León. [1588?] Biblioteca Nacional, varios especiales 3/18355.

Contreras, Jaime, and Gustav Henningsen. "Forty-four Thousand Cases of the Spanish Inquisition (1540–1700): Analysis of a Historical Data Bank." In *The Inquisition in Early Modern Europe,* ed. Gustav Henningsen and John Tedeschi, pp. 100–129. Dekalb, Ill., 1986.

Cueto Ruiz, Ronald. "La tradición profética en la monarquía católica en los siglos 15, 16, y 17." *Arquivos do Centro Cultural Português* 17 (1982): 411–44.

Dedieu, Jean-Pierre. "Les inquisiteurs de Tolède et la visite du district." *Mélanges de la Casa de Velázquez* 13 (1977): 235–56.

———. "The Archives of the Holy Office of Toledo as a Source for Historical Anthropology." In *The Inquisition in Early Modern Europe,* ed. Gustav Henningsen and John Tedeschi, pp. 158–89. De Kalb, Ill., 1986.

———. *L'administration de la foi: L'inquisition de Toledo (xvie–xviiie siècle).* Toledo, 1989.

Domínguez Ortiz, Antonio. "Un testimonio de protesta social a fines del reinado de Felipe II." *Homenaje a Pedro Sainz Rodríguez* 3:219–26. Madrid, 1986.

Dulaey, Martine. *La rêve dans la vie et la pensée de Saint Augustine.* Paris, 1973.

Duplaix, Scipion. *Les causes de la veille et du sommeil des songes et de la vie et de la mort.* Lyon, 1620.

Erickson, Kai. *Wayward Puritans.* New York, 1966.

Escolano, Gaspar. *Decada primera de la historia de la insigne y coronada ciudad y reyno de Valencia. Segunda parte.* Valencia, 1611.

Fernández, Juan Baptista. *Primera parte de las demonstraciones católicas.* Logroño, 1593.

Fernández García, Matias. "Pintores de los siglos xvi y xvii, que fueron feligreses de la parroquia de San Sebastián." *AIEM* 17 (1980): 109–35.

Fischer, Steven R. "Dreambooks and the Interpretation of Medieval Literary Dreams." *Archiv für Kulturgeschichte* 65 (1983): 3–20.

Fox Morcillo, Sebastián. *De naturae philosophia.* Louvain, 1554.

Freud, Sigmund. *The Standard Edition of the Complete Psychological Works.* Ed. and trans. James Strachey. 24 vols. London, 1953–1974.

———. *The Interpretation of Dreams.* Ed. and trans. James Strachey. Harmondsworth, 1982.

The Fugger News Letters: A Selection, 1566–1605. Ed. Victor von Klarwill; trans. Pauline de Chary. London, 1924.

Galen. *Opera omnia.* Ed. Carolus G. Kühn. 20 vols. Hildesheim, 1964–1965.

García Caraffa, Alberto, and Arturo García Caraffa. *Diccionario heráldico y genealógico de apellidos españoles.* 88 vols. Madrid, 1919–1968.

García Carcel, Ricardo. *La germanías de Valencia.* Barcelona, 1981.

García-Villoslada, Ricardo, ed. *Historia de la iglesia de España.* 5 vols. Madrid, 1979–1982.

Gaster, Moses. "The Letter of Toledo." *Folk-lore* 13 (1902): 115–32.

Gerhard, Peter. *The Southeast Frontier of New Spain.* Princeton, 1979.

Gimeno Casalduero, Joaquín. "La profecía medieval en la literatura castellana y su relación con las corrientes proféticas europeas." *Nueva Revista de Filología Hispánica* 20 (1971): 64–89.

Gómez de Castro, Alvar. *De las hazañas de Francisco Jiménez de Cisneros.* Ed. José Oroz Reta. Madrid, 1984.

Gregoire le Grand [Gregory the Great]. *Dialogues.* Ed. Adalbert de Vogüé; trans. Paul Antin. Paris, 1980.

Hart-Davis, Duff. *The Armada.* London, 1988.

Hefele, Karl-Joseph. *Histoire des counciles.* Trans. H. Leclerq. 11 vols. Paris, 1907–1952.

Henige, David. *Colonial Governors.* Madison, Wis., 1970.

Hippocrates. *Works.* Ed. William H. S. Jones. 4 vols. London and New York, 1923–1931.

Historia de la inquisición en España y America. 2 vols. Madrid, 1984.

Horozco y Covarrubias, Juan de. *Tratado de la verdadera y falsa prophecía.* Segovia, 1588.

Huarte de San Juan, Juan. *Examen de ingenios para las ciencias.* Ed. Esteban Torre. Madrid, 1976.

Huerga, Alvaro. "La vida seudomística y el proceso inquisitorial de Sor María de la Visitación." *Hispania Sacra* 12 (1959): 35–96.

———. "La monja de Lisboa y Fray Luis de Granada." *Hispania Sacra* 12 (1959): 333–56.

———. *Historia de los alumbrados.* Madrid, 1980.

Hume, Martin. *The Year After the Armada.* London, 1891.

Ignatius of Loyola. *Spiritual Exercises.* Ed. David L. Fleming. St. Louis, 1948.

Imirizaldu, Jesús de. *Monjas y beatas embaucadoras.* Madrid, 1977.

Irizarry, Estelle. "Echoes of the Amazon Myth in Medieval Spanish Literature." In *Women in Hispanic Literature,* ed. Beth Miller, pp. 53–66. Berkeley, 1983.

Isidoro de Sevilla. *Etimologías.* Ed. José Oroz Reta and Manuel A. Marcos Casquero. 2 vols. Madrid, 1982–1983.

Isidro de Argüello, Gaspar. *Instrucciones del Santo Oficio de la Inquisición.* Madrid, 1630.

Jago, Charles. "Habsburg Absolutism and the Cortes of Castile." *American Historical Review* 86 (1981): 307–26.

Jelsma, Auke. "The Appreciation of Brigit of Sweden (1303–1373) in the 15th Century." In *Women and Men in Spiritual Culture,* ed. Elisja Schulte von Kessel, pp. 163–75. The Hague, 1986.

Jensen, De Lamar. *Diplomacy and Dogmatism.* Cambridge, Mass., 1964.

Josselin, Ralph. *The Diary of Ralph Josselin, 1616–1683.* Ed. Alan Macfarlane. London, 1976.

Kagan, Richard L. *Lawsuits and Litigants in Castile, 1500–1700.* Chapel Hill, N.C., 1981.

———. "Olivares and Education." In *La España de Felipe IV,* ed. Antonio García Sanz. Valladolid, 1990.

Kamen, Henry. "Toleration and Dissent in Sixteenth-Century Spain." *Sixteenth-Century Journal* 19 (1988): 3–23.

Kendrick, Thomas D. *Mary of Agreda: The Life and Legend of a Spanish Nun.* London, 1967.

Kselman, Thomas A. *Miracles and Prophecies in Nineteenth-Century France.* New Brunswick, N.J., 1983.

Lacombrade, Christan. *Synesius de Cyrène.* Paris, 1951.

la Mothe le Vayer, Francois de. *Oeuvres.* 2 vols. Paris, 1654.

Larquié, Claude. "Barrios y parroquias urbanas: El ejemplo de Madrid en el siglo xvii." *AIEM* 12 (1976): 33–63.

———. "L'alphabetisation à Madrid en 1650." *Revue de Histoire Moderne et Contemporaine* 28 (1981): 132–57.

Laud, William. *Works.* 7 vols. Oxford, 1847–1860.

Lea, Henry C. *Chapters from the Religious History of Spain.* Philadelphia, 1890.

Lefèvre d'Ormesson, Olivier. *Journal.* Ed. Adolphe Chéruel. 2 vols. Paris, 1860–61.

Le Goff, Jacques. *L'imaginaire médiéval.* Paris, 1985.

Lenglet, Dufresnoy, Nicolas. *Recueil de dissertations anciennes et nouvelles sur les apparitions, les visions et songes.* 2 vols. Avignon and Paris, 1752.

León Pinelo, Antonio Rodríguez. *Anales de Madrid.* Ed. Pedro Fernández Martín. Madrid, 1971.

Lerner, Robert E. *The Powers of Prophecy: The Cedar of Lebanon Vision from the Mongol Onslaught to the Dawn of the Enlightenment.* Berkeley, 1983.

Llamas Martínez, Enrique. *Santa Teresa de Jesús y la inquisición española.* Madrid, 1972.

Lorca, Bernardino. *La inquisición española y los alumbrados (1508–1667).* Salamanca, 1980.

Llorente, Manuel de la Pinta. *La inquisición española.* Madrid, 1948.

López, Juan. *Historia general de Santo Domingo.* Madrid, 1621.

López Celada, Inocente. *Evolución de las rentas del cabildo de la catedral de Toledo durante el último cuarto del siglo xvi.* Toledo, 1980.

López de Cañete, Cristóbal. *Compendio de los pronósitcos u baticinios antiguos y modernos que publicavan la declinacion general de la secta de Mohama, y libertad de Hierusalem y Palestina.* Madrid, 1623.

López Velaz, Roberto. "Estructura y funcionamento de la burocracia inquisitorial, 1643–1667." In *La inquisición española: Nueva visión, nuevos horizontes,* ed. Joaquín Pérez Villanueva, pp. 159–239. Madrid, 1980.

Lovett, Albert W. *Philip II and Mateo Vázquez de Leca: The Government of Spain (1572–1592).* Geneva, 1977.

———. "The Vote of the Millones, 1590." *Historical Journal* 30 (1987): 1–20.

———. "Philip II, Antonio Pérez, and the Kingdom of Aragon." *European History Quarterly* 18 (Apr. 1988): 131–53.

Luis de Granada. *Historia de Sor María de la Visitación y Sermón de las caidas públicas.* Ed. Bernardo Velado García. Barcelona, 1962.

MaClean, Ian. *The Renaissance Notion of Woman.* Cambridge, 1980.

McDonnell, Ernest W. *Beguines and Beghards in Medieval Culture.* New Brunswick, N.J., 1954.

Mackendrick, Malveena. *Women and Society in Golden Age Spanish Drama.* Cambridge, 1974.

Macrobius. *Commentary on the Dream of Scipio.* Ed. William H. Stahl. New York, 1952.

Magdalena de San Gerónimo. *Razón y forma de la galera, y casa real, que el Rey N.S. manda hazer en estos reinos para castigo de las mugeres vagrantes y ladronas, alcahuetas, hechizeras, y otras semejantes.* Salamanca, 1608.

Mansfield, Bruce. *Phoenix of His Age: Interpretations of Erasmus.* Toronto, 1979.

Marañon, Gregorio. *Antonio Pérez.* 2 vols. Madrid, 1947. Condensed English translation: *Antonio Pérez.* London, 1954.

———. *Los procesos de Castilla contra Antonio Pérez.* Madrid, 1947.

María de la Antigua. *Desengaño de religiosos y de almas.* Ed. Pedro de Valbuena. Seville, 1678.

María de Santo Domingo. *Libro de la oración.* Ed. José Manuel Blecua. Madrid, 1948.

Mariana, Juan de. *Del rey y de la dignidad real.* Madrid, 1961.

Martin, Colin, and Geoffrey Parker. *The Spanish Armada.* London, 1988.

Martínez Kleiser, Luis. *Refranero general ideológico español.* Madrid, 1978.

Martz, Linda. *Poverty and Welfare in Habsburg Spain.* Cambridge, 1983.

Milhou, Alain. "La chauve-souris, le nouveau David et le roi cache (trois images de l'empereur des derniers temps dans le monde ibérique, xiiie–xviie s.)." *Mélanges de la Casa de Velázquez* 18 (1982): 61–78.

———. *Colón y su mentalidad mesiánica en el ambiente franciscanista español.* Valladolid, 1983.

———. "De la destruction de l'Espagne à la destruction des Indes: Histoire sacrée et combats idéologiques." *Etudes sur l'impact culturel du nouveau monde.* 3 vols. Paris, 1984.

Mortier, Daniel A. *Histoire des maîtres généraux de l'ordre des frères prêcheurs.* 8 vols. Paris, 1904–1914.

Mousset, Albert. *Un résident de France en Espagne au temps de la Ligue (1583–1590).* Paris, 1908.

———. *Dépêches diplomatiques de M. de Longlée, résident de France en Espagne (1582–1590).* Paris, 1912.

Nalle, Sara T. "Popular Religion in Cuenca on the Eve of the Catholic Reformation." In *Inquisition and Society in Early Modern Europe,* ed. Stephen Haliczer, pp. 67–87. London, 1987.

———. "Literacy and Culture in Early Modern Castile." *Past & Present* 125 (Nov. 1989): 65–96.

Navarro, Pedro. *Favores del rey del cielo.* Madrid, 1622.

Neame, Alan. *The Holy Maid of Kent: The Life of Elizabeth Barton, 1506–1534.* London, 1971.

Neuman, Francis X. "Somnium: Medieval Theories of Dreaming and the Form of Vision Poetry." Ph.D. dissertation, Princeton University, 1972.

Newman, Barbara. "Hildegard of Bingen: Visions and Validation." *Church History* 54 (1985): 163–78.

———. *Sister of Wisdom: St. Hildegard's Theology of the Feminine.* Berkeley and Los Angeles, 1987.

Niccoli, Ottavia. "Profezie in piazza: Note sul profetismo populare nell'Italia del primo cinquecento." *Quaderni Storici* 41 (1979): 500–539.

———. *Profeti e populo nell'Italia del Rinascimento.* Bari, 1987.

Nolan, Barbara. *The Gothic Visionary Experience.* Princeton, 1977.

Nueva recopilación de todas las leyes de estos reynos. 2 vols. Alcalá de Henares, 1569.

Orozco, Alonso de. *Obras.* 3 vols. Madrid, 1756.

Palley, Julian. *The Ambiguous Mirror: Dreams in Spanish Literature.* Chapel Hill, N.C., 1983.

Parker, Geoffrey. *Philip II.* Boston, 1979; rev. ed. London, 1988.

Pererius, Benedictus. *De magia, de observatione somniorum et de divinatione astrologica libris tres adversus fallaces et superstitiosas artes.* Venice, 1591.

Pérez, Joseph. "Moines frondeurs et sermons subversifs en Castille pendant le premier séjour de Charles-Quint en Espagne." *Bulletin Hispanique* 67 (1965): 5–24.

Pérez Villanueva, Joaquín. "Sor María de Agreda y Felipe IV, un epistolario en su tiempo." In *Historia de la iglesia de España,* ed. R. García-Villoslada, 4:359–417. Madrid, 1979.

———. "Un proceso resonante: Antonio Pérez." In *Historia de la inquisición en España y América* 1:842–76. Madrid, 1984.

———. *Felipe IV y Luisa Enríquez Manrique de Lara, Condesa de Paredes de Nava.* Salamanca, 1986.

Peucer, Kaspar. *Commentarius de pruecipius divinationum generibus.* Wittenburg, 1553. French edition: *Les devins ou commentaire des principales sortes de divinations.* Trans. Simon Coulart Senlisen. Antwerp, 1584.

Pineda, Juan de. *Diálogos familiares de la agricultura cristiana.* BAE, vols. 161–63 and 169–70. Madrid, 1963.

Pinto Crespo, Virgilio. *Inquisición y control ideológico en la España del siglo xvi.* Madrid, 1983.

Pisa, Francisco de. *Apuntamientos para la ii parte de la "Descripción de la imperial ciudad de Toledo."* Ed. José Gómez-Menor Fuentes. Toledo, 1976.

Postel, Guillaume. *Le thresoir des propheties de l'univers* [1564]. Ed. François Secret. The Hague, 1969.

Poutrin, Isabelle. "Souvenirs d'enfance: L'apprentissage de la sainteté dans l'Espagne moderne." *Mélanges de la Casa de Velázquez* 23 (1987): 331–54.

Price, S. R. F. "The Future of Dreams: From Freud to Artemidorus." *Past & Present* 113 (Nov. 1986): 3–37.

Prosperi, Adriano. "Dalle 'divini madri' ai 'padri spirituali.'" In *Women and Men in Spiritual Culture,* ed. Elisja Schulte von Kessel, pp. 71–91. The Hague, 1986.

Quintana, Gerónimo de. *A la muy antigua . . . villa de Madrid. Historia de antigüedad, nobleza y grandeza.* Madrid, 1629; fascimile ed., Madrid, 1980.

Ringrose, David. *Madrid and the Spanish Economy, 1560–1850.* Berkeley and Los Angeles, 1983.

Rivadeneyra, Pedro de. *Obras.* BAE, vol. 60. Madrid, 1868.

Robres Lluch, Ramón, and José Ramón Ortolá. "La monja de Lisboa. Sus fingidos estigmas. Fray Luis de Granada y el Patriarca Ribera." *Boletín de la Sociedad Castellonense de Cultura* 23 (1947): 182–214, 230–78.

Rodríguez Moñino, Antonio, ed. *La silva de romances de Barcelona, 1561.* Salamanca, 1969.

Rodríguez Sánchez, Angel. *Cáceres: Población y comportamientos demográficos en el siglo xvi.* Cáceres, 1977.

Romano, Ruggiero. "Banchieri genovesi alla corte di Filippo II." *Revista Storica Italiana* 61 (1949): 241–47.

Round, Nicolas B. "La rebelión toledana de 1449." *Archivium* 16 (1966): 385–446.

Rubio Pardos, Carmen. "La calle de Atocha." *AIEM* 9 (1973): 81–116.

Sánchez de Vercial, Clemente. *Libro de exemplos por A.B.C.* Ed. John Easton Keller. Madrid, 1986.

Schulte von Kessel, Elisja, ed. *Women and Men in Spiritual Culture.* The Hague, 1986.

Scott, Reginald. *The Discoverie of Witchcraft* [1584]. Ed. Montague Summers. New York, 1930.

Sepúlveda, Jerónimo de. "Historia de varios sucesos del reino de Felipe II, 1584–1603." *Ciudad de Dios* 115 (1918). Reprinted in *Documentos para la historia del monasterio de San Lorenzo el Real de El Escorial,* vol. 4. Ed. Julian Zarco Cuevas. Madrid, 1924.

Serrano y Sanz, Manuel. *Apuntes para una biblioteca de escritoras españolas.* 2 vols. Madrid, 1903.

Shipley, George A. "A Case of Functional Obscurity: The Master Tambourine-Painter of *Lazarillo, Tratado VI.*" *Modern Language Notes* 97 (March 1982): 225–53.

Sieber, Claudia. "The Invention of a Capital: Philip II and the First Reform of Madrid." Ph.D. dissertation, Johns Hopkins University, 1985.

Sieber, Harry. *Language and Society in "La Vida de Lazarillo de Tormes."* Baltimore, 1978.
Silvela, Francisco. *Cartas de la venerable madre Sor María de Agreda y del señor rey don Felipe IV.* 2 vols. Madrid, 1885–1886.
Spearing, A. C. *Medieval Dream Poetry.* Cambridge, 1976.
Speculum laicorum: El espéculo de los legos. Ed. José María Mohedano Hernández. Madrid, 1951.
Spence, Donald F. *Narrative Truth and Historical Truth.* New York, 1961.
Suárez, Francisco. *De juramento fidelitatus.* Ed. L. Pereña. Madrid, 1979.
Swift, Louis J. "'Somnium Vivis' y el 'Sueño de Escipión.'" In *Homenaje a Luis Vives.* Madrid, 1977.
Tarré, José. "Las profecías del sabio Merlín y sus imitaciones." *Analecta Scara Tarraconensia* 16 (1943): 135–71.
Teresa of Jesus. *Complete Works.* Ed. and trans. E. Allison Peers. 3 vols. London, 1946.
———. *The Letters of St. Teresa.* Trans. E. Allison Peers. 2 vols. London, 1980.
———. *Life.* Trans. David Lewis. London, 1911.
Thomas, Keith. "Women and the Civil War Sects." *Past & Present* 13 (1958): 42–62.
———. *Religion and the Decline of Magic.* London, 1971.
Thompson, Colin P. *The Strife of Tongues: Fray Luis de León and the Golden Age of Spain.* Cambridge, 1988.
Thorndike, Lynn. *A History of Magic and Experimental Science.* 6 vols. New York, 1923–1958.
Thornton, Alice. *Autobiography.* Ed. C. Jackson. London, 1875.
Valdés, Juan de. *Diálogo de la lengua.* Ed. Cristina Barbolani. Madrid, 1982.
Vicente Ferrer. "Tratado del cismo moderno." *Biografía y escritos de San Vicente Ferrer.* Ed. José M. de Garganta and Vicente Forcada. Madrid, 1956.
Vilar, Jean. "Formes et tendances de l'opposition sous Olivares: Lisón y Viedma, *Defensor Patria.*" *Mélanges de la Casa de Velázquez* 7 (1971): 263–94.
Villegas, Alonso de. *Flos sanctorum, adiciones a la tercera parte.* Toledo, 1588.
Vives, Juan Luis. *Obras completas.* Ed. Lorenzo Riber. 2 vols. Madrid, 1947.
Weidhorn, Manfred. *Dreams in Seventeenth-Century English Literature.* The Hague, 1970.
Weinstein, Donald, and Rudolf M. Bell. *Saints and Society: Two Worlds of Western Christendom, 1000–1700.* Chicago, 1982.
Wernham, Richard B. *After the Armada.* Oxford, 1984.
Wiltrout, Ann E. *A Patron and a Playwright in Renaissance Spain: The House of Feria and Diego Sánchez de Badajoz.* London, 1987.
Wood, Alfred C., ed. *Memoires of the Holles Family, 1492–1656.* London, 1937.
Zambrano, María, Edison Simons, and Juan Blázquez Miguel. *Sueños y procesos de Lucrecia de León.* Madrid, 1987.
Zarri, Gabriella. "Pietà e profezia alle corti padane: Le pie consigliere dei principi." In *Il Rinascimento nelle corte padane.* Bari, 1977.

INDEX

Library of Congress Cataloging-in-Publication Data

Kagan, Richard L., 1943–
Lucrecia's dreams : politics and prophecy in sixteenth-century Spain / Richard L. Kagan.
p. cm.
Includes bibliographical references.
ISBN 0-520-06655-3 (alk. paper)
1. León, Lucrecia de, b. 1568. 2. Prophets—Spain—Biography.
3. León, Lucrecia de, b. 1568—Prophecies. 4. Inquisition—Spain.
I. Title.
BF1815.L46K34 1990
946′.043′092—dc20
[B] 89-20607

Designer: Sandy Drooker
Compositor: G&S Typesetters, Inc.
Text: 11/13 Ehrhardt
Display: Ehrhardt
Printer: Maple-Vail Book Mfg. Group
Binder: Maple-Vail Book Mfg. Group

Calle de la Greda
Calle de los Iardines
Calle de los Gitanos
Calle del Sordo
DE S. GERONIMO
LXVI
XLIIII
XIV
XXXVI
XXI
Calle del Lobo
Calle del Bauo
Calle de S. Catalina
Calle de la Visitacion
Calle del Principe
Calle de Pardo
Calle del Infante
Calle de Francos
Calle de S. Josephe
XIX
Calle de Cantorranas
Calle de las Huertas
Calle de Leon
XLVIII
Calle de los Treintarios
Calle de S. Maria
Calle del Amor de Dios
Placuela de Matute
XLII
Placuela de S. Iuan
Placuela de Anton Martin
LXI
Calle de S. Iuan
CALLE DE ATOCH
Calle de
Calle del